**Studies of the
Modern World-System**

This is a volume in

STUDIES IN SOCIAL DISCONTINUITY

A complete list of titles in this series appears at the end of this volume.

Studies of the Modern World-System

WITHDRAWN

Edited by

Albert Bergesen

Department of Sociology
University of Arizona
Tucson, Arizona

ACADEMIC PRESS

A Subsidiary of Harcourt Brace Jovanovich, Publishers

New York   London   Toronto   Sydney   San Francisco

ACADEMIC PRESS, INC.
111 Fifth Avenue, New York, New York 10003

United Kingdom Edition published by
ACADEMIC PRESS, INC. (LONDON) LTD.
24/28 Oval Road, London NW1 7DX

Library of Congress Cataloging in Publication Data

Main entry under title:

Studies of the modern world—system.

    Includes bibliographies and index.
      1. International economic relations——History.
I. Bergesen, Albert.
HF1411.S86   337'.09   80—10871
ISBN 0—12—090550—7

PRINTED IN THE UNITED STATES OF AMERICA

80 81 82 83   9 8 7 6 5 4 3 2 1

For Nina

Contents

Chapter **1**

**From Utilitarianism to Globology: The Shift from
the Individual to the World as a Whole as
the Primordial Unit of Analysis**   **1**

Albert Bergesen

Chapter **2**

Imperialism and Development   **13**

Immanuel Wallerstein

Chapter **7**

Regime Changes and State Power in an Intensifying World-State-System   **139**

George M. Thomas and John W. Meyer

Chapter **8**

Trade Dependence and Fertility in Hispanic America 1900–1975   **159**

Michael Hout

Chapter **9**

The Development of Core Capitalism in the Antebellum United States: Tariff Politics and Class Struggle in an Upwardly Mobile Semiperiphery   **189**

Christopher Chase-Dunn

Chapter **10**

Long Waves of Colonial Expansion and Contraction, 1415–1969   **231**

Albert Bergesen and Ronald Schoenberg

List of Contributors

Numbers in parentheses indicate the pages on which the authors' contributions begin.

Albert Bergesen (1, 231), Department of Sociology, University of Arizona, Tucson, Arizona 85721

John Boli-Bennett (77), Department of Sociology, Stanford University, Stanford, California 94305

Christopher Chase-Dunn (189), Department of Social Relations, Johns Hopkins University, Baltimore, Maryland 21218

Michael Hout (159), Department of Sociology, University of Arizona, Tucson, Arizona 85721

John W. Meyer (109, 139), Department of Sociology, Stanford University, Stanford, California 94305

Ronald Schoenberg (231), Laboratory for Socio-Environmental Studies, National Institute of Mental Health, Bethesda, Maryland 20205

George M. Thomas (139), Department of Sociology, Stanford University, Stanford, California 94305

Immanuel Wallerstein (13), Department of Sociology, State University of New York at Binghamton, Binghamton, New York 13901

Robert Wuthnow (25, 57), Department of Sociology, Princeton University, Princeton, New Jersey 08540

Preface

The chapters in this book represent original research on the organization and dynamics of the world-system. Since the publication of Immanuel Wallerstein's *The Modern World-System* (1974), there has been an explosion of interest and research on this topic. The purpose of this collection is to make available a selection of this research.

Just what is the world-system perspective? At the center is the belief that something is going on above and beyond individual societies: There is a collective reality, of one sort or another, at the distinctly world level of analysis. The world-system perspective is not international relations in the sense of multiple states interacting and bargaining as autonomous units. The world-system is a collective reality exogenous to nations. It has its own laws of motion, that, in turn, determine the social, political, and economic realities of the national societies it encompasses. This system emerged during the sixteenth century and has continuously expanded, to include the entire globe by the end of the nineteenth century. The world-system has certain *structural constants* (like the core–periphery division of labor), *cyclical rhythms* (like the boom–bust character of the capitalist world economy), and *long-term trends* (like the growth of the international state system). Each of these properties can be studied as a reality in their own right, or in terms of their effects on the development of national societies.

The hallmark of the world-system perspective is the broader view—large-scale, long-term social change. This outlook is present in these chapters, which cover long periods of historical time, focus on various aspects of social, political, and economic life, critique traditional viewpoints, and put forward alternative ways of conceptualizing classic problems. There are chapters taking a world-system view on theories of social order (Bergesen), imperialism and colonialism (Wallerstein and Bergesen and Schoenberg), the world polity, state strength, and regime stability (Meyer, Boli-Bennett, and Thomas and Meyer), religious movements and science in the seventeenth century (Wuthnow), fertility in Latin America (Hout), and tariff politics in the United States (Chase-Dunn). The breadth of issues and methods employed make these chapters of interest to political scientists, historians, economists, sociologists, and anyone interested in the development of the modern world itself.

The paradigm of the autonomous "society" as the primordial unit of collective reality seems to be passing. Beyond the boundary of sociology is a somewhat blurry image of a collective entity we call the world-system. The chapters in this volume attempt to identify some of its structures and dynamics. They represent different points of view as to just what constitutes the essential world reality, and they employ different methods, from historical analysis to multiple regression. What they all share, however, is the concern with structures and processes at the world level that they assume can be identified and studied. Other than that, each goes its own way. The reader should approach these chapters independently, for although they do share certain assumptions, they also reflect the interests and conceptual framework of each contributor.

**Studies of the
Modern World-System**

From Utilitarianism to Globology: The Shift from the Individual to the World as a Whole as the Primordial Unit of Analysis

I would like to look at the world-system perspective in the context of previous efforts at constructing models of social order. Of particular interest is the trend toward ever-larger units of analysis that begins with the individual-based model of utilitarianism and ends with the present notion of a world-system. During this transition there have been two fundamental paradigm shifts. The first centered on the emergence of sociology in the mid-nineteenth century and the second on the emergence of the world-system perspective in the years after 1945. A third is off in the future—but I think it will come—and will subsume the world-system perspective in a way similar to the sociological absorption of utilitarianism. We will move from conceptualizing the world as a core–periphery division of labor and see it as one collective whole.

The essence of each paradigm shift has been twofold. First a new and higher level of analysis is established and then the causal logic of the previous paradigm is reversed. The assumptions from which social order were derived now become derivations. With utilitarianism, interaction generated social order; with sociology, social order generates interaction. The utilitarian logic is now repeated at yet a higher level of analysis. With the world-system perspective, interactions of core states and peripheral areas result in a world division of labor. Like utilitarianism, interaction precedes order. Although this is our present conceptual framework, it seems reasonable to believe that we will repeat the equivalent of the sociological revolution ex-

1

STUDIES OF THE
MODERN WORLD-SYSTEM

cept on a world scale. We will someday understand the nature of a priori world social relations from which will then derive the core–periphery division of labor. Let us first consider the transition from utilitarianism to sociology.

The Utilitarian Paradigm

The first general paradigm of social order in modern social science is utilitarianism, which emerged in the seventeenth century, and is represented in the works of Hobbes, Locke, Adam Smith, Ricardo, Bentham, and others.

Utilitarianism "was a frame of reference based on the action of the individual, but was extended, in ways that led directly to the conception of 'social system,' to include the interaction of an indefinite plurality of individuals [Parsons, 1968:229]." In this paradigm the basic assumption is that individuals possess wants, needs, goals, or interests—the rational pursuit of which would generate a social system if certain conditions were met. By assuming only wants and rationality, the model would dissolve into Hobbes' "war of all against all" and so two additional assumptions were added that would provide a basis for a utilitarian social system. The idea of the division of labor, introduced by Locke and later developed by Adam Smith, postulated that men would derive enough mutual benefit through exchange that they would not resort to conflict to pursue individual goals. The other notion was Hobbes' contract with the sovereign, in which the individual gave up some natural rights in exchange for collective security. This solution provided for collective order under the direction of the state.

In a very general sense there are three steps in the emergence of the utilitarian concept of collective reality. First comes the individual, the basic unit, who is assigned various wants, needs, passions, interests, or goals that reflect man in the state of nature prior to the contractual emergence of society. The causal logic then moves *upward* to actions of a means–ends character designed to satisfy wants, which are then institutionalized in contract, exchange, and the division of labor. This social system is largely coterminous with the goal-seeking interaction itself. The utilitarian division of labor is not an independent reality, set apart from individual consciousness and behavior, as will later be asserted with sociology. In sum, utilitarian logic goes from (*a*) individual needs and wants to (*b*) action designed to satisfy these wants to (*c*) the creation of a division of labor or contract with the sovereign.

This general paradigm, which emerged during the seventeenth century, was challenged in the nineteenth century by what we call sociology. I conceive of sociology here in the broadest sense to include Marx, Weber, and Durkheim, who, although often having different views from each another, nevertheless stand in common opposition to the earlier utilitarian tradition by asserting that social relations exist prior to, and make possible, the behavioral exchange relations of utilitarianism. Utilitarian thinking, of course, continues, but it is no longer the only, or even predominant, model of social order.

The Sociological Paradigm

The emerging industrial realities of the early nineteenth century appear to have been increasingly difficult to assimilate within the assumptions and logic of the utilitarian model. Social reality seemed more than just the institutionalized interaction of individuals. With the disruptions of the countryside, the overcrowded factory towns, and the wretched conditions of the factory system itself, it must have seemed as if more was involved than just the conscious consent of an infinite plurality of individuals entering contractual relations to further their own ends. Mutual advantage through exchange did not seem to capture the relationship between capital and labor. Certainly the goals of some were furthered, but just as certainly the goals of the great bulk of the population were not.

Social reality took on a new primacy and came to be seen more as a coercive element creating order rather than the natural outcome of the rational pursuit of self-interest. Collective reality, in the form of social relations, became more firm and real than the behavioral web of utilitarian interactions. It came to have a life of its own above and beyond the individuals who participated in it. The causal logic of utilitarianism was also reversed and this, I think, constituted the most fundamental aspect of the sociological revolution. Social relations and social facts, in whatever forms they took, from class relations and modes of production to collective representations and society sui generis, were thought to *precede,* not follow, human interaction. With utilitarianism we argued that given individual wants, people interact and a division of labor emerges. With sociology, we now said that given social relations, people interact and come to have different values, selves, and identities.

Interests and wants were no longer fixed in nature and thought to exist prior to society, but were now, in the form of values people held, thought to be the product of society. This was a complete reversal in our thinking. What was previously derived—the social relations—was now assumed. What was assumed—individual needs—was now derived in the reconceptualized form of values, attitudes, selves, beliefs, and role playing. This a priori nature of social facts and social relations was a common theme for the founders of the new paradigm.

For Marx, class relations and class struggle precede and make possible the division of labor. Economic activity was now determined by relations to the means of production and not by rational acts to realize personal goals. For Weber the central question was one of motives which were the opposite of the utilitarian presocial wants and needs, for their very existence and meaning depended on the social context in which they were embedded. For Durkheim the attack centered on postulating precontractual understandings. Society did not emerge out of contract, but social understandings made contract itself possible. Weber, Durkheim, and Marx introduced numerous social entities—types of authority and domination, collective representations and symbolic orders, and class relations and modes of production— and then proceeded to show their effects upon the interaction and interests of individuals.

The question of the ultimate origin of social order remained, but was now answered at the distinctly societal level rather than being found in our presocial wants and needs. The origin of social life was no longer rooted vertically into our more biological condition—need for food, shelter, security, etc.—but was rooted horizontally, backward at the social level to earlier and earlier forms of social organization. In the new scheme, society begets society. From primitive bands and hunting and gathering societies through settled agriculture and industrial capitalism, the origin of social forms lay in their preceding form; thus the question of transitions, whether by revolution or evolution, became central—from *Gemeinschaft* to *Gesellschaft* for Tönnies; from traditional to rational legal authority for Weber; from mechanical to organic solidarity for Durkheim; and from feudalism and use values to capitalism and exchange values for Marx.

With the sociological revolution accomplished during the second half of the nineteenth and early twentieth centuries, the task shifted to the more normal science of filling in the pieces and resolving some of the contradictory claims of the societal paradigm. Institutional structures were studied, forms of social organization were categorized, society-wide cleavages and dimensions of stratification were articulated, and the links between social structure and individual consciousness were specified. The paradigm emerged in Europe but much of the normal science of research and study occurred in the United States during the first three-quarters of the twentieth century.

There were problems with the sociological paradigm of course, but none sufficient enough to challenge the whole conceptual scaffolding, and none suggesting an even higher level of analysis. While ideas of society and social formations were general in principle and not tied to any particular historical form, in fact, they came to represent national societies. This limitation came to a head after 1945 when the sociological paradigm attempted to account for the underdevelopment of the Third World. For sociology, underdevelopment would provide data it could not assimilate and would generate a crisis similar to the one nineteenth-century industrial realities created for utilitarianism. The resolution of this crisis was similar to the earlier one; a new and higher level of analysis emerged—the world-system.

The World-System Paradigm

With the appearance of many new nations following the decolonization of Africa, India, and Asia, the question of how to characterize them arose. The issue came to be posed as a question of development and underdevelopment, with newer nations being typed as backward, retarded, quasi-feudal, and precapitalist. These distinctions are to a large extent a direct consequence of the assumption of a standard set of stages all societies pass through. The societal model of sociology was predicated on the European experience where most nations had the common heritage of having passed from feudalism to capitalism. The question of differences between societies became a question of where any particular society fit along the evolutionary continuum. In theory, all societies belonged somewhere along this continuum from hunter–gatherer through feudal–agrarian to industrial capitalist.

> It is generally held that economic development occurs in a succession of capitalist stages and that today's underdeveloped countries are still in a stage, sometimes depicted as an original stage, of history through which the now developed countries passed long ago [Frank, 1969:4].

The idea of stages of development is a direct product of the horizontal movement of societal reality. This was the revolutionary break with utilitarianism a century ago, and it is as prevalent in Marxist analysis which can speak of "precapitalist" Latin America and the "feudal regime of the haciendas" (Laclau, 1971) as it is in Rostow's (1960) five stages of development. Since societies were considered the totality of collective reality, their only movement was the transformation of the societal whole from one stage of development to the next.

There were problems with this sort of analysis and they soon came to the surface. If the underdeveloped world lies at an earlier stage of development, then developed nations must have passed through that stage to get to where they are today. But they did not, and that was the crux of the problem. "[D]eveloped countries were never *under*developed, though they may have been *un*developed [Frank, 1969:4].'' If underdevelopment is not a natural sequence of evolutionary stages, what is its origin? It became increasingly clear that underdevelopment was as much, or more, a product of external relations with other developed states than a retarded or backward stage of internal development. During the 1950s Latin American social scientists began developing the idea of dependency theory and locating the problem of underdevelopment with the world market and the needs of the developed nations. With the emergence of ideas about lateral relations between societies as the primary determinant of underdevelopment, the internal development model, predicated upon the sociological paradigm revolt of the nineteenth century, began to crack. The dependency theorists focused largely on Latin America, but once the idea that relations among societies might be *more* central than their own internal relations it was only a matter of time before the argument was made that these relations were regular and patterned and that taken all together constituted a system—a world-system.

What Frank (1969) would call metropolis and satellite and Wallerstein (1974, 1979) core and periphery would come to be understood as the top and bottom of one world—one world-system. Core and periphery were causally interconnected; they were part of one world division of labor and constituted at the level of the world as a whole one social system. Underdevelopment was not a stalled stage of linear development, a question of precapitalism, retarded or backward development, but rather a structural position in a hierarchial world division of labor. One no longer looked to earlier stages of development, but to contemporary relations with other societies to explain underdevelopment.

> national states are *not* societies that have separate, parallel histories, but parts of a whole reflecting that whole. . . . [T]o understand the internal class contradictions and political struggles of a particular state, we must first situate it in the world-economy [Wallerstein, 1979:53].

The essence of this basic paradigm shift can be grasped by using Saussure's (1966) imagery of the sliced twig with which he made his point about diachronic and synchronic analysis. Sociological analysis is diachronic. It focuses upon the replacement of one stage after another in the overtime development of a society. World-system analysis is synchronic. It slices across a number of societies and looks at the structural relations between them. This type of analysis is diagrammed in Figure 1.1.

The individual histories of the United States, Brazil, and Peru can be looked at in terms of their own stages of internal development, or the structural relations of all these societies to each other can be examined. What

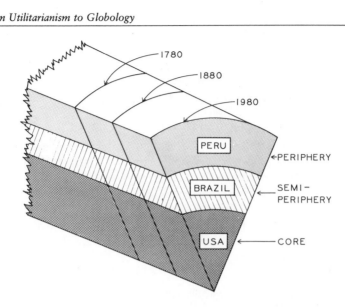

Figure 1.1. *Structural relations of the world-system.*

was linearly the farthest back along the developmental continuum—Peru—
can also be seen as a peripheral position in a system of hierarchial relations.
A country further along the old horizontal continuum—Brazil—is in a
middle, or semiperipheral location. Finally, what would be the farthest
along on the developmental continuum—the United States—can also be
seen as a core position in the vertical hierarchy. It can be done either way.

The principle advantage of the synchronic analysis is that it builds into
the explanation of development and underdevelopment the obvious interre-
latedness of nations in the world-economy. Evolving independently is fine,
except that the world is interconnected and that interconnection should be
built into the paradigm. Also, core, semiperiphery, and periphery are properties of the world-system as a whole and this creates a set of structural relations at the distinctly world level of analysis.

The diachronic—synchronic point also comes out when the system is
examined at different points in time. If it is sliced at 1880, there will be different countries in the core—like Britain, a different semiperiphery, possibly the United States, and Brazil will have joined Peru in the periphery. But
regardless of the occupants of these positions, the structural relations remain the same and *that* is the synchronic point. Slice it at 1780 and now the
United States is in the periphery along with Peru and Brazil. This suggests
that questions of linear societal development can also be seen as issues of
vertical mobility in the world-system.

Utilitarianism on a World-Scale

The question of order in our time is the question of world order, not social order, although of course, that question is still pursued by many. We are, in some sense, in a position similar to the utilitarians; we are formulating a conception of world-order that is based on assumptions about the internal dispositions of societies, their resultant interactions, and the subsequent emergence of a world division of labor. From the world-system perspective, world order, like the utilitarian social order, is a division of labor among interacting units, where the units are societies rather than individuals. The whole level of analysis has been raised so that now societies constitute the basic unit. Like the utilitarians, the collective reality of world order lies in the substance of the exchange relations between the component parts of core and periphery.

> If there is one thing which distinguishes a world-system perspective from any other, it is its insistence that the unit of analysis is a *world*-system defined in terms of economic processes and links, and not any units defined in terms of juridical, political, cultural, geological, etc. criteria [Wallerstein and Hopkins, 1977:137].

In a very general sense the logic is the same as the utilitarian model. The constituent parts—core and periphery—which exist *prior* to the world division of labor come first.

> By a series of accidents—historical, ecological, geographic—northwest Europe was better suited in the sixteenth century to diversify its agricultural specialization and add to it certain industries . . . than were other parts of Europe. Northwest Europe emerged as the core area of this world economy. . . . Eastern Europe and the Western hemisphere became peripheral areas specializing in exports of grains, bullion, wood, cotton, sugar . . . [Wallerstein, 1979:18].

Second comes the interaction among these different areas.

> given slightly different starting points, the interests of various local groups converged in northwest Europe, leading to the development of strong state mechanisms, and diverged sharply in the peripheral areas leading to very weak ones. *Once we get a difference in the strength of these state machineries, we get the operation of "unequal exchange"* which is enforced by the strong states on weak ones, by core states on peripheral areas [Wallerstein, 1979:18; italics added].

The institutionalization of these unequal exchanges and the creation of a hierarchial world division of labor follows. "As a formal structure, a world-economy is defined as a single division of labor within which are located multiple cultures . . . but . . . no overarching political structure [Wallerstein, 1979:159]." This concept of the world economy as a world division of labor represents yet another utilitarian model, this time at the world level. The primordial units are now national societies; the interaction is now the trading and unequal exchange of commodities; and the resultant collective reality is once again the maze of interactions and exchanges that constitutes a division of labor. The logic is again upward, from parts to whole, from the internal characteristics of component units (class coalitions and state strength in core and periphery), through their interaction (trade and unequal exchange) to the resultant world division of labor. In this formulation, though, mutual benefit is not derived by all; rather unequal exchange differentially benefits core over periphery, and functions to reproduce the hierarchial core–periphery division of labor.

To a large extent this conceptualization of the world economy as a division of labor is a direct consequence of clinging to societies as the basic units of analysis. In this sense we are still operating within the conceptual confines of the earlier societal paradigm; we have not gotten beyond the sociological revolution of the nineteenth century. The question now is whether there will be another paradigm crisis that results in the emergence of a model of world social relations that explains the exchange relations between core and periphery in the same way that the sociology of Marx, Weber, and Durkheim subsumed the utilitarian division of labor. I think the answer is yes, for although a globological paradigm does not presently exist, dissatisfaction with the concept of the world economy as a division of labor is growing. The suspicions held by sociologists about utilitarianism—that social order creates patterns of interaction, and not the opposite—is growing about the utilitarian outlook of the world-system perspective. Some critics of the world-system outlook (Laclau, 1971; Brenner, 1977), while emphasizing the need to look at relations of production along with the present emphasis upon exchange relations, are themselves stuck within the old societal paradigm; they see questions of class and modes of production as "internal" issues, as questions about societal infrastructure rather than as social relations that occur on a world level. Brenner (1977), for example, in attempting to identify the determinate relations of the world economy focuses upon the right set of social relations—production rather than exchange—but the wrong level of analysis—societal rather than world. For him the key to understanding the world economy is the identification of class relations. The problem is that he sees class in the compartmentalized form of relations between groups nestled within the societal formations of every nook and cranny of the world. He identifies class relations in sixteenth-century Poland, colonial Virginia, and colonial Pennsylvania. There are these class relations; the problem is that these are the only class relations he articulates. There are also class relations on a world scale between core and periphery as a whole. If some like Laclau and Brenner believe the determinate factors to be "internal," others, like Frank (1978; 1979), see the importance of both internal class relations and external exchange relations, such that, "the 'external' and the 'internal' factors play a combined dialectical role [Frank, 1978:54]."

But whether the determinate relations are composed of external or internal relations, or a mixture of both, all these perspectives still assume that questions of class and production occur at the societal, and not world, level of analysis. The obvious question is why must the analytical idea of a mode of production be limited to only societal units? Why can there not be a world mode of production, and world class relations? I see no reason why not, except for our continued attachment to the societal level of analysis. The final break with the sociological past is not with the world division of labor, for that idea is still predicated upon the primacy of societal units such as core states. The final paradigm revolution will come when we invert the parts-to-whole framework of the world-system outlook and move to a distinctly whole-to-parts paradigm which posits a priori world social relations of production which in turn determine the core—periphery relations of trade and exchange.

The Globology Paradigm: Toward the Idea of a World Mode of Production

The world economy can be as easily conceptualized as a world mode of production as it can a world division of labor. When it is seen as a mode of production, though, it becomes possible to specify distinctly world class relations and not just world exchange relations. As long as the analytical idea of a mode of production is tied to societal units it will be impossible to fully comprehend world class relations and world class struggle.

Speaking from the world-system perspective, Wallerstein argues that, "as a formal structure, a world-economy is defined as a single division of labor," where, "production is for exchange; that is, it is determined by its profitability on a market," such that, "production proceeds as long as it seems more profitable to produce than not produce [Wallerstein, 1979: 159,275]." This formulation, like the utilitarian model overthrown by Marx, Weber, and Durkheim, largely ignores the question of just how these exchange relations arise in the first place. The sale of raw materials on a world market by underdeveloped countries does not occur only because it is "more profitable to produce than not produce." There are a priori world class relations which make the sale of raw materials a necessity. Just as the sale of one's labor is necessary because of the societal class relations involved in the bourgeois ownership of the means of production, so on a world scale, the sale of raw materials is necessary because the core owns and/or controls the world means of production.

By focusing upon unequal exchange as the world economy's primary social relation, the world-system perspective looks at only the outcome, or by-product, of the much more fundamental social relation which precedes exchange and makes its very existence possible. That is, the world class relation of owning–controlling the world means of production, a relation which can only be understood when we conceptualize the world economy as a singular mode of production, with its own distinctive world class relations. Consider Latin America. If unequal exchange is the sole explanatory variable, it is impossible to account for the transition from the Aztec and Inca civilizations to the social infrastructure of underdevelopment. Unequal exchange between Europe and the Aztec and Inca civilizations did not create haciendas, mines, plantations, and the other social arrangements necessary for trade and unequal exchange to come into being. This transformation of Latin America was a direct consequence of the Conquest, that is, of the world class struggle in which peripheral producers were uprooted from their natural economies and divorced from their means of production, to be later reorganized in the plantation, mine, and hacienda under the direct control of the core. Since the inception of the world mode of production in the sixteenth century, colonialism, gun-boat diplomacy, interventionism, foreign investment, multinationals, and military and foreign aid have kept the world means of production under the ownership–control of the core. The present core–periphery division of labor appears self-reproducing only because we have not fully understood the world class relations that make its existence and continuation possible.

The workings of a distinctly world mode of production, with its own class relations and class struggles, is barely understood. The jump from the idea of society to the notion of the world as a corporate whole is a most difficult leap, but we seem to be inching toward a clear break with the past. We must invert the parts-to-whole logic of the idea of a world division of labor and substitute the whole-to-parts reasoning of a globological perspective in which independent world social relations, like world class relations, are seen as determining subsequent patterns of trade and exchange. Then, and only then, will the sociological paradigm truely end, and the globology of the world mode of production begin.

References

Brenner, R.
　1977　"The origins of capitalist development: A critique of neo-Smithian Marxism." *New Left Review* 104(July–August):25–92.

Frank, A. G.
  1969   *Latin America: Underdevelopment or Revolution.* New York: Monthly Review Press.
  1978   *World Accumulation, 1492–1789.* New York: Monthly Review Press.
  1979   *Dependent Accumulation and Underdevelopment.* New York: Monthly Review Press.
Laclau, E.
  1971   "Feudalism and capitalism in Latin America." *New Left Review* 67(May–June): 19–38.
Parsons, T.
  1968   "Utilitarianism." Pp. 229–236 in D. Sills (ed.), *Encyclopedia of Social Sciences.* New York: The Free Press.
Rostow, W.
  1960   *The Stages of Economic Growth.* Cambridge: Cambridge University Press.
Saussure, F. de
  1966   *Course in General Linguistics.* New York: McGraw-Hill.
Wallerstein, I.
  1974   *The Modern World-System: Capitalist Agriculture and the Origins of the European World-Economy in the Sixteenth Century.* New York: Academic Press.
  1979   *The Capitalist World-Economy.* Cambridge: Cambridge University Press.
Wallerstein, I., and T. Hopkins
  1977   "Patterns of development of the modern world-system." *Review* 1(Fall):111–145.

Imperialism and Development*

Our concepts are timebound in two senses: They reflect the conditions of a certain age and they apply to the conditions of a certain age—not necessarily the same one as the one they reflect. When using terms, it is always crucial to perceive both sets of referents, or we shall miss the point of a debate. The term "imperialism" in contemporary usage is a crystal-clear instance of the intellectual problem posed by our failure to note the premises inherent in the term. We are all prisoners—liberals and Marxists alike—of the Hobson–Lenin paradigm, without recognizing how deeply this paradigm is rooted in the *fin de siècle* perceptions of Western intellectuals.

The first use of the word "imperialism," as distinguished from "empire" or "imperial" (both terms deriving from Roman history) seems to be in English in the middle of the nineteenth century. The *Oxford English Dictionary* gives two definitions. As a purely pejorative term, meaning "an imperial system of government; the rule of an emperor, esp. when despotic or arbitrary," it lists five historical usages between 1858 and 1870, the last being a citation from the *Daily News* of September 8, 1870: "That this meeting begs to express its delight at the downfall of Imperialism in France, and the proclamation in lieu thereof of the Republic."[1] Here clearly we are

---

* "Marshall Woods" Lecture at Brown University, February 24, 1977
[1] *The Compact Edition of the Oxford English Dictionary* (Glasgow: Oxford University Press, 1971), I, 1385.

STUDIES OF THE
MODERN WORLD-SYSTEM

still speaking of an analogy to Roman times, inspired by the Napoleonic usage.

The *OED* gives a second definition:

> The principle or spirit of empire; advocacy of what are held to be imperial interests. In recent British politics, the principle or policy (1) of seeking, or at least not refusing, an extension of the British Empire in directions where trading interests and investments require the protection of the flag; and (2) of so uniting the different parts of the Empire having separate governments, as to secure that for certain purposes, such as warlike defense, internal commerce, copyright, and postal communications, they shall be practically a single state.

The *OED* continues in smaller print:

> In the United States, *Imperialism* is similarly applied to the new policy of extending the rule of the American people over foreign commerce, and of acquiring and holding distant dependencies, in the way in which colonies and dependencies are held by European states.

In this latter definition, we find the more contemporary usage. Here, too, the *OED* offers five historical illustrations of the usage, one for 1881 and four others between 1895 and 1899.[2] The French and German dictionaries in turn tell us that the term "imperialism" is taken over from the English.[3]

In 1902, J. A. Hobson published *Imperialism: A Study*.[4] Hobson, a Victorian liberal and a self-styled "religious heretic," was deeply shaken by the Boer War.[5] He started his book, as I have started this paper, by worrying about definitions. He proceeded to describe sympathetically the nationalisms of the nineteenth century—in eastern, southern, northern Europe, and then said:

> It is a debasement of this *genuine nationalism*, by attempts to overflow its natural banks and absorb the near or distant territory of *reluctant and unassimilable peoples*, that

---

[2] *Loc. cit.* Sometimes the term "new imperialism" is used to distinguish the second *OED* definition from the first.

[3] See Paul Robert, *Dictionnaire alphabétique et analogique de la langue française* (Paris: LeRobert, 1975), III, 623; *Der Grosse Duden,* VII: *Etymologie* (Mannheim: Bibliographisches Institut AG, 1963), 283; cf. the series of definitions, from books and dictionaries, cited in Louis L. Synder, *The Imperialism Reader* (Princeton: Van Nostrand, 1962), 19–26.

[4] See J. A. Hobson, *Imperialism: A Study,* with new introduction by Philip Siegelman (Ann Arbor: Ann Arbor Paperbacks, 1965).

[5] Siegelman's introduction cites Hobson: "The Boer War was both a turning-point in my career and an illumination to my understanding of the real relations between economics and politics . . ." Hobson, *op. cit.,* xii. Richard Koebner and Helmut Dan Schmidt remind us nonetheless that Hobson's "revulsion against imperialism" antedated the Boer War, for he wrote about it in *Contemporary Review* in 1898. See their *Imperialism: The Story and Significance of a Political Word, 1840–1960* (Cambridge: University Press, 1964), 221–222, 374. The 1898 articles came before the Boer War but *after* the Spanish–American War.

marks the passage from nationalism to a spurious colonialism on the one hand, Imperialism on the other.[6]

Hobson dated the historic turning-point from true nationalism as 1870.[7] As of 1902, he saw "the process of imperialization" as still far from complete.[8] Hobson found the "taproots" of the new "imperialism," as we all know, in economics. But it is crucial to add that, for Hobson, the economics was bad economics, one that was "clearly condemned as a business policy, in that it has procured a small, bad, unsafe increase of markets, and has jeopardised the entire wealth of the nation in rousing the strong resentment of other nations . . ." Since this is clearly irrational, Hobson asked how this could happen, and he found the answer in the fact: "Although the new Imperialism has been bad business for the nation, it has been good business for certain classes and certain trades within the nation."[9] Here we have Theme No. 1 of the Hobson–Lenin paradigm: There are opposing class definitions of national interests within the imperial state.

What did the supporters of imperialism hope to gain from it? Hobson's answer was straightforward: "Everywhere appear excessive powers of production, excessive capital in search of investment."[10] Why should this have been so? The explanation was the "mal-distribution of consuming power which prevents the absorption of commodities and capital within the country."[11] And, in turn, the reason for maldistribution was "the competitive wage system preventing wages rising *pro rata* with increased efficiency."[12]

There was a remedy for the businessman—the creation of trusts which substituted "regulation of output for reckless over-production." But this, in fact, "dam[med] up the old channels of investment" even further, and led straight to Imperialism, which Hobson saw as "the endeavour of the great controllers of industry to broaden the channel for the flow of their surplus wealth by seeking foreign markets and foreign investments to take off their goods and capital they cannot sell or use at home."[13] There we have Theme No. 2 of the Hobson–Lenin paradigm: Imperialism (at least the "new imperialism") was (is) the expression of the class interests of monopoly capital, a new phenomenon of the late nineteenth century.

---

[6] Hobson, *op. cit.*, p. 6. Italics added. By colonialism, as distinct from imperialism, Hobson meant the phenomenon of white settlers.

[7] See *op. cit.*, p. 19.

[8] *Ibid.*, p. 223.

[9] *Ibid.*, p. 46.

[10] *Ibid.*, p. 81.

[11] *Ibid.*, p. 85.

[12] *Ibid.*, p. 83.

[13] *Ibid.*, p. 85.

Hobson deplored this "remedy." It threatened political and civil freedom; it implied militarism and ruinous wars. However, Hobson offered an alternative remedy—"social reform": "Trade Unionism and Socialism are . . . the natural enemies of Imperialism, for they take away from the 'imperialist' classes the surplus incomes which form the economic stimulus of Imperialism."[14] Here we have Theme No. 3 of the Hobson–Lenin paradigm. Imperialism contradicts the true interests of the working classes of imperial countries.

I have repeatedly talked of the Hobson–Lenin paradigm. Is this fair? Was there no difference between the leader of the October Revolution and a Victorian liberal? Let us see. Lenin, of course, specifically stated in the "Preface to the Russian Edition" of his work on imperialism that he made use of Hobson's book "with all the care that, in my opinion, that work deserves."[15] Lenin, as a Marxist, presumed the existence of different class interests within the nation. He took the theme of monopolies needing to export capital and elaborated it into his "five essential features" of imperialism: These are the decisive role of national monopolies, the rise of "finance capital," the export of capital, the formation of international capitalist monopolies, and the territorial division of the whole world.[16]

Probably the only significant amendment to Hobson's diagnosis—the prognosis to be sure was radically different—was the perception of the role of the working classes in imperial countries. For although Lenin agreed that the interests of the mass of the workers of the imperial countries were not served by imperialism, he explained why leaders of Social Democratic parties nonetheless had often supported imperialism:

> Obviously, out of such enormous *super-profits* (since they are obtained over and above the profits which capitalists squeeze out of the workers of their "home" country) it is quite *possible to bribe* the labor leaders and the upper stratum of the labor aristocracy.[17]

I have said we are all prisoners of the Hobson–Lenin paradigm; some will think I exaggerate. Surely conservative and overtly pro-imperialist elements do not share this analysis. Lenin of course cited the marvelous quotation of Cecil Rhodes which is worth repeating:

---

[14] *Ibid.*, p. 90.
[15] V. I. Lenin, *Imperialism: The Highest Stage of Capitalism* (New York: International, 1939), 7. Indeed, for Lenin, the views of Kautsky and, to some extent, those of Hilferding represented "a step backward compared with the *frankly* pacifist and reformist Englishman, Hobson . . . (p. 13)." And even more bitingly, Lenin argued that Kautsky had "labelled as Marxism what Hobson, in effect, described as the cant of English parsons (p. 117)."
[16] See *ibid.*, p. 89.
[17] *Ibid.*, p. 13.

I was in the East End of London yesterday and attended a meeting of the unemployed. I listened to the wild speeches, which were just a cry for "bread," "bread," "bread," and on my way home I pondered over the scene and I became more than ever convinced of the importance of imperialism. . . . My cherished idea is a solution for the social problem, i.e., in order to save the 40,000,000 inhabitants of the United Kingdom from a bloody civil war, we colonial statesmen must acquire new lands to settle the surplus population, to provide new markets for the goods produced by them in the factories and mines. The Empire, as I have always said, is a bread and butter question. If you want to avoid civil war, you must become imperialists.[18]

But this statement was made in 1895, and since then, imperialists have become less frank.

The real issue is whether there exists any widely accepted alternative paradigm to that of Hobson–Lenin to explain the phenomenon. A conservative paradigm must essentially be based on the eternal inevitability of imperialism as a sort of "law of nature"—a variety of social Darwinism. Veblen, for example, in talking of German imperialism discussed the "loss of moral perspective" that results from "an overwhelming sense of power." He cited various cases from the Huns to the Children of Israel to the Spanish conquistadors and observed: "It is the moral attitude of the pot-hunter towards the fur-bearing animals. One does not keep faith with the fur-bearing animals."[19]

Once again, we turn to Schumpeter for the most sophisticated conservative analysis. Schumpeter explicitly sought to refute the "neo-Marxist theory" which "views imperialism simply as the reflex of the interests of the capitalist upper stratum, at a given stage of capitalist development."[20] Schumpeter sought to demonstrate that, although there have always been imperialisms,[21] the phenomenon within modern capitalism is different.[22]

[18] *Ibid.*, p. 79.

[19] T. Veblen, *Imperial Germany and the Industrial Revolution* (Ann Arbor: Ann Arbor Paperbacks, 1966), 256 fn.

[20] J. A. Schumpeter, "The Sociology of Imperialism," in *Imperialism and Social Classes* (New York: Meridian, 1951), 7. "Neo-Marxist" refers to Bauer and Hilferding, not to Lenin. Schumpeter probably was unaware of Lenin's text, since his was published in 1919, whereas Lenin's text, although written in 1916, does not appear in a language other than Russian before 1920. See Paul A. Sweezy, "Schumpeter on 'Imperialism and Social Classes,'" in S. E. Harris (ed.), *Schumpeter, Social Scientist* (Cambridge: Harvard University Press, 1951), 120, fn. 7. Since however, Lenin borrowed much from Hilferding, this can be seen as a relatively direct confrontation.

[21] The title is mistranslated in English. The German original is "Zür Soziologie den Imperialismen." The plural form is essential to Schumpeter's argument.

[22] Lenin does not disagree with the observation of *difference:* "Colonial policy and imperialism existed before this latest stage of capitalism, and, even before capitalism. . . . But 'general' arguments about imperialism . . . inevitably degenerate into absolutely empty banalities. . . . Even the colonial policy of capitalism in its *previous* stages is essentially different from the colonial policy of finance capital." *Ibid.*, pp. 81–82.

However for Schumpeter, the difference was that, under capitalism, for the first time, imperialism "is atavistic in character." Or, he added, "put in terms of the economic interpretation of history, [modern imperialism stems] from past rather than present relations of production."[23] He used this conception to sustain the general perspective that "the application of the economic interpretation of history holds out no hope of reducing the cultural data of a given period to the relations of production of that same period."[24] Modern Imperialism was atavistic because capitalism and war were considered by Schumpeter to be fundamentally antithetical to each other, since war interferes with rational production, and therefore "capitalism is by nature anti-imperialist."[25]

Here, then, seems to be the opposite of the Hobson–Lenin paradigm. Yet Schumpeter, writing in 1919, could scarcely ignore such minor exceptions to his thesis as the "scramble for Africa" or the First World War. How did he explain them? It turns out that there in fact existed

> within a social group that carries great political weight, a strong, undeniable, economic interest in such things as protective tariffs, cartels, monopoly prices, forced exports (dumping), an aggressive economic policy, an aggressive foreign policy generally, and war, including wars of expansion with a typically imperialist character.[26]

With this admission, Schumpeter more or less accepted at least the Hobson variant of the Hobson–Lenin paradigm, and was reduced to "warning [us] against overestimating it," and reasserting that despite the conflicts "born of an export-dependent monopoly capitalism," *true* capitalism will one day win out. "Deep down, the normal sense of business and trade usually prevails."[27]

Nonetheless, despite this theoretical consensus, there are bothersome aspects of the Hobson–Lenin paradigm. First of all, if colonialism is the inevitable outcome of the rise of monopolies, how can we explain the post-World War II phenomenon of "decolonization?" For "monopolies" persist, but colonialism seems to have disappeared. One can make this logically consistent by attributing this phenomenon to the victory of anti-imperialist, anticolonialist forces. But if this is the explanation, we cannot then think of the result of "decolonization" as "neocolonialism." For "neocolonialism" as a

---

[23] Schumpeter, *op. cit.*, p. 65.
[24] *Ibid.*, p. 172.
[25] *Ibid.*, p. 73.
[26] *Ibid.*, pp. 83–84.
[27] *Ibid.*, p. 84. The difference with Lenin, as between Hobson and Lenin, is prognosis. Since "it is a basic fallacy to describe imperialism as a necessary phase of capitalism, or even to speak of the development of capitalism into imperialism," it follows that "in the end the climate of the modern world must destroy [the precapitalist elements in our social life, i.e. export monopolism]." *Ibid.*, pp. 89, 98.

concept suggests that strong capitalist forces had an active, affirmative interest in decolonization, as indeed they did.[28]

Second, the Hobson–Lenin paradigm makes it impossible for us to analyze the politico-economic role of the U.S.S.R. and other socialist states in
the contemporary world-economy. Some of course feel there is nothing to
discuss, that the socialist internationalism of the U.S.S.R. is the very antith-
esis of American imperialism. The Chinese clearly did not agree. Yet they
too felt constrained by the paradigm. They showed it by inventing a new
term, "social imperialism," whose theoretical content is far from being
clear.[29]

Third, it is highly questionable how much export of *capital* there has
been in the twentieth century from "imperial" countries to either direct colonies or independent peripheral states. In any case, it is far from clear that
U.S. export of capital in the mid-twentieth century or British export of capital in the late nineteenth was *proportionately* any greater or economically
more significant than Dutch export of capital in the late seventeenth and
eighteenth centuries.[30]

In any case, by stressing what is said to be *new* in the capitalist world-
economy after 1870, Hobson and Lenin have seriously misled us. They have
separated capitalism and imperialism into two separate phenomena, leading
us to construe imperialism as a "stage" of capitalist development, as a *foreign policy* of given states at given points of time. This diagnosis has led to
two prognoses—neither of which has worked.

Hobson's prognosis of social reform has in fact inspired a sort of
worldwide network of quasi-pacifist liberals, who have argued that virtue is
the best policy. No doubt those inspired by such views played a salutory role
at the time of, say, the Vietnam War, but who can doubt that it was Vietnamese resistance that was the crucial element in the struggle?

Lenin's prognosis has inspired a series of national revolutions, which
have doubtless helped to strengthen worldwide anti-systemic forces. But
today we are more inclined to worry about how much these states have been

---

[28] Catherine Coquery-Vidrovitch explicity tries to salvage Lenin by dropping his fifth essential element, colonialism, saying that "the colonial phase was . . . capable of being transcended when it began to contradict the very objectives of imperialism." "De l'impérialisme
ancien à l'impérialisme moderne: l'avatar colonial," in A. Abdel-Malek (ed.), *Sociologie de
l'impérialisme* (Paris: Ed. Anthropos, 1971), 94.

Kwame Nkrumah showed his implicit discomfort with the paradigm by naming his book
Neo-Colonialism: The Last Stage of Imperialism (New York: International, 1965).

[29] Johan Galtung has made an effort to translate this term into systematic constructs. See
"Social Imperialism and Sub-Imperialism: Continuities in the Structural Theory of Imperialism," paper delivered at VIII World Congress of Sociology, Toronto, 1974.

[30] For a discussion of some of the conflicting evidence on this, see A. C. Carter, *Getting,
Spending and Investing in Early Modern Times* (Assen: Van Gorcum & Company B.V., 1975).

reincorporated into the capitalist world-economy than to celebrate the effi-
cacy of their disentanglement and "development."[31]

Let me try to suggest an alternate paradigm of "imperialism and development," or rather of "imperialism and capitalism." Capitalist producers produce in order to obtain profit, thereby expanding their capital.
They do this by producing commodities sold in the market, which is a
world market. Pursuing their economic interests, they relate to the politico—
cultural environment in two ways. Insofar as it constrains the maximization
of their individual profit, they seek to throw off its fetters. Insofar as it aids
the maximization of their individual profit, either directly or because it constrains competitors, they utilize it and sustain it.

Individual capitalist firms are juridically quartered in particular states.
However, the circuit of their capital in all its moments—the procurement of
the means of production, the transformation of the materials into commodities, the distribution and sale of these commodities, and the investment of
the profit as accumulated capital—is accomplished in whatever part of the
world-economy is most profitable, given any particular politico–economic
conjuncture.

If we think of the circuit of capital as a chain of economic activities,
which may all be under the aegis of a single firm—whether the Fuggers in
the sixteenth century or Exxon today—or which may be the work of a set
of market-linked companies (not usually all that fortuitously linked), there
is little reason to believe that such chains were more likely to cross state
boundaries after 1870 than before. Indeed, I would go so far as to assert
that *proportionately* the number of transstate chains has been quantitatively
and qualitatively roughly the same from the early days of the capitalist
world-economy in the sixteenth century to the mid-twentieth century. Obviously, the amount of transstate economic activity has expanded absolutely, but that is because the overall amount of economic activity has expanded.

The state structures intervene in the capitalist world-economy at each
of the moments of the circuit of capital. They alter the cost of procurement
of the means of production by affecting their flow across boundaries,
whether we are talking of material resources or of labor power. Imperialism
here normally refers to conquest or semiconquest in order to obtain raw materials or human beings (e.g., slaves or the brain drain).

States alter the process of transformation by their direct effect on wage-

[31] For a detailed review of this problem, see A. Gunder Frank, "Long Lives Trans-ideo-
logical Enterprise: The Socialist Economies in the Capitalist International Division of Labor,"
Review, I, 1, Summer 1977, 91–140.

levels as well as by subsidies. The political ability of workers in core countries to obtain, sustain, and expand real wage levels (at given levels of productivity) constitutes the so-called historical element in wage-structures, which explains the phenomenon of unequal exchange. The theory of "imperialism" takes into account at this point the ambiguous attitude of these workers of the core countries. On the one hand, the world division of labor is precisely what makes it possible for them to have higher real wages than parallel workers in peripheral countries. On the other hand, and precisely for this reason, they are constantly threatened by the generic phenomenon of the runaway shop, as common four centuries ago as it is today, and as likely to cross state boundaries then as now.

States clearly affect the process of realization of value by the imposition of barriers to trade. Imperialism here refers to the securing of markets by the (forcible) lifting of barriers that do not serve capitalists located in a particular exporting state and the creating of barriers in one's own favor (e.g., colonial mercantilism).

Finally, states affect the process of investment of money profit by ensuring or preventing its "repatriability" and by keeping borders open to permit the free flow of capital pursuing its paths as required by the tendency to equalize the rate of profit. Imperialism here ranges from its familiar, contemporary neocolonial form of World Bank loan requirements to the "export of capital" chasing after cheaper labor as observed by Hobson and Lenin to the plunder of the buccaneers in the seventeenth-century Caribbean.

Imperialism is not a stage of capitalism. It is simply a reference to those activities of stronger states towards weaker states that derive from one of the fundamental antinomies of capitalism: the existence of an economic division of labor that has boundaries far larger than any particular state structure. What Hobson and Lenin observed was not a new stage in the process of capitalism but rather a cyclical phenomenon. As particular hegemonies in the world-economy are challenged—in 1870 we are talking of British hegemony—two things happen simultaneously. On the one hand, the challenging states try to create mercantilist protected zones to weaken the commercial and financial advantages of the hegemonic power. These attempts, along with the responses of the hegemonic power, take the form of the colonial division of peripheral zones. On the other hand, one of the reasons the challenging states are indeed able to challenge the erstwhile hegemonic power is that the latter's relative productive efficiencies have been falling, both because of relative aging of fixed capital and the relative rise of real wages. This means that productive capitalists located in the hegemonic country will be more likely than previously to find optimal investment opportunities outside their state boundaries. This is the so-called "export of capital," which is in fact a measure of a changing set of costs of the factors of production at home.

Since this is a *cyclical* phenomenon, it does not last eternally. Decolonization comes about in inverse circumstances, the full achievement of an alternate hegemony, in this case the United States from 1945–1967. During the U.S. rise to hegemony, let us say 1873–1945, the "export of capital" on a large scale would scarcely have made much sense, as it was a period of rising relative productive efficiencies within the United States.

When I say that the "new imperialism" was not new but cyclical, I am *not* thereby suggesting that capitalism has *no* stages, no secular developmental processes. Indeed it does. The danger of the Hobson–Lenin paradigm is that by mislabeling a cyclical phenomenon for a secular one they have diverted our attention from the secular ones. This is not merely an abstract danger at the level of diagnosis. It is a concrete danger at the level of prognosis.

To understand what is going on, we have to put together the cyclical constants and the secular variables. The attempts to create monopolies and to destroy them, the pressures to colonize and decolonize, the rise and fall of hegemonies—these are cyclical constants resulting from the basic contradictions of capitalism. The secular variables are (*a*) the steady commodification of the factors of production, and hence the steady transformation of the multiplicity of actual productive relations at points of production towards the capitalist ideal-type of surplus-producing labor coming from lifetime true proletarian households; (*b*) the steady mechanization of the factors of production, increasing the proportion of fixed to variable capital; (*c*) the steady increase of antisystemic political organization of "lower strata"; (*d*) the steady reapportionment of surplus-value from ruling strata to their agents, what might be called the "janissarization" of the capitalist system.

All these trends are trends of the capitalist world-economy taken as a whole, and not of individual states within the capitalist world-economy. These trends are leading to new and more sophisticated forms of class consciousness within the world-system, and class alliances that are forged in a more knowing and intelligent fashion.

What is crucial for our prognosis, however, is not to assume that these trends, which all move towards asymptotes, have come near reaching them yet. The curves are going upward, but have still some way to go. Insofar as we hope to affect history and not merely to suffer it, we must be able to distinguish between cyclical and secular tendencies. We may use the former, but it is in order to affect the latter. If we only affect the cyclical tendencies, we shall be playing musical chairs, rotating who shall exploit whom. If we affect the latter, we shall hopefully end the exploitation.

Hobson and Lenin were not wrong. They shouted *cris de coeur* that were efficacious in their time. But if we are to pursue the struggle today we must go beyond their timebound formulations to the critical issues of our era. We must recognize "imperialism" as a constant, not a variable, thrust in a capitalist world-economy. We must organize against its changing forms, and we must remember that it is merely one aspect of a wider system of human exploitation that is capitalism.

The World-Economy and the Institutionalization of Science in Seventeenth-Century Europe

The great achievements of modern science in the technological realm have strongly reinforced the assumption that science is a uniquely adaptable mode of arriving at truth. I do not wish to quarrel with this assumption here, except to point out that it often obscures understanding the evolution of science. For in regarding science strictly as truth, it becomes tempting to explain its evolution as the simple unfolding of an inner intellectual logic. According to Barry Barnes (1974), this point of view is in fact the one currently taken by most historians of science of both Popperian and Kuhnian persuasion.

At present, efforts to examine the institutionalization of science with reference to larger social conditions are in full retreat. At the same time, however, it is hard to deny that institutionalization is a social process—even when it involves science. Joseph Ben-David (1971), who has recognized this fact more clearly than most, puts it well when he says that certain aspects of science are "eminently sociological phenomena." To say this in no way jeopardizes the importance of examining the internal unfolding of scientific ideas. But it poses the importance of also investigating the institutionalization of science in relation to social conditions.

Though institutionalization has been defined in various ways, a rather simple definition will probably suffice for our purposes. If a social institution is a pattern of roles that (*a*) receives resources from its environment sufficient to be sustained over time, (*b*) enjoys autonomy from other institu-

25

STUDIES OF THE
MODERN WORLD-SYSTEM

tions in setting and pursuing its goals, (c) is deemed legitimate by the surrounding society, and (d) is internally integrated through communication and organization, then institutionalization may be defined as the process by which these characteristics come into being.

To date, the two leading attempts to account for the institutionalization of modern science (though neither was intended as a full explanation) have been the so-called "Merton thesis" and the Marxian explanation. The Merton thesis, set forth in Robert K. Merton's doctoral dissertation (published in 1938 as *Science, Technology and Society in Seventeenth-Century England*), follows a Weberian line of reasoning, arguing that certain values in Puritanism contributed to the legitimacy of the scientific role. These values included reason, service, and the glorification of God through study of his handiwork. The effect of these values, as they became prominent in England during the second quarter of the seventeenth century, was to enhance the likelihood of science being chosen as a vocation.

The Marxian explanation, as formulated by Edgar Zilsel (1942), J. D. Bernal (1971), Boris Hessen (1971), and others, suggests that the gradual rise of bourgeois capitalism during the late sixteenth and seventeenth centuries contributed decisively to the institutionalization of science. Capitalism created (among other things) new technological problems, particularly in mining, transportation, and ballistics. These problems raised the status of artisans and technicians in relation to academic philosophers, became the focus of scientific experimentation, and produced discoveries which stimulated new theories of the natural universe.

Even the harshest critics of the Mertonian and the Marxian theories have stopped short of suggesting that Puritanism and capitalism had *no* effect on the institutionalization of science. Both were such prominent features of the seventeenth century that science could scarcely *not* have been affected by them, at least indirectly. But with the accumulation of better historical evidence in the decades since each theory was formulated, two things now seem clear.

First, neither the effects of Protestantism nor of capitalism appear as direct or as straightforward as they once did. The Merton thesis has been re-examined in light of more extensive data on early members of the Royal Society and a comprehensive study of British scientists of the eighteenth century. The former revealed that only one-fourth of the members of the Royal Society were Puritans and that religious and political expediency was more the rule than firm commitments (Mulligan, 1973). The latter discovered that less than five percent of eighteenth-century scientists had graduated from the Protestant dissenting academies (Hans, 1951). Intellectual historians have also shown that the "elective affinity" between Puritan ideals and scientific values breaks down at a number of points upon closer scrutiny of these concepts (Hall, 1963; Greaves, 1969; Hooykaas, 1972).

The Marxian explanation has similarly come under attack. Recent work by economic historians has generally suggested that technological inventions of the seventeenth century owed little to scientific research nor that scientific research was greatly stimulated by technological problems (Hall, 1967, 1972; Clark, 1970:63–64; Braudel, 1973:321). For example, John Nef concludes, "The more one considers the direct connections between the scientific and the early industrial revolution, the more they seem to be superficial [1964:320–21]." Other research has called into question the Marxian assumption that scientists were recruited primarily from bourgeois backgrounds (Hans, 1951).

Second, it is now evident that neither theory accounts for some of the more interesting developments associated with the institutionalization of science. The Merton thesis fails to explain the significant degree of institutionalization that took place in Italian science prior to similar developments in England. The prosperity of French science also poses a particular embarrassment to the Merton thesis. Even if the Huguenots were a significant force in French science, their success amidst presumably alien religious conditions and the continued success of French science after their expulsion remain to be explained. Nor will it do to argue that science on the Continent merely diffused there from England. While it is true that there was substantial diffusion, there was equally as much infusion from the Continent to England. Dutch science presents an embarrassment of a different sort. Its marked decline after the middle of the seventeenth century squares poorly with the continued prominence of Calvinism there. The Merton thesis also falters, insofar as it is focused primarily on individual motivation, to account for the other social requisites that contributed to the emergence of science as an institution.

Spokesmen for the Marxian theory, for their part, have been noticeably silent about the virtual absence of scientific activity in the two countries where problems of transportation, metallurgy, and ballistics were particularly important—Spain and Portugal. Nor does the Marxian theory explain why other absolutist states, which remained very much in the hands of the aristocracy (as Perry Anderson, 1974, has recently shown), should have become major patrons of the fledgling sciences. The Marxian theory also proves unsatisfactory once comparisons are made between Europe and China. Until the end of the sixteenth century, China remained technologically superior to Western Europe in a number of important respects (Needham, 1954). Yet contrary to the Marxian assumption that technology produces science, Chinese technology failed to promote anything like the institutionalization of systematic scientific experimentation that occurred in Western Europe.

The point of this litany is not to suggest that the Mertonian and Marxian theories should be packed off to the scrapheap—only that the last word on the institutionalization of science has hardly been spoken. As with any complex and precarious social process, the institutionalization of science in seventeenth-century Europe does not lend itself to monocausal explanations. The religious explanation yields considerable mileage in accounting for certain aspects of the institutionalization process, as does the economic explanation. But neither in itself, nor the two together, fully accounts for the connections established between science and its social milieu. A large amount of historical research remains to be done. And, perhaps more importantly, there exists a serious need for new perspectives to guide this research.

In the pages that follow, I shall attempt to outline a theoretical framework that, in my opinion, offers some promising insights into the institutionalization of science. I have relied heavily on recent work of various sorts in economic history which stresses the organic or systemic character of the European region. Immanuel Wallerstein's (1974) research on the evolution of capitalist agriculture in the sixteenth century is a prime example of this kind of work. In borrowing from this research I do not mean to imply full agreement with its conclusions. Nor do I assume that what applies to the economic sphere necessarily applies to events in the realm of science. My only assertion is that certain general concepts emerge from viewing the European region as a single social system which correspond to several of the important characteristics of seventeenth-century science. Before turning to a specific consideration of the institutionalization of science from this perspective, it may be worth commenting briefly on these points of correspondence.

In the first place, one can argue on the basis of the historical evidence that science in the seventeenth century was highly integrated across the European system. There were important differences in the character of science from one country to the next, to be sure, but science was European-wide, bound together by an international network of communication, and concerned with problems that transcended national boundaries. As A. Rupert Hall, in speaking of English science, has remarked,

> The current problems in these various sciences tackled in England were the current problems over all Europe—science was international, critical, competitive in the seventeenth century as it is now. There was no separate little English world of science isolated from the universe and playing the game according to private rules, as though science were a form of cricket [1972:44].

Both Merton and the Marxian theorists, I suspect, recognized this fact in their choice of explanatory conditions that, like science, were variously distributed throughout Europe. Still, the emphasis has been upon "distribution," as if science consisted of so many beans in a bottle, whereas in reality science was much more organically interconnected than this. What I am suggesting, then, given the systemic character of science, is that an appropriate context in which to examine the institutionalization of science would appear to be one that emphasized the systemic nature of European social structure as well.

Second, one is forced to view European authority structure in an appropriately different manner, once one takes the entire European system as an organic unit of analysis. Decentralized political authority has been discussed in a number of contexts as a positive factor in the development of science (or intellectual innovation more generally). For example, Max Weber saw the importance of a lack of authoritarianism during the Period of Warring States in China, the first period during which "a hundred [intellectual] flowers bloomed," and likened it to the political conditions in antiquity that fostered Greek science and philosophy (1951:152). More recently, for another example, Joseph Ben-David (1971) has stressed political decentralization as a factor in the institutionalization of science in Germany and the United States in the nineteenth century. Political decentralization has also been emphasized implicitly in discussions of the compatibilities between science and democracy (Barber, 1962; Polanyi, 1964; Merton, 1973).

As far as the seventeenth century is concerned, it has been difficult to reconcile the growth of science with the prevailing political conditions of Europe. The traditional view, formulated from looking at individual societies, has been that the late sixteenth and early seventeenth centuries constituted an age of absolutism and oligarchy. In comparison with late medieval feudalism, the obvious fact about absolutism and oligarchy was that they represented a great concentration of *centralized* authority. From the standpoint of the larger European system, however, the relevant comparison is with other territorially large social systems, of which the chief cases prior to the seventeenth century had been politically unified empires. In this comparison, the important thing about authority in Europe is not that it was centralized, but that it was *decentralized*—divided among competing sovereign states. These two views of authority, it should be noted, are less incompatible than they may appear at first sight. Wallerstein (1974) has presented evidence suggesting that the growth of centralized authority within states was partly nurtured by the decentralization of authority between states—a fact that we shall return to later. But the important implication that derives from viewing Europe as a larger social system is that political decentralization may, after all, have contributed to the institutionalization of science in the seventeenth century, as in other periods. What this contribution may have been seems worthy of investigation.

The other conceptual advantage one gains by regarding Europe as an organic unit is probably less obvious. Some accounting has to be made for the fact that science became institutionalized in differing degrees in different parts of Europe—or at least did so at different times and, accordingly, grew at different rates. One of the reasons that the Mertonian and Marxian theories have enjoyed such popularity, despite the objections surveyed here, is probably that both predict a high degree of scientific institutionalization in England—where it did, in fact, occur. Yet if one takes the previously mentioned objections seriously, as I believe one must, then some other manner of describing the variation in European social structure that corresponds better with the variation in scientific instutionalization must be found. Without entering fully into the details at this point, I believe a strong case can be made that the distinction between "core" (or dominant) and "periphery" (or dependent) areas of territorially large social systems, as Raul Prebisch (1959), Edward Shils (1972:355–371), Immanuel Wallerstein (1974), and others have conceptualized it, affords a useful way of doing this.

Having hinted briefly at the relevance of the framework to be outlined, we can now turn to an examination of the institutionalization of seventeenth-century science from this perspective. It will have to be left to the historian of science to supply empirical detail of the kind needed to fully test the utility of this perspective. But some tentative indications of its utility can be provided from even a cursory survey of the available historical material. Let us consider each of the four aspects of institutionalization listed near the beginning of this chapter: autonomy, resources, legitimacy, and internal communication and organization.

Scientific Autonomy

Institutional autonomy, insofar as science is concerned, means, above all, autonomy from any body capable of arbitrarily restricting the freedom of scientific inquiry, which in nearly all practical instances means government. But no one would argue that autonomy implies total independence (let alone isolation) from government. For science has been heavily indebted to the protection and patronage of government. One might suggest, therefore, that scientific autonomy consists of a special form of relation, in which science and government interact for mutual gain, but where checks are present to limit the arbitrary extension of government control over science (cf., Shils, 1962; Price, 1965; Ravetz, 1971).

As previously mentioned, it is difficult to explain how institutional autonomy for science could have developed during the age of absolutism and oligarchy, since these highly centralized and expansive forms of political organization appear inimical to scientific autonomy. But if science is viewed

within the context of the larger European "world-economy," to borrow
Wallerstein's term, the presence of competing sovereign states emerges as a
means by which the arbitrary intrusion of any single government could be
circumvented or controlled.

How might this have worked in practice? One possibility is that scientists were able simply to migrate from one jurisdiction to another in order to
escape politically undesirable conditions. There is indeed a great deal of evidence that this was the case. Kepler, for example, was persecuted in Tübin-
gen but was able to escape to Austria. Descartes is alleged to have voluntar-
ily exiled himself from France because of his disenchantment with the
political conditions there. The scientific movement in Flanders was able to
survive by fleeing north (Geyl, 1932:273–274). During the 1630s large
numbers of students from England went to Leyden to study in order to escape the political turmoil in England (Hackmann, 1976:93). The entire
group of scientists that had gathered around the Duke of Northumberland
and that later became instrumental in the formation of the "invisible college" fled England during the revolutionary period and received patronage
in France (Brown, 1934). Newton's mentor, Isaac Barrow, who was a firm
supporter of the king, for which he felt certain of being excluded from becoming Regius Professor of Greek during the Cromwellian period, spent
four years touring the Continent, returning to England only upon the Restoration of Charles II. Joseph Priestly fled to America avowedly because of
his political views. Countless other examples could be added. The obvious,
yet by no means trivial, point is that a politically centralized Europe could
have guaranteed no such autonomy.

Of course it is impossible to assess, except in individual cases, how
much the political decentralization of Europe contributed to the political
autonomy of scientists. It is worth noting, however, that the same conditions promoting autonomy in the larger European system seem to have also
been present in the Italian city-state system. For example, Galileo's criticisms of an invention proposed by a member of the Medici family temporarily placed him in disfavor with the Grand Duke of Tuscany who controlled
his appointment at the University of Pisa. Fearing for his appointment, Galileo turned to the Venetian Republic where he obtained an appointment at
the University of Padua, avoiding an early termination of his career (Geymonat, 1965:15–16). For another example, Borelli found himself accused
of sedition after an uprising at Messina. Rather than standing trial, the outcome of which seemed particularly uncertain, he took refuge in Rome where
he was received into the Academy of Queen Christina of Sweden who was
residing there.

These examples may have been more the exception than the rule. But
they illustrate that some of the same conditions that may have facilitated the

institutionalization of science in seventeenth-century Europe may have also facilitated this process within Italian science. Insofar as this may have been the case, the hypothesis of a relation between political decentralization and scientific autonomy appears to be capable of some degree of generalization. In contrast, the Mertonian theory, and to a lesser extent the Marxian theory, appear to be of limited applicability to the Italian situation.

The other way in which political decentralization may have contributed to the autonomy of seventeenth-century scientists is by invoking political competition for their services, thereby enhancing the bargaining power of scientists with their particular governments. That there was such competition between governments seems to be well evidenced at least among the more prominent scientists of the period. A number of courts competed to attract the medical skills of Vesalius and Harvey. France competed successfully for Huygens, Homberg, Viviani, Cassini, and Roemer, among others, by offering handsome stipends. The Dutch also competed actively to attract foreign scientists, offering high university salaries as incentives, apparently with considerable success, so that in the seventeenth century at Gronigen, for instance, 34 of its 52 professors were foreign (Hackmann, 1976). And England drew a number of foreign scientists both through patronage and by promoting a climate of toleration and appreciation of scientific inquiry (Nef, 1964:324).

Clearly the fact that governments competed at all for the services of eminent scientists indicates that science already enjoyed a certain degree of respectability. This is not the point at issue. The point, as any scientist who has participated in the "job market" knows, is that one's autonomy goes up measurably if there are multiple sources of employment competing for one's talents. In the seventeenth century there was competition within countries as there is today (though on a smaller scale, of course). But the evidence suggests that there was also significant competition among countries.

The main comparison case which illustrates the importance of political decentralization for scientific autonomy in the seventeenth century—by virtue of its absence—is the Hapsburg empire. Although Charles V, whom Napolean came to greatly admire, nearly succeeded in bringing Europe under the central control of the Hapsburg regime in the early part of the sixteenth century, these ambitions lay unfulfilled and largely beyond hope of repair by the beginning of the seventeenth century. Castile was rapidly becoming incorporated into the larger European world-economy as a peripheral member dependent on foreign exchange and foreign diplomatic agreements. Yet in domestic economic and political structure Castile remained organized as a closed imperial state. Culturally it continued to be the most educated society in Western Europe. But in comparison with other areas having the necessary educational prerequisites it developed no autonomous scientific tradition. According to Richard Kagan (1974), who has studied extensively the Castilian universities of the seventeenth century, the major cause of this failure was not so much Catholicism, as usually alleged (although this may have been an indirect factor), but the degree of government intervention in the selection of instructors, curricula, students' career choices, and academic standards (cf., Ortiz, 1971:235). Not only did the crown take a strong interest in salary raises, appointments, academic decisions, and student conduct, but books from the outside world were strictly prohibited and almost all students were forbidden to attend universities outside Castile. There was neither opportunity nor much incentive—given the reward system of the Castilian university—for scientists to bargain or migrate in hopes of gaining greater intellectual autonomy.

Of course it is true that autonomy can be gained from even the most centralized empire if one is willing and able to emigrate. The difference with the decentralized European system was that one could emigrate but still remain within the larger system where there was contact and communication with other scientists. In short, autonomy could be negotiated within the European social system itself.

There appears to be some evidence, then, suggesting that the institutional autonomy of science in the seventeenth century was facilitated by the political decentralization of the European world-economy. However, I do not wish to overemphasize the importance of autonomy and decentralization. At most, autonomy is but a passive condition in the development of an institution. Other social and intellectual conditions no doubt played a much more active role in the overall growth of seventeenth-century science. Furthermore, the political autonomy that scientists enjoyed—to the extent that it was important—can only be attributed in part to political decentralization. Even if decentralization provided a lever against political interference, one must ask why this lever was permitted to be used as it was. The role of autonomy, therefore, goes only part way in explicating the effects of the world-economy on the institutionalization of science.

Patronage

In the seventeenth century, science was infinitely less costly to maintain than it is now, but even then it had to obtain material resources in order to become established as a social institution. In particular, the livelihoods of interested and talented individuals had to be secured in order for them to devote time to scientific experimentation rather than to more gainful careers. Beyond this, support was also a frequent necessity for the procurement of expensive scientific apparatus.

In virtually every European country scientists received financial assistance from persons of wealth and from those in positions of power. Tycho Brahe received assistance from Holy Roman Emperor Rudolf II. Kepler's observatory was built at the expense of the King of Denmark. Galileo received advances from the Medici and from the Florentine firm Giucciardi Corsi (Braudel, 1972:320). Benedetti, who was known primarily for his work in mathematics and physics, served as court mathematician to the Duke of Farnese in Parma and received financial support from the Duke of Savoy. Bonaventura was supported by the Duke of Urbino. In Italy the most consistent supporters of scientists were Ferdinand II, Grand Duke of Tuscany and his brother Prince Leopold, founders of the Accademia del Cimento (Middleton, 1971). In France the Academy of Sciences provided royal pensions of 1,500 *livres* annually for 14 scientists; in addition, a number received patronage from private sources (Hahn, 1962). In England similar sources of support were provided by a variety of individuals in private life.

Patronage was also bestowed indirectly in the form of public offices. In France these included the office of tax collector (occupied by Lavoisier), treasurer (occupied by Montigny), postmaster general (occupied by d'Onsenbray), director of the Royal Observatory, and numerous court physicians, apothecaries, surgeons, and tutors. Similarly, in England government positions were occupied by a number of the more prominent scientists, including Gilbert, Wilkins, Bacon, Brouncker, and Newton. One estimate has suggested that nearly one-third of the original members of the Royal Society were "high servants of the Crown and state officials [McKie, 1960:35]."

In addition to supporting scientists, a number of the nobility and officers of the state also took a personal interest in scientific experimentation. Rudolf II amassed a rich collection of scientific and artistic curiosities at his court in Prague (Holborn, 1976:284). Charles II had his own chemistry laboratory as did Louis XIV's brother, the Duc d'Orleans. Other amateur scientists in France included the Duc de Luynes, the Duc de Roannes, and Melchisadec Thevenot (founder of the Academy Thevenot and patron of a number of scientists including Steno and Frenicle). Prince Rupert, according to his biographer, had an "inexhaustible interest in forge and laboratory." The ninth Earl of Northumberland earned the appellation "wizard of earl" for his experiments in anatomy, alchemy, and cosmography (Stone, 1967:326). Other amateur scientists in England, who had either their own laboratories or who took an active role in experimentation, included the Earl of Cork, the Duke and Duchess of York, the Bishop of London, the second Earl of Cumberland, fifth Lord Dudley, the Duke of Buckingham, Lord Willoughby, Sir Robert Moray, and Sir Robert Hale.

Noblemen and great officers promoted the rise of applied sciences, not only as patrons but sometimes also as active researchers. Cuthbert Tunstall, Master of the Rolls under Henry VIII and later Bishop of London and Durham, wrote a textbook on arithmetic (in Latin); in Thomas More's large household mathematics and astronomy were considered to be principal subjects of study, and the noted mathematician Nichols Katzer tutored More's children in astronomy. When John Dee in the third quarter of the sixteenth century assembled a large scientific library in his house near London, it became a center not only for scholars and instrument makers who looked for advice, but also for the great merchants who sought his counsel before voyages, and for members of Elizabeth's court and council who came to study chemistry with him. Lord Burghley, Elizabeth's chief minister, tried to promote both the sciences and scientists. On his request, William Bourne wrote a short treatise on the properties and qualities of glasses for optical purposes. Digges, one of the greatest mathematicians of his time, was called into the service of his country as a military engineer, first to supervise the fortifications at Dover, later as Muster-Master-General of the English forces in the Netherlands [Fischer and Lundgreen, 1975:544].

In Italy Ferdinand II and Prince Leopold were not only patrons of science but active experimenters as well, as was Count Federigo Cesi, founder of the Accademia dei Lincei, and a number of other Italian notables (Burke, 1974:73–74). Members of both the Medici and the Fugger families dabbled in science. Amateur scientists in Germany included the Duke of Magdeburg, Tschirnhausen, Hevelius, and Otto von Guericke. To the extent that scientists received patronage from persons of power, therefore, it seems reasonable to conclude that this patronage was given out of genuine interest in, and typically with some knowledge of, the nature and purposes of science.

In total amounts, the patronage that scientists received was seldom a major expense on the part of its benefactors. For example, in France where stipends were perhaps more generous than anywhere else the total amount of pensions to scientists added up to approximately 30,000 *livres* a year during the 1670s and for the 25 year period from 1664 to 1690 totalled 1.7 million *livres* plus another .7 million *livres* if the cost of the royal observatory is included (King, 1948:289; Hahn, 1976:131). Yet during this period government receipts from the *taille* alone amounted to between 40 million and 50 million *livres* annually (Anderson, 1974:98). Thus, the amount given over to scientific activities represented only a tiny fraction of the state's finances. However, this financial support was of considerable value to those receiving it, making it possible to devote time to experimentation that would otherwise probably have been spent in more gainful activities, and providing instruments for the conduct of these experiments.

The importance of obtaining financial assistance was often evident in the activities of even the leading scientists. As Roger Hahn explains

The financial problem became the central issue in the soliciting of governmental assistance by the more dedicated members of the learned circles. On one level, their needs stemmed from the cost of constructing improved instruments (especially the expensive ones for astronomical observations) and of purchasing raw materials to carry on chemical and biological experiments. Without substantial sums, it was also impossible to initiate large-scale enterprises such as scientific expeditions [1971:7].

And in a similar vein, Martha Ornstein (1975:67) has argued that the high cost of instruments and laboratories was one of the important reasons why the aristocracy was so heavily represented among the early scientists and why gradually the scientists began to form organizations to allow greater cooperation in the procurement and use of instruments.

But why was patronage given to the sciences? The Mertonian theory offers no explicit explanation. One can perhaps infer from the Mertonian theory that patronage was granted because science was thought to be of value to the general welfare and that concern for the general welfare had been promoted by certain doctrines of the Protestant reformers. But this explanation fails to account for the extensive patronage that scientists received in Catholic countries and from Catholic monarchs. The Marxian discussions have also failed to give any explicit explanation of scientific patronage. It is not inconsistent with the Marxian approach to assume that the rise of commercial capitalism was an important stimulus to this patronage. Indeed, there are instances of patronage being given directly by members of the new commercial classes and of state-sponsored research connected with commercial ventures. What does not square well with the Marxian interpretation is the high involvement of the aristocracy and the absolutist state in providing patronage to the sciences.

Whatever their general limitations, the Mertonian and the Marxian theories do stress one motivation that seems to have been present among the early patrons of science. Both theories suggest that science was of utilitarian value, chiefly in promoting technological innovation. And there is certainly anecdotal evidence suggesting that science was patronized for this purpose. Bacon's utilitarian defense of science clearly seems to have been widely appealing. Charles II repeatedly admonished the Royal Society to study things that were useful. Colbert's interest in science rested heavily on utilitarian considerations. "Among the noblemen and gentlemen who were conspicuous as scientific dilettanti at this time," writes G. N. Clark, "it is easy to see that the excitement of study was mixed with the hope of gain [1970:9]."

The case could probably be argued that both Protestantism and capitalism reinforced a general "ethos" in seventeenth-century Europe in which utilitarian interests in science could surface. But there also seems to be evidence that this utilitarian interest in giving patronage to the sciences, especially insofar as much of this patronage seems to have been associated with the state, may have been reinforced by the political and economic competition that prevailed among the leading members of the European world-system. More explicitly, one of the social conditions that probably helped to motivate patronage of the sciences in the seventeenth century was the decentralized character of the European world-economy and the rivalry that existed among these multiple centers of power. This is a condition that emerges as a dominant feature of the seventeenth century once one adopts a world-system perspective on the period.

By the end of the sixteenth century, the fact that Europe could not be politically unified, but would consist of a system of multiple competing powers had become apparent to contemporary statesmen. Hopes of religious unification had been destroyed by the firm footholds that Protestantism had gained in Germany, Holland, Scandanavia, and England. Militarily, the efforts of the Hapsburgs to restore unity to Europe had dissipated with the defeat of the Spanish armada, the success of the revolt in the Netherlands, and the continuing effectiveness of France as a counterpoise against Hapsburg expansion.

The fact of political decentralization had also begun to be regarded as normative. Schemes emphasizing the doctrine of equilibrium or "balance," rather than unification, began to gain favor in political theory. This doctrine was evident in Machiavelli and later became pronounced in the writings of Harrington and Cromwell and in the Duke of Sully's "Great Design." "That Europe should be unified through the hegemony of any one power, be it Hapsburg or be it Bourbon," Goeffrey Barraclough has written, "was rejected on all sides as unthinkable [1963:28]." In place of unification, the new schemes argued that *interdependence* among the European powers was preferable; indeed, that it was inevitable, since the various states were endowed with different abilities, climates, and resources. If interdependence was inevitable, the important problem, therefore, was to maintain a balance of power among the major contending states sufficient to ensure a steady flow of exchange without any one state gaining an unfair advantage over the others.

Along with the political doctrine of equilibrium, the economic theory, later to become known as "mercantilism," stressed the necessity of each state cultivating its own unique resources and developing its full potential strength in relation to the others (see Schmoller, 1896; Knorr, 1944; Hecksher, 1955; Wilson, 1958). The assumption upon which this theory rested was that the European states, though interdependent, coexisted competitively in what would now be called a "zero-sum game" in which one could gain only at the expense of another. As Bacon put it, "whatsoever is somewhere gotten, is somewhere lost" (quoted in King, 1948). If any one state failed to maintain its strength, it was thought that the result would be unwarranted gains on the part of other states, the ultimate consequence of which might be the destruction of the precarious European equilibrium. Thus, a politically and economically powerful corporate state was deemed to be important both for its own domestic security and for the well-being of the larger international system.

The situation in the seventeenth century, therefore, resembled in many respects the political situation in the contemporary world, especially in the importance that was attached to the power of competing states, and in the degree to which this power was evaluated, perhaps less in terms of control over subject populations, but in comparison with other states occupying similar positions in the world-system. Both in reality and in normative understandings, the world-economy of seventeenth-century Europe was characterized by competition among states to develop their political, social, and economic resources to the fullest possible extent.

Evidence has already been presented of the extent to which states competed to attract and retain eminent scientists. In mercantilist theory science was regarded, like material resources, as a storehouse of strength with which each country had been differently endowed and it was up to the officials of each country to develop this potential.

> Laffemas, the earliest of the French economic writers who attempted to work the scattered mercantilist ideas into a complete system, proposed the organization of *Chambres des manufactures* which should instruct youth in "sciences" and teach them to study scientific treatises. In his *Economies royales* . . . the Duc de Sully, who had been the principal finance minister of Henry IV, proposed an industrial museum like that suggested by Descartes; there should be set up in the Louvre a collection of models of machines used in industries. A. de Montchretien, who had traveled in Holland, Germany, and Switzerland, proposed the establishment in France of the sort of elementary industrial training which he had seen abroad [Artz, 1966:24].

Not only the domestic good of the nation, but the collective good of the entire region depended upon the responsible cultivation of the sciences. As one observer of the times wrote in 1646,

> Each climate receives its particular influences; these influences communicate divers qualities, and the qualities create divers talents of the mind, and by consequence divers kinds of sciences and industries among men. Some are suited for Philosophy, others for mechanics, others to some arts and particular exercises: the Author of nature distributing thus unequally his gifts and his talents to men, in order to render them reliant on one another, and to oblige them to share what they have in particular [quoted in King, 1948:135].

It is difficult to know how much the political and economic competition of the mercantilist period may have contributed to the provision of patronage to the sciences. One thing that seems clear is that this competition carried over into the realm of science, as we have seen, and that it was typically the countries that provided the greatest patronage and resources, either in the form of royal stipends as in France or in the form of private support and state offices as in England, that attracted the most eminent scientists. One thing that also seems clear is that the competitive spirit of the age was not wholly lost upon scientists themselves. For example, it is easy to see the undercurrent of this spirit in the following appeal to Louis XIV on behalf of a proposal to found a national observatory:

> Its *Project* is so great, and may be so glorious for the state, and so useful for the public, if it is executed in all its details, that it is impossible not to be persuaded that Your Majesty, who has designs so vast and so magnificent, should not approve and favor it; and I can declare that all the neighboring nations have been for some time in an incredible expectation of so great an establishment [quoted in Brown, 1934:145].

The observatory was built at a cost of 700,000 *livres*.

While much of the incentive for patronizing the sciences may have been rooted in strictly utilitarian considerations, it should probably be acknowledged that this patronage may have also been motivated by expressive or "ceremonial" concerns. The seventeenth century was the great age of ceremony. In the arts, in architecture, and in learning, it was the age of the baroque, of Versailles, of the richly ornamented facade and the ornamental garden, the heroic tragedy, great operas and orchestras, punctilious court etiquette, the King James Bible, and St. Paul's Cathedral (Ogg, 1972:36–38). The seventeenth century was also the age of high ceremony and protocol in diplomatic relations and it was the age of what G. N. Clark (1947:139–143) has called "speculative wars", which dramatized state boundaries by testing the military strength of opposing forces.

It is perhaps not surprising that ceremony should have been as pronounced as it was in the seventeenth century, given what has already been said about the European world-economy. Lacking a central authority capable of defining and legitimating the membership and status of states in the European system, ceremonial activities may have served as an alternative means of dramatizing the strength and status of states to one another. These activities may have also served as a means of demonstrating each state's ability to maintain and defend its position in the European system and of manifesting each state's subscription to norms and expectations common to members of the system. In a somewhat parallel context, for example, Meyer and Rowan (1977) have observed that formal organizations in competitive environments often develop formal structures that, among whatever other functions they may fulfill, dramatize the status and purposes of the organization to its competitors.

There are several reasons for suspecting that science may have been patronized, though perhaps not in any deliberate or systematic fashion, because of its ceremonial value. For one, the arts were just as likely to be the recipients of patronage as the sciences (Wolf, 1951; Foss, 1971)—something that one would not expect had utilitarian concerns been the sole motivation for patronage. For another, the scientists who received patronage and who were elected to the royal academies were more often men of eminence, whose sponsorship added prestige to the state, than men of proven practical accomplishments. For example, in describing the members of the Academy of Sciences, Roger Hahn observes:

> Among them were men of considerable cultural attainments and erudition, such as Pierre Carcavi and Christiaan Huygens, the polymath Marin Cureau de La Chambre, the Oratorian theologian Jean-Baptiste Du Hamel, the magistrate Bernard Frenicle de Bessy, and Charles Perrault's equally famous brother, the architect and physician Claude Perrault. Though many were intimately concerned with the practical applications of scientific studies, none was selected for his technical prowess alone. . . . A tacit understanding almost seems to have existed that a sound liberal education rather than apprenticeship in a trade was a proper qualification for admission. Hence, from the outset, there was a certain social and intellectual bond in the Royal Academy which ran counter to the hopes of the framers of the Company. Artisans were clearly excluded [1971:14–15].

A similar picture is given in Maurice Ashley's description of the Royal Society:

> One is particularly struck by the versatility of the members of the Royal Society. They included John Aubrey, the author of the *Brief Lives* of his contemporaries . . . John Evelyn, botanist and numismatist, and Samuel Pepys, the naval administrator, . . . John Locke, metaphysician, educationist, political philosopher, theologian, physician, and man of affairs; Sir William Petty, who contends with Captain John Graunt for the distinction of being the first English statistician or 'political arithmetician'; Dr John Wallis, who wrote books on arithmetic as well as English grammar; John Dryden, the poet; Wren, the architect; Dr John Williamson, the politician; the Duke of Buckingham and the Earl of Sandwich; Sir Kenelm Digby, the Roman Catholic, who collected book bindings and invented the 'powder of sympathy' to heal wounds; and even the Moroccan ambassador who was admitted as an honorary member. Besides them stood scientists whose names are still universally honoured: Robert Boyle, the "father of modern chemistry" and inventor of Boyle's law; Isaac Barrow, the mathematician and clergyman; Robert Hooke, city surveyor, mathematician, physicist, and a great inventive genius; and Jonathan Goddard, one of the first English makers of telescopes [1973:156].

Many of these individuals, as we shall see later, were also placed in diplomatic positions where their eminence could serve directly to dramatize the prestige of their sponsoring governments.

It has also been observed that patronage continued to be granted to the sciences even when it was evident that few scientists were especially concerned about practical problems and few practical solutions seemed to be directly attributable to the work of scientists. It seems doubtful that patronage would have been as consistent in the absence of more pronounced practical accomplishments had patronage been given only for utilitarian considerations. But even when science wasn't of practical value, it may have functioned as a locus of erudition. Thus, by supporting the sciences—even nominally as Charles II did in chartering the Royal Society—representatives of state could demonstrate their commitment to learning, rationality, and modernity.

In short, the decentralized and competitive social structure of the larger European system in the seventeenth century may have contributed to the interest that representatives of state showed in patronizing the sciences, perhaps for both utilitarian and ceremonial reasons. Patrons also supported the sciences for a host of personal reasons; many probably supported the sciences sheerly because of personal fascination. Had it been strictly a matter of personal whim whether or not the sciences received patronage, however, this aspect of the institutionalization process might not have developed to the extent that it did. What the social structure of the larger European system did was to create a competitive situation, both practically and normatively, that encouraged the leading states to develop their national resources, among which was scientific experimentation.

Legitimation

Traditional explanations have paid more attention to the legitimation of early scientific activities than to the other aspects of scientific institutionalization that have just been considered and they have been relatively more successful at explaining legitimation than these other aspects. It is probably reasonable to say that Protestant and capitalistic values, insofar as both stressed the practical realities of this life and of nature, helped to legitimate science even beyond those specific areas where Protestantism and capitalism were most successful. It is probably reasonable as well to suppose that Protestantism and capitalism were pervasive enough that their values "filtered down" sufficiently to individual scholars to have some direct motivating potential in the direction of scientific careers, as Merton in particular has stressed.

To this discussion of scientific legitimation can be added the suggestion that science may have also received a significant share of legitimation from its relation to the state. In an age when even religious claims were coming to be subordinate to the ideology of *raison d'etat* and when enterprises ranging from trading ventures to societies of literature looked to the state for justification, it would be surprising if science did not also receive legitimation from the state. We have already seen that there was, indeed, a close relation between science and the seventeenth-century state—(*a*) in the numbers of scientists who received patronage from the state, (*b*) in the numbers of scientists who occupied positions within state bureaucracies, and (*c*) in the numbers of state officials who took a personal interest in science as amateur experimenters. There is also evidence suggesting that scientists, for their part, were aware of the importance of receiving official sanctioning of this nature.

It has been said that Galileo's willingness to recant his views to the Church was less a sign of any weakness of character as it was an indication of his conviction that good relations with the Church, as the most powerful authority in his immediate milieu, were critical to the legitimacy and survival of the fledgling sciences (Geymonat, 1965). It was this same conviction, allegedly, that motivated him to devote over 20 years of his life to dialogue with representatives of the Church on behalf of his discoveries and to make every effort to enlist the powerful Medici in his struggle.

In England the members of the invisible college, though by no means of exclusive royalist persuasion, were quick to agree on the importance of soliciting a royal charter for their society from Charles II. It has been more generally argued that royal legitimation, even before the founding of the Royal Society, was one of the decisive influences that attracted scientists to England and permitted science to flourish there to the extent that it did.

> On the Continent, except perhaps in Holland and Denmark, there was no country where the learned man who wanted to try new methods of scholarship and research, without any practical purpose, could count as much as in England on sympathetic recognition and authoritative support. For several generations the universities and the ecclesiastical foundations, including the churches set up by the Reformers, had been generally hostile to revolutionary intellectual innovations. Queen Elizabeth's patronage of Gilbert was a symptom of a new attitude among the mighty toward the experimenter and his efforts. Isaac Casaubon (1559–1614), the French classical scholar, could not find satisfactory conditions for his work either at Geneva or at Paris, and in 1610 he finally sought asylum at the English court and became a naturalized Englishman. Casaubon's biographer, Mark Pattison, tells us that the court of James I, for all the king's pedantry, was the only court in Europe where the learned professions were in any degree appreciated. It is significant that Kepler, who must have known of James I's visit to the observatory of Brahe in Denmark in 1590, should have thought enough of the king's scientific interests to dedicate to him *De harmonice mundi,* a work published at Augsburg in 1619, in which the great scientist announced his third law of motion. During James I's reign, with Francis Bacon in office as solicitor-general and later as attorney-general, the outlook on experimental inquiry by learned men was more liberal in England than in other parts of Europe. So the English court provided new experimental work with official approval such as could be obtained almost nowhere else [Nef, 1964:324].

The relation between this sort of legitimation and the decentralized character of the European world-economy is indirect, of course. If it can be argued, as attempted in the previous section, that the actual and normative political competition that characterized the mercantilist world-economy of the seventeenth century was an inducement to the patronage of science, both for utilitarian and for ceremonial reasons (although in varying degrees in different countries), then this aspect of the larger European social system also contributed indirectly to the legitimation that came with patronage from the state. It is perhaps useful to mention at least two specific consequences of this legitimation. First, to the extent that official approval of the sciences on the part of the state fulfilled ceremonial functions as well as strictly utilitarian interests, science was afforded an a priori form of legitimation which did not depend on the production of immediately useful knowledge. As we have seen, science continued to receive support even though its practical accomplishments were as yet of perhaps minimal importance in comparison with those being made outside of science. This support and approval was probably of special value in the period when science was first becoming institutionalized—that is, before its legitimacy became independently rooted in discoveries and technological contributions.

The second consequence of receiving legitimation from the state that may have been of particular importance to the development of science was the fact that this legitimation gave science additional autonomy from the established universities. It was important for the state to function as a corporate unit, according to mercantilist philosophy, especially in the eyes of its rivals in the European system. As far as the universities were concerned, however, they had, following the decline of the church's influence, become a force increasingly associated with local interests (Lytle, 1974; Morgan, 1974; Stone, 1974). By supporting scientific activities outside the universities, the state was able to circumvent the power of the universities to some degree and, in turn, science received from the state a strong voice in overcoming resistance from within the universities to the new methods and discoveries it sought to propound (cf., Ben-David, 1971).

Communication and Organization

The remaining aspect of institutionalization that was mentioned earlier has to do with the fact that any institution must manifest a minimal degree of communication among its members and must organize its activities into stable patterns of organization if it is to survive. The two most notable developments along these lines in seventeenth-century science were the institutionalization of an extensive international communication network among scientists and the organization of scientists into national academies. The latter has been carefully described in studies by Harcourt Brown, (1934), Roger Hahn (1971), W. E. Knowles Middleton (1971), Martha Ornstein

(1975), and others. The former has been studied less systematically, but there is ample evidence of the extensive communication that existed among European scientists from at least the middle of the sixteenth century onward.

For example, Henry Oldenberg carried on an extensive correspondence with scientists throughout Europe from his home in England. A similar network was established in France through the efforts of Mersenne. Galileo appears to have kept informed of Kepler's research through personal correspondence. Galileo is also alleged to have first learned of the Dutch telescope from correspondence with a French nobleman, Jacques Badovere (Drake, 1957:28–29). Besides correspondence, scientists also learned of one another's work through extensive foreign travel. For example, 44 of the 65 eminent sixteenth- and seventeenth-century scientists discussed in Taton's *History of Science* had been educated abroad, had traveled extensively, or had worked in countries other than those in which they had been born.

Had Europe in the seventeenth century consisted simply of a set of relatively autonomous countries, as textbook history has often portrayed it, it would likely have been less conducive to the kind of international communication that developed within the scientific community. The fact was, however, that the various countries of Europe by the seventeenth century had become highly interconnected economically and politically. Regular shipments of naval stores from the Baltic to the Mediterranean by way of the German trading cities, or grain from Poland to England via the Netherlands, or wool from England to the Netherlands in return for finished cloth had become commonplace, ensuring that correspondence and informal flows of information would occur on a routine basis (Wallerstein, 1974).

With increasing economic interdependence also came attempts to institutionalize diplomatic relations (Mattingly, 1955). These especially appear to have augmented the flow of information among scientists. For example, most of the extensive international correspondence of the Accademia del Cimento was carried on by resident ministers of the Grand Duke of Tuscany, such as Lorenzo Magalotti in France, and other persons in diplomatic service (Middleton, 1971). For another example, Sir Francis Bacon spent 4 years at the French court in the retinue of the English ambassador where he came into contact with a number of French scientists. William Harvey visited Germany in 1636 in the company of the English ambassador and made observations which served importantly in the writing of his *Anatomical Exercises on the Generation of Animals* (1651). Sir John Finch, a noted English astronomer, became the resident minister of Charles II in Florence. The French diplomat Frenicle, a protegé of Melchisadec Thevenot, is said to have been an important link between experimenters in Italy and experimenters in France. Thevenot himself, founder of one of the forerunning academies to the Academy of Sciences, was both scientist and diplomat and maintained close contact between scientists in France and Italy during the 1650s. Leibniz, of course, was also both scientist and diplomat. Perhaps Dorothy Stimson (1948) has described the situation most clearly:

> Though there were no newspapers as yet, even then a net-work of communications linked England with the European countries. Men went abroad on government or on private business and brought back European books as well as news. Students wandered from university to university in Italy, France, Holland. Men, exiled to foreign cities, when restored to favor, brought back with them new tastes, new ideas, new interests learned abroad [p. 146].

Scientists, in a sense, were welded into a single transnational community through their correspondence, travel, and common interests. However, no single scientific body emerged of the kind that might have eventually stifled creativity and diversity of opinion. Instead, separate scientific academies developed in the various European states. The circumstances surrounding the founding of these academies have been studied extensively. What is of interest in the present context is that the political and economic competition that characterized the European state-system in the seventeenth century also seems to have been reflected in competition among the scientific academies themselves. The rivalry between the Royal Society and the Academy of Sciences is well know. Such rivalry, it appears, also characterized some of the earlier academies in Italy. Indeed, one theory of the founding of the Accademia del Cimento in Tuscany—the theory espoused by the distinguished Italian historian Riguccio Galluzzi—suggests that its founding may have been at least partly motivated by the founding of an Academy of Belles Lettres in Vienna a year previously (1656).

Middleton (1971) discounts this theory on the grounds that the Academy was short-lived and had nothing to do with scientific experimentation. Yet the fact remains that the founders of the Accademia del Cimento were aware of the other academy and that the two were organized along similar lines in their respective states. Middleton's research has also uncovered evidence in letters from the 1650s showing the rivalry then beginning to exist between the Montmor Academy in Paris and the scientists associated with Prince Leopold in Tuscany. For example, a letter from Constantyn Huygens to his brother Christiaan remarks

> We have had a good laugh at that fine assembly at Monsieur de Montmor's, and what happened in that meeting of fools when you were there hardly makes us respect the intelligence of these academicians, who patiently listen to pedants jawing for hours on end about nothings. To tell you what I think, it seems to me that those gentlemen in Florence are worth much more than these Parisians and treat things with fore-thought and modesty [pp. 298–299].

Rivalry such as that expressed in Huygen's letter may have contributed to the multiplicity of academies that developed across Europe in the seventeenth century, and these in turn, may have afforded greater intellectual freedom than might have been present had a single academy, capable of imposing its opinion on all, developed. Rivalries between scientists in different states may have also reinforced skepticism and criticism of the kind useful for the advancement of scientific knowledge. It has been suggested, for example, that there were probably not more than three or four people in all of Europe capable of understanding Newton's *Principia* at the time it was published (Wolf, 1951:224). Among these were Halley in England, Huygens in France, and Leibniz in Germany. It may not be entirely coincidental that, of the three, only Halley accepted Newton's work without reservation; Huygens and Leibniz by comparison raised important criticisms, some of which were not answered until the nineteenth century.

What these pieces of evidence suggest is that the structure of the larger European world-system—integrated yet decentralized—was reproduced in the scientific community. Scientists not only interacted with one another across national boundaries, but organized themselves into competing bodies. There was within the scientific community already in the seventeenth century, therefore, the making of an integrated yet flexible institution capable of expanding and adapting as its own discoveries and the growth of modern political and economic conditions dictated.

Core and Periphery in the Institutionalization of Science

Thus far, the important differences that existed among the various European countries in their contributions to scientific activity have been overlooked in the interest of discussing some of the general implications for the institutionalization of science of the decentralized social structure of the European system. With this background, some suggestions can now be formulated from the same perspective about the sources of national differences and similarities. An important distinction that informs work on the early modern world-system is that between *core* areas, which are politically and economically dominant, and *periphery* areas, which are politically and economically dependent. From the perspective of the world-system as a whole, core areas occupy *structurally similar* positions that differ from those occupied by the periphery. Core areas can be expected to generate some of the same kinds of activities, therefore, merely because of their structurally similar positions, despite the fact that they may differ greatly from one another on other political, religious, or economic characteristics. Similarly, certain activities would be expected to be common to periphery areas, despite other domestic differences in these areas.

The implication of this argument for the institutionalization of science is that scientific activity might be expected to manifest similarities in areas occupying structurally similar positions in the world-system, regardless of other differences in these areas. In particular, the hypothesis might be put forth that science should show similar overall patterns of growth in core areas of the world-system, despite political and religious or other differences, because of certain advantages accruing to core areas due to their central position in the world-system. These advantages might include (a) the flow of economic resources toward the core, making it possible for the core to support a larger educated elite from whom scientists and patrons of science could be recruited and a larger state bureaucracy providing offices and patronage to scientists; (b) the central position of the core in relation to channels of trade, diplomacy, and communication; and (c) the greater role of ceremonial activities for the purpose of legitimating the power and position of states in relation to one another in the core (cf., Shils, 1972; von Gizycki, 1973).

It is possible to test this hypothesis, at least indirectly, not only by comparing the scientific activity of core and periphery areas, but also by examining the changes in scientific activity that occur as countries move in or out of the core over time. Two generalized indicators of scientific activity are available for the period 1500 to 1850: (a) the number of scientists living in selected countries as calculated from Marquis' *Who's Who in Science,* and (b) the number of discoveries in selected countries listed in Darmstädter's handbook of scientific and technical discoveries.

The data on numbers of scientists (see Figure 3.1) show the relative dominance of the Hapsburg domains (Spain, Italy, and Germany) in 1500 and the increasing shift away from these domains as the core of the European world-economy moved toward northern Europe, particularly to England and France, with the eventual inclusion of Germany. What is noteworthy about the patterns for the latter countries is their similarity. Despite great differences in religion, population, and form of government, the numbers of scientists and the trends in these numbers are virtually the same in England and France and, after 1700, in Germany.

In contrast to the growth manifested in northern Europe, the precipitous decline in the status of Spain during the sixteenth century is accompanied by a concurrent decline in its number of scientists. The general shift in the status of Italy from a core power to a semiperipheral area is reflected in the arrest of its scientific growth after about 1600 and its increasing displacement as a center of scientific activity by England, France, and Germany. The Netherlands also affords a particularly interesting case. Its posi-

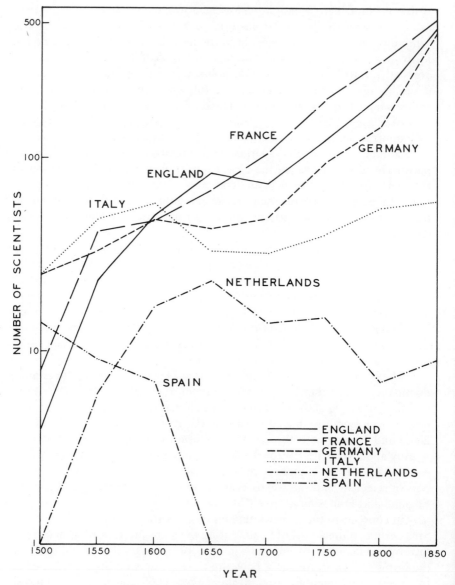

Figure 3.1. *Scientists by country, 1500–1850.*

tion of economic hegemony in the early seventeenth century along with England and France is reflected in the rapid increase in its number of scientists until approximately 1650, after which its declining power, owing to its various military defeats at the hands of England and France, is also reflected in the decline of its scientific activity. This decline, it might be noted, has been linked directly to the declining status of the Dutch in relation to England, especially in the eighteenth century (Levere, 1970).

As far as the periphery countries were concerned (not shown in Figure 3.1), they contained virtually no scientists. For example, one scientist is recorded in Poland in 1500; one in 1550; three in 1600; none in 1650; none in 1700; one in 1750; four in 1800; and twelve in 1850. Denmark had none in 1500; none in 1550; four in 1600; six in 1650; five in 1700; three in 1750; nine in 1800; and fourteen in 1850. Portugal showed a similar pattern. In contrast, it is interesting to observe that a quite different pattern obtained in those countries that became semiperipheral areas to Britain in the eighteenth and nineteenth centuries. For example, the United States, Ireland, and Scotland all had steep growth curves accompanying their inclusion into the world-economy after about 1750.

Figure 3.2 shows the data on scientific discoveries. Again, there are differences between core and periphery areas that closely resemble the differences in the numbers of scientists. Spain and Italy are again prominent at the beginning of the sixteenth century, but the position of Spain declines markedly after 1550 and discoveries in Italian science appear to level off after 1600. From 1600 onward, approximately the same number of discoveries are made in England, France, and Germany—with Germany taking a slight lead around 1850. Scientific discoveries in the Netherlands rank nearly equal to England, France, and Germany in 1600 and grow at nearly the same rates until 1700, after which they lag increasingly behind the numbers made in the core countries. Again, scientific discoveries are virtually absent in the periphery countries.

These indicators, of course, mask important differences in the kinds of scientific work being done in the various countries at different times—differences in style, subject matter, and quality of research, owing both to differences in cultural traditions and in the talents of individual scientists. But they suggest a crude correspondence between levels of scientific activity and countries' positions in the larger European world-economy. The reasons for this correspondence undoubtedly include social conditions indigenous to particular countries preceding both their position in the world-economy and their level of scientific activity. Apart from these conditions, however, the similarities in levels of scientific activity in countries occupying similar positions in the larger European system suggest that influences of this larger system cannot be ignored.

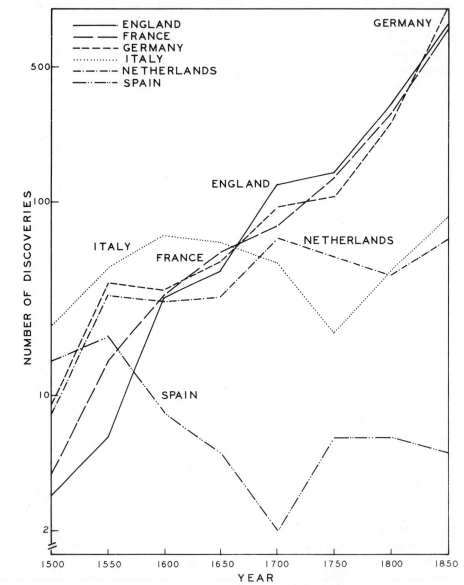

Figure 3.2. *Discoveries by country, 1500–1850.*

Some Implications

In concluding, some implications of the foregoing for the analysis of contemporary science may be suggested. First, it seems evident that there continue to be similarities in the scientific activities of countries occupying similar positions in the world-system, despite gross differences in the domestic structure of these societies. Contrary to the argument that science and totalitarianism are mutually exclusive, for example, the Soviet Union has emerged as a major competitor of the United States in scientific research. The achievements of both in science and technology not only serve to maintain their status as core nations in the modern world but to dramatize this status to one another and to the other nations of the world. Manifestations of these achievements, whether in explorations of outer space, military hardware, or consumer products, dramatize not only the powers of science but of the societies sponsoring them. Nobel prizes especially, as Harriet Zuckerman (1967;1977) has shown, become cherished tokens of national wisdom in much the same way that Olympic medals symbolize national fitness or physical prowess. However different in domestic social structure, the core countries of the world have felt compelled to participate in this ceremonial scientific competition and have allowed this competition to influence their scientific activities.

Second, it appears that periods of intense national competition such as that which prevailed in the seventeenth century (though not necessarily war) have been particularly conducive to the rapid development of science. The great steps forward in atomic research during World War II cannot be fully explained without taking account of the conflict present in the larger world-system, nor can the rapid buildup of scientific research in the 1960s be explained apart from the Cold War competition between the two leaders of the post-war world. Despite the universalistic norms and the cosmopolitan attachments of the scientific community, science has frequently been the beneficiary of rivalries among core nations.

Finally, the foregoing discussion suggests certain continuities in the history of science. Contrary to popular arguments distinguishing between the contemporary problems associated with "big" science and the historic opportunities associated with "little" science, there appear to be some similarities in the social factors conditioning the institutionalization of science throughout the entire modern era. In particular, it seems worth emphasizing that the close relation between contemporary science and the state is not entirely new, but can be illustrated, as we have seen, in as early a period as the seventeenth century.

It is perhaps worth restating that my aim in this chapter has not been to present a thorough analysis of the relations between the European world-economy and the institutionalization of modern science in the seventeenth century but rather to suggest what some of these relations may have been and, thereby, to illustrate some of the possibilities that the world-system perspective may entail for the historical analysis of scientific development. Nor have I suggested that conditions at the level of the larger European system are *more* important for understanding the institutionalization of modern science than conditions internal to particular countries or internal to science itself; only that these larger conditions should not be ignored.

References

Anderson, Perry
1974   *Lineages of the Absolutist State.* London: Humanities Press.
Artz, Frederick B.
1966   *The Development of Technical Education in France, 1500–1850.* Cambridge, Mass.: MIT Press.
Ashley, Maurice
1973   *England in the Seventeenth Century.* London: Penguin Books.
Barber, Bernard
1962   *Science and the Social Order.* New York: Collier Books.
Barnes, Barry
1974   *Scientific Knowledge and Sociological Theory.* London: Routledge & Kegan Paul.
Barraclough, Goeffrey
1963   *European Unity in Thought and Action.* Oxford: Basil Blackwell.
Ben-David, Joseph
1971   *The Scientist's Role in Society.* Englewood Cliffs, N.J.: Prentice–Hall.
Bernal, J. D.
1971   *Science in History,* 4 vols. Cambridge, Mass.: MIT Press.
Braudel, Fernand
1973   *Capitalism and Material Life, 1400–1800* (Miriam Kochan, trans.). New York: Harper & Row.
Brown, Harcourt
1934   *Scientific Organizations in Seventeenth Century France (1620–1680).* Baltimore: Johns Hopkins University Press.
Burke, Peter
1974   *Venice and Amsterdam: A Study of Seventeenth-Century Elites.* London: Temple Smith.
Clark, G. N.
1947   *The Seventeenth Century,* 2nd. ed. London: Oxford University Press.
1970   *Science and Social Welfare in the Age of Newton.* Oxford: Clarendon Press.
Drake, Stillman
1957   *Discoveries and Opinions of Galileo.* Garden City, N.Y.: Doubleday.
Fischer, Wolfram, and Peter Lundgreen
1975   "The recruitment and training of administrative and technical personnel." In Charles Tilly (ed.), *The Formation of National States in Western Europe.* Princeton: Princeton University Press.

Foss, Michael
    1971   *The Age of Patronage: The Arts in Society, 1660–1750.* London: Hamilton.
Geyl, Pieter
    1932   *The Revolt of the Netherlands, 1555–1609.* London: Williams & Norgate.
Geymonat, Ludovico
    1965   *Galileo Galilei: A Biography and Inquiry into His Philosophy of Science.* Stillman
            Drake, (trans.), New York: McGraw-Hill.
Greaves, Richard L.
    1969   "Puritanism and science: The anatomy of a controversy." *Journal of the History of
            Ideas* (July):345–368.
Hackmann, W. D.
    1976   "The growth of science in the Netherlands in the seventeenth and early eighteenth
            centuries." In Maurice Crosland (ed.), *The Emergence of Science in Western Europe.*
            New York: Science History Publications.
Hahn, Roger
    1962   *The Fall of the Paris Academy of Sciences During* the French Revolution. Cornell
            University: Unpublished Ph.D. Dissertation.
    1971   *The Anatomy of a Scientific Institution: The Paris Academy of Science, 1666–1803.*
            Berkeley and Los Angeles: University of California Press.
    1976   "Scientific careers in eighteenth century France." In Maurice Crosland (ed.), *The
            Emergence of Science in Western Europe.* New York: Science History Publications.
Hall, A. Rupert
    1963   "Merton revisited: Science and society in the 17th century." *History of Science* 11:1–
            16.
    1967   "Scientific method and the progress of techniques." In E. E. Rich and C. H. Wilson
            (eds.), *The Cambridge Economic History of Europe,* Vol. IV: The Economy of Ex-
            panding Europe in the Sixteenth and Seventeenth Centuries. Cambridge: Cambridge
            University Press.
    1972   "Science, technology and Utopia in the seventeenth century." In Peter Mathias (ed.),
            Science and Society, 1600–1900. Cambridge: Cambridge University Press.
Hans, Nicholas
    1951   *New Trends in Education in the Eighteenth Century.* London: Routledge & Kegan
            Paul.
Hecksher, Eli F.
    1955   *Mercantilism,* 2 vols. London: Allen & Unwin.
Hessen, Boris
    1971   *The Social and Economic Roots of Newton's 'Principia.'* New York: Howard Fertig.
Holborn, Hajo
    1976   *A History of Modern Germany,* Vol. I: The Reformation. New York: Alfred A.
            Knopf.
Hooykaas, R.
    1972   *Religion and the Rise of Modern Science.* Grand Rapids, Mich.: Eerdmans.
Kagan, Richard L.
    1974   "Universities in Castile, 1500–1810." In Lawrence Stone (ed.), *The University in So-
            ciety,* Vol. II: *Europe, Scotland and the United States from the 16th to the 20th Cen-
            tury.* Princeton: Princeton University Press.
King, James E.
    1948   *Science and Rationalism in the Government of Louis XIV, 1661–1683.* Baltimore:
            Johns Hopkins Press.
Knorr, Klaus
    1944   *British Colonial Theories, 1570–1850.* Toronto: The University of Toronto Press.

Levere, Trevor H.
  1970   "Relations and rivalry: Interactions between Britain and the Netherlands in eigh-
         teenth-century science and technology." *History of Science* 9:42–53.
Lytle, Guy F.
  1974   "Patronage patterns and Oxford colleges, c. 1300–1530." In Lawrence Stone (ed.),
         The University in Society, Vol. I: *Oxford and Cambridge from the 14th to the Early
         19th Century.* Princeton: Princeton University Press.
Mattingly, Garrett
  1955   *Renaissance Diplomacy.* Boston: Houghton Mifflin.
McKie, Douglas
  1960   "The origins and foundation of the Royal Society of London." In Harold Hartley
         (ed.), *The Royal Society: Its Origins and Founders.* London: The Royal Society.
Merton, Robert K.
  1970   *Science, Technology and Society in Seventeenth-Century England.* New York:
         Harper & Row.
  1973   *The Sociology of Science.* Chicago: University of Chicago Press.
Meyer, John W., and Brian Rowan
  1977   "Institutionalized organizations: Formal structure as myth and ceremony." *Ameri-
         can Journal of Sociology* 83: 340–363.
Middleton, W. E. Knowles
  1971   *The Experimenters: A Study of the Accademia del Cimento.* Baltimore: Johns Hop-
         kins Press.
Morgan, Victor
  1974   "Cambridge University and 'the country,' 1560–1640." In Lawrence Stone (ed.),
         The University in Society, Vol. I: *Oxford and Cambridge from the 14th to the Early
         19th Century.* Princeton: Princeton University Press.
Mulligan, Lotte
  1973   "Civil War politics, religion and the royal society." *Past and Present* 59: 92–116.
Needham, Joseph
  1954   *Science and Civilisation in China,* Vol. I: *Introductory Orientations.* Cambridge:
         Cambridge University Press.
Nef, John
  1964   *The Conquest of the Material World.* Chicago: University of Chicago Press.
Ogg, David
  1972   *Europe in the Seventeenth Century.* New York: Collier.
Ornstein, Martha
  1975   *The Role of Scientific Societies in the Seventeenth Century.* Chicago: University of
         Chicago Press.
Ortiz, Antonio D.
  1971   *The Golden Age of Spain, 1516–1659.* New York: Basic Books.
Polanyi, Michael
  1964   "The republic of science: Its political and economic theory." In Edward Shils (ed.),
         Criteria for Scientific Development: Public Policy and National Goals. Cambridge,
         Mass.: MIT Press.
Prebisch, Raul
  1959   "Commercial policy in the underdeveloped countries." *American Economic Review
         Papers and Proceedings* (May).
Price, Don K.
  1965   *The Scientific Estate.* Cambridge, Mass.: Harvard University Press.
Ravetz, Jerome
  1971   *Scientific Knowledge and Its Social Problems.* Oxford: Oxford University Press.

Schmoller, Gustav
1896 *The Mercantile System and Its Historical Significance.* New York: Macmillan.
Shils, Edward A.
1962 "The autonomy of science." In Bernard Barber and Walter Hirsch (eds.), *The Sociology of Science.* New York: Free Press.
1972 "Metropolis and Province in the Intellectual Community." In Edward Shils (ed.), *The Intellectuals and the Powers.* Chicago: University of Chicago Press.
Stimson, Dorothy
1948 *Scientists and Amateurs: A History of the Royal Society.* New York: Henry Schuman.
Stone, Lawrence
1967 *The Crisis of the Aristocracy, 1558–1641.* Oxford: Oxford University Press.
1974 "The size and composition of the Oxford student body, 1580–1909." In Lawrence Stone (ed.), *The University in Society, Vol. I: Oxford and Cambridge from the 14th to the Early 19th Century.* Princeton: Princeton University Press.
von Gizycki, Rainald
1973 "Centre and periphery in the international scientific community." *Minerva* 11: 474–494.
Wallerstein, Immanuel
1974 *The Modern World-System.* New York: Academic Press.
Weber, Max
1951 *The Religion of China.* New York: Free Press.
Wilson, Charles
1958 *Mercantilism.* London: Routledge & Kegan Paul.
Wolf, John B.
1951 *The Emergence of the Great Powers, 1685–1715.* New York: Harper & Row.
Zilsel, Edgar
1942 "The sociological roots of science." *American Journal of Sociology* 47: 544–562.
Zuckerman, Harriet
1967 "The sociology of Nobel Prizes." *Scientific American* 217: 25–33.
1977 *Scientific Elite.* New York: Free Press.

World Order and Religious Movements

Against all the predictions of nineteenth-century sociologists, religious movements have survived and flourished in the modern world. We need not seek their causes in benighted minds or in abnormal personalities. Nor need we posit superhuman charismatic leadership to explain their persistence and frequency. For religious movements have emanated from the central social processes of the modern world itself. Groups whose lives have been intruded upon by the expanding world-economy have sought refuge in the security of religion. Rising cadres have legitimated their new status with religious creeds. Basic changes in the structure of world order have characteristically produced, and in turn have been nurtured by, exceptional outpourings of religious activity.

But religious movements have been distributed neither evenly nor at random in space and time. The early sixteenth century stands out as a time of great religious experimentation. The early seventeenth century also is notable, less as a time of sweeping reform, than as a time for a vast number and variety of new religious movements. The period in between was one of intense religious activity, but did not spawn religious movements in the numbers or magnitude of either the preceding or succeeding periods. In the eighteenth century, definitions of ultimate reality were fundamentally transformed by the Enlightenment, much as they had been by the Reformation. But it was not until the 1830s and 1840s that religious movements began again to multiply in large numbers. From the 1860s to the end of the nine-

57

STUDIES OF THE
MODERN WORLD-SYSTEM

teenth century, there was a period of relative calm in religious movements, although the seeds of another world-shaking redefinition of ultimate reality were being sown in the gradual evolution of Marxism. In the twentieth century, every decade has witnessed religious movements, but these movements have varied greatly in kind and in location. Few decades have given rise to as many religious movements as the late 1960s and early 1970s. By the early 1970s, in fact, some estimates suggested that the number of local new religious groups in America might number in the thousands, with some of the larger movements claiming adherents in the hundreds of thousands (Wuthnow, 1978).

In light of their uneven occurrence, it has been tempting for social scientists to seek the causes of modern religious movements in some form of rapid social change and its accompanying tensions and strain (cf., Glock and Stark, 1965:242–259; Wilson, 1970). Efforts have been made to classify the various religious responses to social strain and to show that different kinds of strain produce different kinds of religious movements. But these efforts run into trouble when confronted with historical reality.

They fail to explain, for example, why the rapid industrial changes of the 1880s and 1890s in the United States produced relatively *few* religious movements in comparison with the 1830s and 1840s. They fail to explain why the disruptions of two world wars produced fewer religious movements than the 1960s, or why Britain experienced more religious movements in the 1840s than it did in the 1780s during the Industrial Revolution. They also fail to explain why different periods have nourished wholly different types of religious movements. There have been profound reformations and there have been ephemeral cults. There have been great religious revivals and sweeping religious defections. Movements have developed within the churches as well as outside of the churches and against the churches. Conventional accounts of religious sects and cults have said little about many of these kinds of movements.

Religious Movements and World Order

My reading of history convinces me that modern religious movements can be understood better in conjunction with major changes in *world order* than they can be by looking only at changes within societies. By "world order," I mean simply the presence of a transnational division of labor in which societies and members of societies participate, necessitating recurrent, patterned exchange (economic, political, and cultural) across national boundaries. World orders are stratified into dominant, "core" areas and dependent, "periphery" areas. As with societies, the status of these areas and the relations among them tend to be patterned and legitimated by broad definitions of reality.

The modern world order had its origins in sixteenth-century Europe as the various local and regional economies of the Mediterranean, the Hanse, France, England, and the Baltic came to be integrated into a single system of production and exchange (Wallerstein, 1974). At the outset of the sixteenth century, the European world order was politically dominated by the expanding Spanish Hapsburg dynasty. But what distinguished the European world order from the various world-systems that had flourished in antiquity, and from contemporaries such as the Ottoman Empire, was that the Hapsburg dynasty failed in its attempts to bring the European world order under the hegemony of a centralized political empire. By the middle of the seventeenth century, a new system of world order, which later critics would call "mercantilism," had come into being, dominated by a politically decentralized core (England, France, and to a lesser extent the Netherlands), and encompassing all of Europe (but not Russia), colonies throughout much of North, Central, and South America, and trading centers in coastal parts of West Africa, India, China, and the Indonesian Archipelago (Schmoller, 1896; Chirot, 1977). As the colonial and protectionist trade policies of this system became increasingly cumbersome, a system of free trade dominated by the British empire gradually superseded the mercantilist system, resulting in a world-economy which included nearly all parts of the globe by the end of the nineteenth century (Polanyi, 1944; Fieldhouse, 1966; Hobsbawm, 1969). In the twentieth century, after the experience of two world wars, the establishment of a communist sector, and numerous nationalist movements throughout the Third World, the capitalist world-economy has continued to prevail and expand, but within a provisional diplomatic framework characterized by military tensions and economic uncertainty.

The main religious movements in modern history have been closely associated with periods of crisis and transition in the expanding capitalist world order so defined. Three kinds of periods, in particular, have given rise to intense religious activity: (a) periods in which the dominant world order has expanded rapidly to the point of producing strain in the basic institutions linking together core and periphery areas; (b) periods of overt polarization and conflict between core and periphery; and (c) periods in which newly stabilized patterns of world order are being reconstituted.

The first—expansionary periods—are best illustrated by the first half of the sixteenth century, in which the Hapsburg dynasty expanded to its farthest reaches; by the early eighteenth century, which saw the first wave of colonial expansion under the mercantilist system; and by the years sur-

rounding the turn of the present century, in which the second wave of colonial expansion took place. The second—periods of polarization—are most
evident in the late sixteenth, the late eighteenth, and the early twentieth centuries, all of which were dominated by international wars involving both
core and periphery powers. The third—periods of reconstitution—are
most clearly evidenced in the early seventeenth century, in the early nineteenth century, and in the period following World War II, in which the mercantilist, free trade, and contemporary (provisionally known as "detente")
forms of world order, respectively, were in the process of formation. The
differences in the political and economic processes prevailing in these three
kinds of periods have led to major differences in the kinds of religious activity characterizing these periods.

The kinds of religious activity generated in each period also differ
depending on whether it occurs among groups whose relation to power is
rising or among groups whose relation to power is declining (cf., Tilly,
1969). In expansionary periods, the main groups whose power increases are
new political and economic cadres in periphery areas, and the main groups
whose power decreases are members of the lower orders in periphery areas
who lose traditional rights vis-á-vis these cadres. In periods of polarization,
representatives of periphery areas struggling to secure independence from
the dominant core have tended to gain power, while representatives of the
core have typically lost power. In periods of reconstitution, strata associated
with emergent patterns of international exchange within each society have
been most likely to gain power, while strata associated with decaying patterns of international exchange have been likely to lose power.

The perspective afforded by regarding the context of religious movements as world order, rather than societies, makes it possible to better identify the major forms that modern religious movements have taken, and to
specify the important social conditions that have produced them. This identification is based on a simple argument: A population's place in the larger
world order strongly affects the manner in which it defines the major problems of its existence, and therefore, the nature of its religious orientations.
These religious orientations, for their part, channel the kinds of actions that
people take, and therefore, affect their influence upon the world order.
Without too much difficulty we can place the forms of modern religious
movements in the following categories: revitalization, reformation, religious
militancy, counter-reform, religious accommodation, and sectarianism. In
the pages that follow I shall attempt to outline briefly the social conditions
at the level of world order that have facilitated the formation of each of
these kinds of religious movements. This will serve as a context then for
some brief observations about the relations between world order and contemporary religious movements.

Revitalization

The term "revitalization" is Anthony Wallace's (1956). However, I would like to give it a more restrictive meaning which is both more in keeping with the movements with which Wallace was most concerned and more useful for discriminating among kinds of movements. Revitalization movements are attempts involving some form of religious ideology to collectively restore or reconstruct patterns of life that have been radically disrupted or threatened. The main varieties of revitalization movements include (*a*) nativistic movements, which attempt to purify their members from the influences of alien persons or customs; (*b*) revivalistic movements, which attempt to rediscover simple or natural styles of life perceived as being threatened by modern culture; (*c*) cargo cults, which attempt to import advantages supposedly available from alien persons or ideas; (*d*) millenarian movements, which attempt to prepare their members for the coming of an apocalyptic world transformation; and (*e*) messianic movements, which attempt to prepare for the coming of a divine saviour. Periods of revitalization may combine a number of these responses.

Conventional accounts of revitalization movements have emphasized social disruption as their source, but not all sorts of disruption produce revitalization. Natural disasters have displaced entire communities, but seldom have they been the source of revitalization movements. During World War II, much of Europe fell victim to devastation, yet largely without such movements developing. The kind of disruption that has produced revitalization movements most often has come from contact between traditional populations and a dominant cultural system (cf., Worsley, 1968). Such contact occasionally has been disruptive because of forced migration and resettlement, or because of violent conquest. But these disruptions usually have not produced revitalization movements, because they themselves impose new forms of social organization (e.g., Wolf, 1959:176–201). The kind of cultural contact that has most often produced revitalization movements is that which creates cleavages between local elites and the mass majority.

Cleavages of this sort have occurred on the widest scale during periods of rapid expansion in the modern world-economy. As trade flourishes and new markets become integrated into the world-economy, local elites who have previously been dependent upon local economies participate in the benefits of broader markets. Their new prosperity gives them greater power vis-a-vis subject populations, whose traditional rights can now be curtailed or neglected. Cleavage between local elites and subject populations is not only economically disadvantageous but socially disorganizing for these populations, since local elites in such settings typically remain in charge of distributing social services and enforcing the regulations that affect daily life.

Revitalization movements provide hopes that transcend immediate deprivations and inspire new modes of social organization.

These conditions are clearly illustrated in the origins of the Anabaptist movements of the early sixteenth century, which developed during a period of rapid expansion in trade, population, prices, political hegemony, and capitalist agriculture throughout Europe. This expansion brought to the territorial landlords and city magistrates of the German states, the Swiss Confederation, and Hapsburg Austria new opportunities for production and exchange beyond the local market, permitting and encouraging the erosion of seigneurial obligations. The sale or division of common lands, the replacement of land tenure with contractual relations, and the centralization of judicial functions resulted from this growth. In the wake of these infringements of traditional rights under the old "common" law, the Anabaptist movements occurred first and most extensively among those peasants who had enjoyed the greatest prosperity and freedom under these customs and, therefore, were most disinherited by their erosion (Williams, 1962).

Similar effects are again apparent in the early eighteenth century during the commercial and colonial expansion of the mercantilist system; for example, in the early Methodist movement among the miners at Bristol, in the religious awakening among the urban poor in Scotland, and in the various prophet cults among the Indians of North America. The same effects are also evident during the early years of the twentieth century in areas newly incorporated into the free trade system; for example, the Watchtower movement in South Africa, the widespread influence of Pentecostalism among the Toba Indians in Northern Argentina, the spiritualist movement in Singapore, and the cargo cults in Melanesia (Wilson, 1973).

The distinctive diversity of revitalization movements is a function, first, of the fact that these movements are aimed at restoring disparate local customs in the face of an expanding world-economy, and second, of the different forms in which this expansion becomes manifest. For example, revivalistic movements that stress individual salvation and piety, such as early Methodism, have been more common where individuals have been displaced from traditional groups and incorporated separately into new economic contexts. In contrast, cargo cults and nativistic movements have been more likely where whole groups have been collectively displaced, as among the North American Indians.

The evolution of revitalization movements has also varied with the kind of expansion experienced. Where commercial expansion has been accompanied by settlement colonies, revitalization movements have tended to be short-lived due to the reorganization or extinction of native populations. Where expansion has occurred through the incorporation of domestic lower classes into new occupational roles, these movements have generally evolved into established religious organizations, as in the evolution of Methodism in England. Revitalization movements have persisted as such on the widest scale among populations exposed to the dominant world order but not fully incorporated into its rights or style of life, as evidenced by the continued spread of these movements in the Third World.

Reformation

It has been suggested on numerous occasions that there have been three ideological reformations of unparalleled significance since the inception of the modern world order: the Protestant Reformation, the Enlightenment, and the growth of Marxism. Each successfully institutionalized a fundamental redefinition of ultimate reality. Of all religious movements, reformations have been the most distinctively international and can be understood only in the context of world order.

Reformations have been carried by rising elites in periphery areas during periods of rapid expansion in the world-system. Overall economic expansion incorporates these elites into wider markets and, as previously suggested, increases their freedom relative to subject populations. In the extreme, economic and political expansion has also created greater administrative burdens for core areas than for periphery areas, significantly increasing the competitive advantages of periphery elites in relation to the core. The correlative decentralization in the distribution of world power has afforded opportunities for the growth of new ideas, especially ones that challenge the hegemony of the core and legitimate the rising status of the periphery.

The Protestant Reformation occurred in the context of rapid population growth, a long-term rise in grain prices, great expansion in the volume and circulation of money due to the importation of bullion from America, naval and military innovations, and an intensification and broadening of trade. This expansion greatly benefited the German and Polish nobility, the Swiss city magistrates, and the Dutch and English merchants, all of whom prospered from the expanding trade between the Baltic and the Mediterranean. It was among these peripheral cadres that the Reformation first became institutionalized. The reformers' attacks against the Church implicitly desacralized the Hapsburg empire, whose legitimacy rested heavily in the defense of universal faith, and broadened access to legitimate authority. In the periphery the Reformation prompted the secularization of church lands, giving elites revenues independent of church and other taxes, and encouraging land reform beneficial to commercial agriculture. The net effect of this placed the periphery in a more favorable trading position in the world-economy. After the middle of the sixteenth century, owing significantly to the financial burdens which Spain incurred in combating the Protestant heresies, the core of the European economy shifted increasingly to the north, and with it the Reformation became firmly established.

Like the Reformation, the Enlightenment and the institutionalization of Marxism also took place during periods of demographic, economic, and territorial expansion, the first during the years in which the mercantilist system had spread to its farthest reaches through commercial, industrial, and colonial expansion, the second during the global explosion of trade and imperialism after the turn of the present century. The Enlightenment attracted the rising commercial and industrial classes in peripheral sectors of the world-economy, such as Manchester, Scotland, and North America, and was only later institutionalized in areas such as France and Prussia. Marxism was also most successfully institutionalized in areas peripheral to the European metropolis. Both challenged the legitimacy of prevailing patterns of world order and encouraged successful economic reforms, respectively of labor and capital, in the periphery. In all three cases, these were reformations from above, gaining institutionalization before achieving mass popularity.

The distinctive ideological coherence of each global reformation inhered in its opposition to the sacred assumptions underlying the prevailing world order. These assumptions were made the explicit objects of profanation: Church as Harlot, mercantilist protection as inimical to national wealth, bourgeois culture as false consciousness. Each reformation most vigorously attacked the rituals binding people to their most sacred institutions: the sacraments (for which Luther was excommunicated), the laws and tariffs of the mercantilist state, the fetishism of commodities in the free market. At the same time, each reformation posed a new definition of ultimate reality that liberalized access to the sacred: salvation by faith, freedom in reason, justice through proletarian revolution. The success of each reformation was determined by the conjunction of these ideas with the rising status of the elites that were attracted to new definitions of reality.

Religious Militancy

Relatively little attention has been paid to religious militancy as a type of social movement; yet, some of the most familiar of modern religious and quasi-religious experiments—Calvinists, Jacobins, Bolsheviks—have been of this kind. I shall define religious militancy as any diffuse movement which in the guise of an ultimate definition of reality actively attempts to overthrow an established social order through violent or forceful means. Though the offspring of reformations, these movements have typically espoused a more radical doctrinal departure from received definitions of reality, have believed in a more avenging God, and have championed the authority of the minority over the majority. They have generally been highly organized into tightly knit, strictly disciplined struggle groups.

Although many religious movements have taken militant stands, the broadest and most successful outbreaks of religious militancy have been among cadres in the periphery during periods of deep polarization and conflict in world order. These have been periods in which widespread economic instability and stagnation have produced divisive political strain within core areas, especially where these areas have been politically decentralized. Instability and strain of this sort have typically resulted in efforts on the part of the core to effectively tighten control over economically or politically strategic periphery areas. But these restrictions have seldom been received lightly in the periphery, particularly among elites having grown strong in autonomy during times of expansion and prosperity. The usual consequence has been conflict between periphery and core, as, for example, in the revolt of the Netherlands against Spain, the American revolution against England, and the various anticolonial revolts of the twentieth century.

The emergence of radically militant religious groups has been a function of the distinctive state of world order during periods of polarization. The weakened position of the core due to economic reversals and increasing military and bureaucratic expenditures has inhibited its ability to crush the formation of militant movements in the periphery. This has particularly been so when the resources of the core have been preoccupied with internal factionalism and war. Militant movements have been facilitated further by the social disorganization accompanying war, once war has emerged between core and periphery. An overwhelming number of the Dutch Calvinists who revolted against Spanish domination in the late sixteenth century, for example, were exiles from earlier purges in the Netherlands and elsewhere throughout Europe (Geyl, 1932). Beyond these conditions, a decisive circumstance contributing to the rise and spread of religious militancy has been the fact that periods of polarization in world order have usually followed upon the heels of successful reformations which have left the world divided ideologically and politically. The important consequences for militant religious movements have been twofold. First, these movements have been able to gain strength through international alliances and, indeed, have typically espoused highly internationalistic orientations (a fact that Troeltsch, 1960, emphasizes in his discussion of Calvinism, for example). Second, international political divisions have tended to promote competing domestic factions benefiting from, and therefore supporting, alternative foreign policies (the War of the Three Henrys being an extreme example). Internal rivalry of this sort has necessitated disciplined loyalty within the ranks of such factions. Militant religious devotion has been of strategic value to political mobilization in such periods of polarization.

Counter-Reform

Counter-reforms may be characterized as movements among institutionalized representatives of ultimate reality to strengthen the moral obligations that bind individuals to the corporate order. The beliefs of these movements conceive of ultimate reality in corporate terms and stress the immanence of ultimate reality in institutions representing the corporate order. Attainment of a relation with ultimate reality is made contingent upon participation in corporate sacraments and ceremonies. Examples include the renewal of Thomism in sixteenth-century Spain, the Gallican revival in eighteenth-century France, and the religious nationalism of the interwar years in the present century.

Counter-reforms have tended to occur in core areas during periods of polarization in world order, usually at least partly in reaction to the challenge of reformations and militant movements. It was in the context of the Protestant revolts, military setbacks, price inflation, and imperial bankruptcy that the Counter-Reformation experienced its greatest successes in the Hapsburg domains. It was in the period of colonial revolt against the mercantilist system, accompanied by growing disaffection among the lower classes and increasing rivalry and conflict among the core powers, that the romantic reaction against the Enlightenment emerged with its Rousseauean emphasis upon the authority of the general will. Similarly, it was in the aftermath of World War I, followed by the collapse of the balance of power system and the international gold standard which had undergirded the free market world order, that fascist ideologies commanding quasi-religious devotion spread throughout much of Europe.

In each case, the geopolitical conditions were much the same. Increasing military and administrative expenditures on the part of the core, together with declining export markets and enlarged foreign debts, produced an unfavorable balance of trade for the core, weakening further its domestic economy. To maintain the traditional system of stratification under these circumstances placed greater burdens, especially in the form of taxation, upon the lower strata. Declining economic opportunities among the upper strata also produced pressures upon the polity to absorb excess members of these strata into the administrative bureaucracy, especially through the bestowal of honorific titles, military pensions, and—where available—ecclesiastical offices.

The incentive for counter-reform came most directly from the need to reinforce the loyalties of the lower strata to the social order in the face of declining material rewards. Thus, the activities of counter-reforms, while including proselytizing activities toward the periphery, have been focused for the most part on the lower strata within the core, directed especially at undermining local, family, and ethnic ties providing alternative sources of identification to the social order. The capacity for such reforms to be carried out successfully has been enhanced greatly by the influx of new personnel into the central bureaucracies representing the established order.

Religious Accommodation

I shall employ the term "religious accommodation" to indicate movements that adapt mainstream religion to prevailing social conditions. The main varieties include (*a*) liberal reform movements within established religious organizations; (*b*) movements within these organizations to alleviate social problems; (*c*) the incorporation of minority or sectarian movements into the religious mainstream; and (*d*) movements of defection which strip religious organizations of certain traditional obligations.

Movements of these kinds have been particularly prominent in times when new patterns of world order were in the process of institutionalization. The emergence of the mercantilist system was accompanied, among other religious movements, by the Arminian movement in Holland, by the charitable movement initiated by Vincent de Paul in France, and by the incorporation of the Separatists and Independents in England. Similarly, the rise of the free trade system coincided with the Liberal-Catholic movement in France and Belgium and the great theological reforms of Schleiermacher, Hegel, and Strauss, the French monastic renewal oriented toward ministering to the poor, the incorporation of Protestant dissenters in England through the repeal of the Test and Corporation Acts, and with what Eric Hobsbawm (1962) has aptly called "the secularization of the masses" in speaking of the widespread religious defection that took place among the middle and lower classes during this period—to list but a few of the more prominent examples.

The social contexts nurturing these movements are far too complex to summarize in a few paragraphs, but at the level of world order the following conditions have contributed significantly to the prominence of these movements. These are the declining status of formerly dominant core areas during periods of reconstitution, the rising status of new core powers, new relations with periphery areas, and the temporary absence of a stable international monetary and diplomatic order. The major consequence of these conditions is an erosion of economic groups whose power has been protected by former patterns of international exchange and a strengthening of economic groups oriented to new patterns of international exchange.

This realignment, together with the overall economic instability deriving from the absence of an embracing international monetary order, generates civil conflict frequently resulting in some degree of political reform. This process occurs within the limits imposed by the interests of other nations and is conditioned by the presence of similar conflicts elsewhere. The net result consists typically not only of a change in the position of domestic interest groups but of a redefinition of government policy and of national role in the world-system. For established religion, especially where it has been in some measure subordinated to the polity, the consequences have usually included rising legitimacy for minority religions formerly critical of existing social arrangements, defection on the part of groups dissatisfied with the ossification of religious organizations, and efforts on the part of others to reform religious organizations in keeping with new political and moral climates. These have typically included social service activities functioning to alleviate hardships brought on the lower strata by the economic and political instability of the times.

As a brief example, the religious situation in England during the first half of the nineteenth century may be considered. By 1815 the mercantilist system of protective tariffs, colonial bilateralism, and state monopolies had been rendered obsolete by the successes of the American and French Revolutions, the high costs of the Napoleonic Wars, and the popularity of Enlightenment ideology. A new system of world order organized along principles of free trade was emerging, creating pressures for changes in domestic social organization. Most urgently needed was reform of the protective tariff policies on shipping and grain which kept British food prices unnaturally high in view of cheaper sources from the United States and Prussia, thereby preventing wage levels from sinking to internationally competitive levels, creating unrest among the working classes, and maintaining undue privileges among the landed aristocracy (Knorr, 1944). Conflict between the landed aristocracy and the rising industrial, commercial, and financial interests came to a head in a series of Parliamentary clashes between the Whigs and Tories, culminating in the repeal of the Corn Laws in 1846 (Kammen, 1970). In religion the changing climate of political power and opinion led to increasing legitimacy for those minority bodies (largely Evangelicals and Dissenters) that had been early advocates of political reform and that could be counted upon for further support of the new government policies. It also led to the reforms of the 1830s, the purpose of which was to effect changes in the Anglican church, both in theology and organization, making it more compatible with the views and interests of the new commercial classes, many of whom had defected from the church over its support of aristocratic privileges. Finally, this period saw increasing efforts on the part of the church—especially among its more evangelical elements—to minister to the needs of the urban poor. Similar movements took place throughout the European system during this period.

Sectarianism

The final kind of religious movement to be discussed is sectarianism, also most prominent in periods of reconstitution in world order, but occurring more among groups whose relation to power is declining than among groups whose relation to power is increasing. Sectarianism includes what might be called "backlash" movements, which occur in response to efforts on the part of religious organizations to accommodate themselves to new social circumstances, sects that arise among the lower classes, and the radical and utopian movements that typically arise among intellectuals and students. Sectarianism encompasses a variety of doctrinal styles and orientations, as Bryan Wilson (1970) and others have pointed out.

I have already traced the processes leading to liberal reforms within established religious organizations. The accomplishment of these reforms characteristically occurs in the face of opposition from those whose interests were better protected by previous patterns of world order and domestic policy. When this opposition contains moral as well as political dimensions, it frequently results in religious schism and, if not contained, the formation of new minority religious bodies. The *devot* movement in France, arising in opposition to Richelieu's policy of cooperation with the German Protestants, affords a clear instance of this kind of movement during the early mercantilist period. The Oxford Movement which developed in reaction to the liberalization of the Church of England in the 1830s provides a similar case during the early free trade period. It was largely contained within the church. Among those movements that could not be contained were the "great dispute" in Scotland in 1843, the secession of "Old Lutherans" in Prussia, and the birth of the Christian Reformed Church in the Netherlands. In each instance, these movements were predominantly populated by interest groups whose privileges were being undermined by the emergence of new patterns of international exchange.

The conditions leading to the rise of sects among the lower classes during these periods result in the largest sense from a lack of stable international monetary and political relations. These precipitate and worsen domestic economic crises which create temporary unemployment and economic hardships for the lower strata. These deprivations are aggravated by the efforts of both rising and declining elites to maintain their share of scarce economic resources. In addition, the likelihood of new sects emerging among the lower strata is enhanced by their physical migration away from established religious organizations due to economic difficulties and changing opportunities for employment. The kinds of movements that result are illustrated by the diffuse spread of what G. L. Mosse (1970) has termed "popular piety" among the peasants of England, Holland, and Germany during the early mercantilist period, and by the efflorescence of Baptists, Methodists, and Adventists in the new grain-growing regions of North America and among the new industrial workers of Britain during the early free trade period. The diffusion of these movements is significantly enhanced by the presence of political and economic instability *throughout* the world-system during such transitional periods.

This instability, together with the fluctuating moral climates it produces, is also an important factor contributing to the radical and utopian sects that have frequently developed among intellectuals and students during these periods; for example, the Cambridge Platonists and the Rosicrucians in England and the Socinians in Poland during the seventeenth century, and the Christian Socialists in England and the Transcendentalists in America during the nineteenth century. In each case, consciousness among intellectuals of domestic injustices to the lower classes and of foreign struggles for political reform were significant factors in the inspiration of these movements.

The Contemporary Period

Only some of the relations between religious movements and world order have been sketched here. It should be apparent even from this necessarily condensed discussion that religious movements in the past have been deeply conditioned by the prevailing state of world affairs. To an even greater degree this has been true of the contemporary period.

By the end of World War II the basic institutions undergirding the free trade system of the nineteenth century—the international gold standard, the British dominated balance of power, *laissez faire* government, and extensive colonial dependencies—had been mortally weakened (Polanyi, 1944). In their place a nascent system of world order dominated by the United States and the Soviet Union has emerged. But the operating principles of world order have yet to be fully reconstituted. Repeated attempts to create a stable international monetary system have met with only limited success (Block, 1977). The threat of nuclear war has proven only marginally capable of maintaining a stable international balance of power. Relations between the superpowers themselves have changed markedly, especially with the emergence of China as a nuclear force. In the Third World, the re-percussions of anticolonial revolts are still being felt.

The result of these instabilities has been a nearly continuous succession of domestic crises and political realignments in the world's major nations. In the United States, the more vivid of these adjustments have included the Korean War, the McCarthy era, the Cuban missile crisis, and the Vietnam war. Less visible, but perhaps equally important, have been the United States' changing relations with Japan and Western Europe, with China, and the changing relations between the government of the United States and its multinational corporations. For other parts of the world—for Vietnam, Czechoslovakia, Israel, Cuba—the consequences of a world order in transition have been dramatically more pronounced.

This period of reconstitution has been highly conducive to the kinds of religious movements that America has experienced in the past quarter century. Successive shifts in the relations among nations have created successive shifts in the statuses and ideologies of domestic interest groups which, in turn, have occurred amidst a chorus of responses at the level of our deepest spiritual and moral convictions. There have been reform movements within religious organizations and sectarian reactions against these reforms. There have been religious defections, social service and civil rights campaigns, and radical and utopian movements. These have been deeply conditioned by the instabilities present in the larger world-system. This is perhaps most evident in the crisis of the 1960s.

The crisis of the 1960s was, in an immediate sense, the Vietnam war. But it was also a crisis in world order and in the positions of domestic interest groups connected to that order. Insofar as the United States was concerned, the world order of the 1950s and early 1960s was oriented chiefly toward military containment of the Communist bloc and the strengthening of America's stabilizing influence within the free world (Schurmann, 1974). This system was predicated upon the monopoly of effective nuclear strike capabilities by the United States and by the Soviet Union, the dominance of the Soviet Union in the Communist world and its ability to exert control over member nations, the ability of the United States to maintain security within its sphere of influence, and the tacit agreement on the part of both superpowers as to the boundaries of their respective spheres.

The containment system also meshed neatly with the interests and ideologies of America's major power groups, even to the extent of limited wars. In the South, strong military commitments to the defense of the free world strengthened the political power of old-guard hawks, fed money into Southern military training camps, provided career opportunities for both blacks and whites, and wedded the conservative religious orientations of the South to the national interest. For agriculture, the same forces that kept Southern politicians strong also helped ensure a stable farm subsidy program which, in the short-run, appeared better than the vagaries of an open international market, and again coincided with the religious and moral convictions of farmers and townspeople in the rural areas.

For the largest corporations, containment politics were scarcely essential to their prosperity. But for many of the weaker corporations (and in turn, labor) continuous demands for new weapons systems, the role of a large standing army in minimizing unemployment, and formal encouragement of foreign subsidiaries and joint ventures with Japan and Western Europe were by no means without importance. Even for the larger corporations, and certainly the universities, the scientific and technological efforts inspired by the arms race, and increasingly by the space race, contributed significantly to their overall wellbeing.

Vietnam was both symptom and cause of the changes in world order that witnessed the demise of containment politics. Included in these were the rise of China as a nuclear power, the Sino–Soviet split, economic tensions among the Western allies, and postcolonial instabilities in the Third World. Under these circumstances Vietnam became the catalyst which precipitated far-reaching realignments among domestic interest groups. For the South the increasing costs of the war, and hence its growing unpopularity, undermined the power of the old-guard and facilitated the rise of the so-called new Southern politician. Increasingly the war divided the interests of blacks, who saw the Great Society usurped by the costs of defense, from those of the white establishment, further eroding the traditional base of Southern politics.

Ideologically, the war drove a wedge between the more liberal advocates of containment and the more conservative champions of a rollback policy. For the corporate community, the worsening balance of foreign payments as the war dragged on precipitated a reevaluation of its commitment to a firm containment orientation. In the universities, the war brought to a crisis the basic inconsistency of interests wedded to the export of military technology and ideology espousing universal humanitarian ideals. In short, the 1960s witnessed a major realignment of domestic interests, not just because of internal unrest, but because of larger conditions in world affairs associated ultimately with the breakup of the free-trade system and the transition to a new pattern of world order.

In religion, the most immediate consequences of this realignment were the radical and utopian cults that emerged among intellectuals and students, generally espousing antiwar and antitechnological orientations, and deriving popularity from their rejection of Western religious traditions. But the religious repercussions of Vietnam ran far deeper than these. The shifting moral climate and definitions of national purpose associated with the protests and realignments of the 1960s nourished liberalizing and social reform movements within the mainstream churches, including Christian—Marxist dialogue, civil rights activism, antiwar efforts, experiments in liturgy, and reevaluations of traditional political and moral postures. They also contributed to widespread defection from the churches among the better educated classes for whom the events of the 1960s symbolized a growing gap between world conditions and the traditions of the church.

As in the past, religious accommodation of this sort brought forth other movements in reaction among those for whom the emerging pattern of world order meant declining power—new denominations in the South and in the Midwest, such as the National Presbyterian Church and the reconstituted Missouri Lutherans; movements among Vietnam hardliners within the churches (the Presbyterian Laymen's Association, for example); and diffuse defection from mainline denominations into the more politically circumspect evangelical churches (cf., Kelley, 1977). Though generalized affluence and the welfare state prevented the kind of extreme hardships that had given rise to widespread sectarianism among the lower classes in the past, those caught at the margins of society during this transitional period, particularly minorities and less privileged young people, followed predictable patterns in their attraction to movements such as the Children of God, Pentecostalism, the Unification Church, the Black Muslims, and the Black Christian Nationalist Movement.

The religious accommodation and sectarianism of the contemporary period, like that of the early seventeenth and the early nineteenth centuries, has been a product of the transitional state of world order. Though the current transition has not produced civil conflict anything like the English Civil War or the revolutions of 1848, the social unrest brought to a climax by the Vietnam war was part of a major realignment in the relations between domestic interest groups and world affairs. The contemporary unrest in religion, both in America and abroad, has been symptomatic of the extensiveness of this realignment.

Periods of religious unrest like the one through which America has recently passed have, of course, been regarded as portents of change—as historical watersheds—at least since Herodotus. There has been much speculation about what the present religious unrest may signal for the culture. And, in this sense, this chapter must also remain speculative. Typological approaches like the one adopted here are of necessity limiting and a great deal more historical work would be required to demonstrate how well or how poorly specific historical events may correspond to these typological distinctions. Let me suggest in closing, however, that the principle value of considering religious movements in the context of world order, as I have attempted to do here, is that it affords a systematic basis for comparing the kinds of watersheds that religious movements may portend.

References

Block, Fred L.
    1977   *The Origins of International Economic Disorder: A Study of United States International Monetary Policy from World War II to the Present.* Berkeley and Los Angeles: University of California Press.
Chirot, Daniel
    1977   *Social Change in the Twentieth Century.* New York: Harcourt Brace Jovanovich.
Fieldhouse, D. K.
    1966   *The Colonial Empires from the Eighteenth Century.* New York: Delta.
Geyl, Pieter
    1932   *The Revolt of the Netherlands, 1555–1609.* London: Williams & Norgate.
Glock, Charles Y., and Rodney Stark
    1965   *Religion and Society in Tension.* Chicago: Rand McNally.
Hobsbawm, Eric J.
    1962   *The Age of Revolution, 1789–1848.* New York: New American Library.
    1969   *Industry and Empire.* London: Penguin Books.
Kammen, Michael
    1970   *Empire and Interest: The American Colonies and the Politics of Mercantilism.* New York: Lippincott.
Kelley, Dean M.
    1977   *Why Conservative Churches Are Growing,* 2nd. ed. New York: Harper & Row.
Knorr, Klaus E.
    1944   *British Colonial Theories, 1570–1850.* Toronto: The University of Toronto Press.
Mosse, G. L.
    1970   "Changes in religious thought." Pp. 169–201 in J. P. Cooper (ed.), *The New Cambridge Modern History,* Vol. IV: *The Decline of Spain and the Thirty Years War, 1609–48/59.* Cambridge: Cambridge University Press.
Polanyi, Karl
    1944   *The Great Transformation.* Boston: Beacon Press.
Schmoller, Gustav
    1896   *The Mercantile System and Its Historical Significance.* New York: Macmillan.
Schurmann, Franz
    1974   *The Logic of World Power: An Inquiry into the Origins, Currents, and Contradictions of World Politics.* New York: Pantheon.
Tilly, Charles
    1969   "Collective violence in European perspective." In Hugh David Graham and Ted Robert Gurr (eds.), *Violence in America.* New York: Bantam.
Troeltsch, Ernst
    1960   *The Social Teachings of the Churches.* New York: Harper & Row.
Wallace, Anthony F. C.
    1956   "Revitalization movements." *American Anthropologist* 58: 264–81.
Wallerstein, Immanuel
    1974   *The Modern World-System.* New York: Academic Press.
Williams, George H.
    1962   *The Radical Reformation.* Philadelphia: Westminster Press.
Wilson, Bryan
    1970   *Religious Sects: A Sociological Study.* New York: McGraw-Hill.
    1973   *Magic and the Millennium.* London: Heinemann.

Wolf, Eric
  1959 *Sons of the Shaking Earth.* Chicago: University of Chicago Press.
Worsley, Peter
  1968 *The Trumpet Shall Sound.* New York: Schocken Books.
Wuthnow, Robert
  1978 *Experimentation in American Religion.* Berkeley and Los Angeles: University of California Press.

Chapter **5**   *John Boli-Bennett*

Global Integration and the Universal Increase of State Dominance, 1910–1970

We can consider the power of the state from both an external and an internal viewpoint. The external power of the state is an issue primarily of its power relative to other states in the world system. The internal power of the state is an issue of its power relative to economic and labor organizations, political parties, and social movements operating within the sphere of state jurisdiction; in short, it is the power of the state relative to "society." Most discussions of state power have the external power of the state as their object. In this chapter I focus instead on internal state power, to which concept I apply the term *state dominance*. State dominance is the degree to which the state controls and regulates economic and social activity in its associated society; put another way, it is the degree of effective implementation of the state's organizational apparatus. My concern here is to explain state dominance throughout the world system in the twentieth century by means of a crossnational, longitudinal analysis.

Figure 5.1 shows how much state dominance has increased in the period from 1910 to 1970. The means of two indicators are plotted here:

1. *Government revenue as a percentage of national income* (GR/NI) is the best available indicator of state dominance. It directly measures the degree to which the state controls or regulates all economic activity in society. By extension one can interpret it as a measure of the degree to which the state controls or regulates social life in general. National income estimates

STUDIES OF THE
MODERN WORLD-SYSTEM

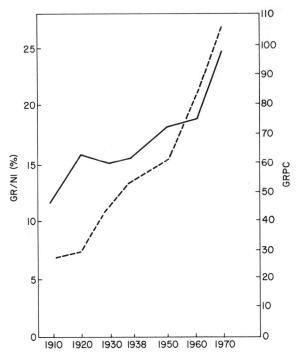

Figure 5.1. *Government revenue as a percentage of national income and government revenue per capita, 1910–1970 (mean values of 3-year averages for each time; independent countries only). GR/NI (left-hand scale) is represented by* ____; *GRPC (right-hand scale) is represented by* _ _ _ _. *GRPC is constant 1947–1949 United States dollars.*

Number of cases							
GR/NI	23	23	26	29	56	94	112
GRPC	51	53	55	55	65	102	132
Independent countries	56	66	68	67	82	113	142

are available for only one-third to one-half of all countries before 1950, so relatively few of the less developed nations are in the data base until that time.

2. *Government revenue per capita* (GRPC) is a measure I use for illustrative purposes only. It is available for nearly all cases over my period but it is too highly confounded with economic development to be a conceptually adequate measure of state dominance. It is moderately correlated with GR/NI (around .5 to .6 between 1910 and 1970, with a peak of .8 in 1938; 3-year averages are used for each variable).

Figure 5.1 shows that the state has become much more dominant since

1910. Both indicators rise considerably, especially after 1930. The mean for GR/NI goes from 11.5% to 24.3% over the period, while GRPC increases by a factor of four, from $26.81 to $106 (constant dollars). These increases are even more significant when we recall that they occur in a period of very extensive state-formation in the world system, the number of independent countries more than doubling in 60 years.

Three general perspectives must be distinguished to explain the increasing dominance of the state. The first perspective derives from conventional economic and sociological theory and considers only the internal development of societies. The second perspective draws upon dependency theory and more recent "world-system" theory to explain variations in state dominance by the positions of countries in the world political economy. The third perspective develops two additional arguments concerning the world system's impact on state dominance. One argument considers the degree of integration of countries into the world system and leads to a position at odds with that of dependency theory. The second shows how properties of the world system as a whole, the degree of integration of the system and the pluralization of power in the center of the system, help account for the expansion of the state observed in Figure 5.1

The Internal Development Perspective

Economic accounting systems, international regulatory agencies, military alliances, and most social researchers have viewed nations as the largest social units in the world. Nations are viewed as largely autonomous, affected by events outside their borders only to a small degree (e.g., Inkeles and Rossi, 1956; Kerr *et al.*, 1960). The extent to which the state dominates society is therefore a reflection of internal processes, which can be either structural (the technicizing economy) or political.

The Structural Argument

Much of the theory of neoclassical economics (e.g., Samuelson, 1964; Rostow, 1960) says that the state expands in order to manage economic growth (cf. Galbraith, 1973). At a different level of analysis organization theorists point to a corresponding process: To manage the increasing complexity ("differentiation") of an expanding organization, the organization's "administrative component" must also expand (Blau, 1970; Rushing, 1967). Parsons (1966) and Eisenstadt (1963) extend this thinking to societies as large-scale, highly differentiated organizations, arguing that the rising level of development necessitates increasing governmental power and scope. Ellul (1954, 1977) develops the argument in detail, showing how the application of "technique" to an increasing range of human activities (for example, human relations, sex, sports and leisure, as well as more traditional activities such as commodity production and military organization) prompts the state to expand its jurisdiction and assume control of the technicized activities. The state integrates them into the technical system as part of its general managerial function in society, and to an increasing extent the state is itself a factor in the generation of technique. This line of argument leads to the following proposition:

1. *State dominance directly depends on economic and technical development.*[1]

The Political Argument

The most important political argument focuses on class struggle as the motive force in political structures. The dominance of the state depends on which class, bourgeoisie or proletariat, controls the state, with the former restricting state power except as it is needed to ensure economic expansion while the latter expands the state to curb the abuses of economic control by the bourgeoisie (Boli-Bennett, 1976). By Marx's original analysis, economic development should increase state dominance (because the proletariat eventually comes into control) and then state dominance should diminish as the state "withers away" (Marx and Engels, 1922).

I am convinced, however, that Marx's class analysis cannot be applied to the contemporary world. In both developed societies and less developed societies, until recently under colonial rule, we have a 'new class' (Djilas, 1957) of technocrats (state bureaucrats, *techniciens,* corporate executives, experts) that rules in the interests of both itself and technical development as a whole and has superseded the historically important classes that are now of secondary importance only (Ellul, 1967; Touraine, 1971; Bell, 1973; Galbraith, 1973). This class is defined by its relation to the means of production but the issue of ownership is now secondary. The technocracy *controls* the means of production but it need not *own* them (cf. Burnham, 1941).[2] In particular, it controls these means of recently dominant importance: production of knowledge, information processing methods, organizational management techniques, propaganda, and so on.

The technocracy supports an expanding state because overall system

---

[1] The evidence from organizations research suggests a proportionately smaller role for the administrative component as differentiation increases (Blau calls it a decelerating relationship). But Bendix (1956) finds that the industrial sector of technicizing societies displays the opposite relationship: The ratio of administrative to production personnel as a whole increases with technical development. Proposition 1. follows this.

[2] "Need not," *not* "does not." The technocracy owns a disproportionate share of the wealth, but it controls far more than it owns and often its individual members have little control of what they own.

management requires close coordination of all social sectors, a perennial function of the state. Under the impact of different histories and political ideologies, the form of state–society relationship that best serves increasing coordination needs may vary: In "socialist" nations, the state takes formal control of all of society and the distinction between state and society disappears; in "capitalist" nations the fiction of private ownership is maintained but the operating distinction between state and society blurs.[3] In both cases it is primarily technical considerations that determine the rate of expansion of the state and its internal and external activity. (Ellul, 1954)

This argument requires one amendment. A sizeable portion of the technocrats staffing the state bureaucracy view it as their sole source of power and status. They have few links to economic and party power sources and they seek autonomy for the state; hence they may attempt to expand the state more than is technically necessary. However, the degree to which they will succeed in this attempt is dependent on the previously established dominance of the state that is in turn (from the internal view) dependent on the level of development. This line of reasoning thus affirms the first proposition given above: State dominance depends on the level of development. Political analysis, then, leads to the same position as the structural argument.[4]

The World Stratification Perspective

The internal development perspective is misleading in its implicit assumption that national economic and political development is independent of external forces in the larger world system. Much sociological and economic theory of the post-World War II period has emphasized the impact of the world system on internal development, stressing the different roles assumed by nations in the system and the interactions among nations that determine the development within them. The most significant tradition of such studies is dependency theory, which originally came to focus under the direction of Prebisch at the UN Economic Commission for Latin America in the 1950s (Chase-Dunn, 1976, has succinctly summarized the dependence literature on economic development). In this tradition the world stratification structure is the starting point of analysis.

[3] E.g., Lockheed and General Dynamics are "private" while the Dept. of Defense is a state agency ("public"); the technostructure ignores the formal distinction and circulates freely between the two spheres (Domhoff, 1967). Also: IBM is private and the Cabinet is public, while four of Carter's Secretaries are directors of IBM (*Grapevine*, 1977).

[4] The implications for state dominance of "pluralist" political theory are less clear. Classes do not exist, and politics consists of the struggles among interest groups, no one of which dominates the system as a whole (Rose, 1967; Dahl, 1961). The state is an independent arbiter of the political process. As such, each interest group acts to influence the state in its favor, seeking state action that will enhance its own success and restrict that of other groups. In this push–pull process, whether or not the state will expand is hard to determine.

Centrality in the World System and Economic/Technical Development

The world stratification perspective explains state dominance as a function of a country's centrality in the world system. Drawing on historical studies of the genesis of the modern world system (especially those by Braudel and others of the *Annales* school), this perspective argues as follows.

Far from having emerged at different times in different countries, the process of continually advancing economic/technical development (what has been called "self-sustaining economic growth," Rostow, 1960; the "great transformation," Polanyi, 1944; the "great transition," Boulding, 1964) is a unitary, transnational phenomenon that first sprang up in prenational Europe under the impact of gradually increasing long-distance ("foreign") trade (Pirenne, 1937). Later, the "age of exploration" saw the colonization of much of the non-European world and its incorporation as subsidiary areas under the control of the European powers—especially Spain, England, and France. Very rapidly there developed a worldwide division of labor based on the following principles (Bukharin, 1929; Frank, 1967; Wallerstein, 1974):

1. Exchange of primary products and raw materials (initially: timber, wheat, furs, wax, gold, and other luxuries) from the periphery for *relatively* highly processed goods (initially: textiles, worked iron, luxury manufactured goods) from the core or center of the world system.

2. Economic dominance by the center over the periphery: control of the exchange process by central countries and correspondingly disproportionate control of economic surplus ("profits") by the center.

3. As a result of the preceding, a cycle of continuing economic advantage to the center by virtue of its command of capital and correspondingly greater capacity for more efficient production and its military superiority based on technical supremacy.

In essence, development depends on centrality in the world system. But this is a reciprocal relationship: The countries that constitute the center of the world system are those that have reached the highest level of development; possession of a central role makes further development more certain and rapid. Countries in the periphery can move toward or into the center, but to do so they must either rely mainly on internal exploitation (e.g., the USA in the late nineteenth century) or isolate a portion of the world for external exploitation (e.g., Japan in the twentieth century).[5]

---

[5] Indeed, I hold that most of the economic surplus generated in our era resulted from internal rather than external exploitation for all but a handful of countries (e.g., the Low Countries). Centrality aids development largely in structural terms, not so much in terms of capital.

To complete the argument, centrality affects state dominance. Central countries both require and have the resources necessary to finance more dominant states. They require them in order to manage demanding external relations (trade and warfare) and to help restructure society around the needs of development—especially in the competitive economic system of our world (Moffett, 1971). The necessary financial resources derive from center control of the terms of trade and the consequent appropriation of surplus from peripheral areas. Also, states in central countries assert their external power (which heavily depends on their internal dominance) to prevent the emergence of powerful peripheral states that could challenge their control. This argument leads to the second proposition.

2. *State Dominance Directly Depends on Centrality in the World System.*[6]

Centrality in the World System and Class Alliances in Control of the State

Turning to the political argument of the world stratification perspective, we again focus on the role of classes. Frank (1967), Wallerstein (1974), and Chase-Dunn and Rubinson (1979) discuss the economically based class alliances that take control of the state in different sectors of the world system. By their analysis, in the center it is an alliance of commercial, industrial, and financial groups that dominates the state: first, rather directly as the main source of state revenue (Braun, 1975); later, through staffing the bureaucracy or illegally seizing the state (Soboul, 1962, so interprets the French Revolution); still later, through influence, control of voting, and propaganda (Mueller, 1973).

These groups ("capitalist," "bourgeois") support a strong state that will ensure their success in the global economy and spread the risks of investment at home. In the periphery it is an alliance of the export-oriented, usually landed groups in control of primary production that have the upper hand (nobility, encomenderos, Junkers, warlords). They have no interest in a strong state, relying on their relationship to the center for protection in the world system and fearing that a strong state would attempt to assert national independence through policies in support of indigenous merchant and industrial groups. The externally oriented elites in the periphery thus seek states only strong enough to maintain internal order [see Frank's (1967) dis-

---

[6] In data analysis, I will abandon Wallerstein's (1974) scheme of identifying three distinct spheres of the world system (core, periphery, and "semiperiphery") by conceiving a nation's place in the stratification structure as a continuous variable ("centrality"). It will nevertheless be useful to retain his terms for theoretical simplicity throughout the paper.

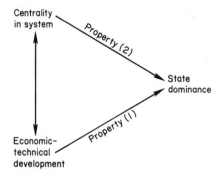

Figure 5.2. *Initial model explaining state dominance.*

cussion of successful efforts throughout Chile's history to prevent the state from taking the lead in reducing Chile's dependence on the metropolitan center].

My criticism of this argument is essentially the same as that presented with respect to the internal development argument about the role of classes in determining state dominance. Technocratic elites have come to power in most peripheral countries as well as in central countries, and I find the traditional class explanations very limited with respect to the present situation. Nevertheless, centrality in the world system may well affect state dominance through the mechanisms described previously.

Figure 5.2 combines propositions 1 and 2 as an initial model explaining state dominance. Note that the figure has very different implications from 1 alone: States expand not simply because of economic and technical development but also because, if central in the world stratification system, they have both the capacity and the need to expand in order to maintain their central position. Thus central states should become more dominant internally as they marshal resources to compete successfully; peripheral states, however, should either become less dominant or maintain a constant but rather low level of dominance.

Inadequacy of the Internal Development and World Stratification Perspectives

According to Figure 5.2, we should expect to find strong relationships among economic/technical development, centrality in the world system, and state dominance. More peripheral countries should be less developed and have significantly less dominant states. Further, we should expect to find increasing differences between peripheral and central states with respect to state dominance, if the dependency theory of the self-reinforcing cycle of de-

velopment in the center and underdevelopment in the periphery is correct.
What do available data show concerning these claims?

Consider Figure 5.3. Using GR/NI as the indicator of state dominance, I
present here the means for central, semiperipheral, and peripheral countries
at 10-year intervals over the 1910–1970 period. I distinguish these three
categories of countries according to the percentage of world trade controlled by each country. An examination of the distribution of this variable
shows a quite "natural" breakpoint at 3% of world trade for most analysis
times, with seven to ten of the major economic powers above this figure. I
therefore designate this group as the central countries. The division between
semiperiphery and periphery is more arbitrary, though for some analysis

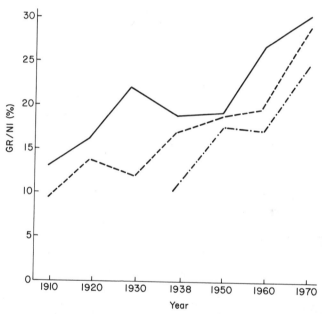

Figure 5.3. *Government revenue as a percentage of national income, 1910–1970, for central,
semiperiphery, and peripheral countries (mean values of 3-year averages for each time; independent countries only). Central countries (_____) (with more than 3% of world trade) in 1970
in descending order of centrality: United States, West Germany, France, Japan, United Kingdom, Italy, U.S.S.R., Netherlands, Canada, Belgium. Semiperipheral countries (_ _ _ _)
(1–3% of world trade) in 1970 in descending order of centrality: Austria, Australia, Czechoslovakia, Denmark, East Germany, Poland, Spain, Sweden, Switzerland. Peripheral countries
(_ _ _ _ _) those with less than 1% of world trade.*

Cases							
Central	9	9	7	7	8	10	10
Semiperipheral	9	9	13	12	12	10	9
Peripheral				(10)	36	74	96

times there is a fairly obvious breakpoint around 1% of world trade. I designate countries controlling less than 1% of world trade as peripheral, and the semiperipheral category lies between these two points. Despite the apparent arbitrariness of this procedure, the way it divides the world accords very well with our intuitive notions about the structure of the world system, as can be seen by examining the lists of nations in the central and semiperipheral categories for 1970 at the bottom of Figure 5.3.

Figure 5.3 at best only partially supports the initial model of state dominance. We know that there has been extensive economic/technical development in the center and semiperiphery, and this development is reflected by increasing state dominance for these two categories. This finding is in accord with the internal development perspective and the first proposition. Further, Figure 5.3 shows that central countries have the most dominant states and peripheral countries have the least dominant states, a finding in accord with the world stratification perspective and the second proposition.

However, neither of these perspectives can account fully for the results in the figure. Centrality and development go hand-in-hand (see the Appendix for correlations among indicators of the two concepts), but state dominance does not follow: Peripheral countries are much less developed than central countries, but their states are only moderately less dominant, especially in 1970. Semiperipheral countries are also less developed than central countries, but their states are just slightly less dominant than central states. Given the really huge differences in centrality and development between the center and the periphery, we should find much greater differences in state dominance than appear here. Further, the gaps among the three sets of countries are not clearly increasing. Particularly between 1960 and 1970 we see a great deal of narrowing of the gap between the center and the periphery; yet this was a period of rapid development in the world system as a whole, precisely the type of period that by Frank's (1967) analysis should result in the strengthening of central control of the periphery and a weakening of peripheral states. The state has become much more dominant everywhere, and there is much more convergence in the degree of state dominance throughout the world system than the internal development and world stratification perspectives suggest.

The Global Integration Perspective

The world stratification perspective considers both internal development and external position in the world system, but it omits two important factors concerning the world system's impact on state dominance. First, we must consider not only a country's centrality in the system but also the degree of integration of the country into the system. By integration into the system, I mean the degree to which the local economy is oriented to the world economy, the degree to which local politics reflect developments in world politics, the degree of penetration of "world culture" (Meyer *et al.,* 1975) into the local culture, and so on. The degree of integration into the world system is essentially unrelated to the degree of centrality in the system;[7] both central and peripheral countries may be strongly or weakly integrated into the system.

The second omission of the world stratification perspective is direct consideration of properties of the world system as a whole that affect the subunits that comprise it (cf. Bergesen, pp. 231–277 in this volume). In particular, we must look at the effects of the increasing integration of the world system on state dominance. In this section, then, the focus is on two aspects of global integration: first, the degree of integration of individual countries into the world system; second, the integration of the system as a whole; and how these factors affect state dominance throughout the world system in this century.

INTEGRATION INTO THE WORLD SYSTEM

The world system contains a fairly coherent and uniform set of ideological and organizational standards for national behavior (cf. the discussions in Meyer *et al.,* 1975; Meyer, Chapter 6 in this volume; Boli-Bennett, 1976, 1979). There are, first, standards that define external success in the system: economic predominance, geopolitical influence, national autonomy. Second, there are standards that define the meaning of internal success: rising GNP per capita (regardless, to some extent, of the specific forms of production and services that make up GNP), rising real per capita income, a schooled and literate population, a high level of citizen participation in political matters, restrained use of official violence and little violation of "human rights," some degree of advanced technological development, and highly polished forms of cultural expression (whether avant-garde or traditional) that contribute to national prestige in the world system. These standards are highly institutionalized, but it is only in this century that they have become universally established. There is still considerable variation in the degree to which they have penetrated local elites and ideologies.

A third set of standards are the ideologies defining the mechanisms to be used to achieve internal and external success. The mechanisms are implicit in the standards themselves: a mass educational system, a mobilized

[7] Correlations between centrality and integration into the system are very near zero or weakly negative over the 1910–1970 period, where the measures correlated are the proportion of world trade controlled and trade as a proportion of national income, respectively; see the Appendix.

citizenry, considerable investment in research and development, strong identification with national goals and priorities on the part of citizens. Stated in these terms, it is obvious that the chief underlying mechanism for national success must be an increasingly dominant state that organizes society around projects that will satisfy world standards. That the dominant state is seen as the "obvious" mechanism for internal and external success reflects two, partly independent processes.

First there is the ideological triumph of state socialism ("statism") in the twentieth century (Ellul, 1973; Acton, 1957; Berger *et al.*, 1973). Almost everywhere elites express strong rhetorical support for "socialism," "revolution by and for the proletariat" (whether there is a local proletariat or not), "people's democracy," and other once impotent doctrines of the left intelligentsia. Even many military governments now proclaim themselves socialist, no matter how "reactionary" they may appear to outside observers. In only a handful of countries (mainly the USA and some of its client countries) is there serious ideological opposition to the expanding power of the state, and even in these places the general movement is toward greater acceptance of state dominance in society.

Second, at the level of practical achievement we find that it is precisely those countries in which the state has become most dominant that have best met the standards of success in recent decades. Where the state is controlled by the Communist Party more rapid economic growth has occurred, at least since World War II (Meyer *et al.*, 1975). These countries have also made very rapid gains in education, industrialization, health care, and the like. Until the 1950s the Soviet Union was the leading "demonstration case" because of its startlingly rapid development into one of the two "great powers" after the war; since that time both China (for large countries) and Cuba (for small countries) have taken on the image of very successful nations, and in these two places the role of the state is extremely expanded. The other major models of success are the Scandinavian countries, especially Sweden, but these are nothing other than the Western "capitalist" countries in which the state is most dominant. Hence both ideology and organizational implementation of ideology support the expanded dominance of the state as the primary mechanism for achieving success.

Where is employment of the mechanism of the dominant state most eagerly sought? Return to the ideological level for a moment, and let me emphasize that this discussion is specific to the twentieth century and the particular content of world culture at this time. The more fully integrated into the world system a country is, the more deeply will the ideology of statism have penetrated. As a country becomes better integrated into the world system, its political and economic elite groups become more thoroughly imbued with the entire corpus of world ideology. This ideology is carried partly by economic organizations, especially multinational corporations based in central countries. These organizations operate under the assumptions of statism (typically quite strong in central countries) even though a portion of their motivation for investment in other countries is a desire to escape the often confining action of the state. Multinational corporations impose their ideological assumptions on host country elites, partly consciously and partly unwittingly, seeking to use the host state in the way they use their home states to further economic/technical development. This process leads to increasing local elite acceptance of statism. It is important to remember that this process applies to relations among central countries as well as relations between central and peripheral countries.

World ideology also travels through the mass media and global intellectual movements; increasing integration into the world system exposes local elites increasingly thoroughly to the ideological assumptions underlying these media. Integration also brings local elites into training programs in central countries' universities and technical schools. Hence integration into the world system leads to the diffusion of central country ideologies; in particular, the ideology of statism, and the degree to which statism takes hold in the various countries depends on their respective degrees of integration into the larger system.

The same process operates at the more concrete organizational level. Training in central countries teaches not only the ideologies of state dominance and mobilization (cf. Deutsch, 1961) but also the specific organizational forms and techniques for implementing these ideologies. Similarly, multinational corporations impose organizational forms and techniques in the economic sector that can be transferred to the political realm and employed by the state. Again, the more highly integrated into the system a country is, the more broadly and deeply will these forms and techniques penetrate both the economy and the state.

This perspective contrasts sharply with dependency theory and the world stratification perspective. Peripheral countries highly integrated (but weak) into the world system may have relatively dominant states because they have been penetrated by the ideologies and organizational structures of dominant central countries. This is not to say that they can be expected to have highly developed economies, for dependence leads to the structural immobilization of their economic sectors; however, their political sectors are not subject to this same immobilization. This latter fact demands explanation; though central countries may diffuse the ideologies and organizational forms of the dominant state, this is not enough in itself to ensure their actual implementation in the periphery. The proper political context must exist for the state to extend its power and authority over society, an issue I take up in a moment.

With respect to central countries, the integration perspective suggests that less highly integrated centers may also have less dominant states than we would otherwise expect. Those few centers (such as the USA and Canada) that are less highly integrated into the world system[8] are less subject to statist ideology and organization than the more highly integrated centers; they can more easily pretend (as did ancient China) that they are the whole of the universe and the standards and mechanisms prevailing in the larger system are mostly irrelevant. Of course, their high level of development leads (by the internal development argument) to a fairly high level of state dominance, but it would be even higher if they were more fully integrated into the system.

To explain the political context that permits high state dominance in peripheral countries that are highly integrated into the world system, we should look first at the internal political situation in the periphery. Compared to central countries, peripheral countries are characterized by relatively weak political organizations other than the state. This is particularly true for peripheral countries that have become independent only since World War II; only the former colonial administrative apparatus embodied the powerful technical forms of political organization of the twentieth century. Political, parties, indigenous economic organizations, labor unions, and traditional political forms were quite weak. The most powerful nonstate organizations in these countries have been the externally controlled corporations and their subsidiaries. Hence efforts to expand the state meet relatively little internal resistance in the periphery.

Furthermore, those portions of the peripheral-country elites who are most thoroughly committed to the standards of the world system have been generally aware of the weakness of nonstate power centers and have recognized the importance of taking command of the state both for success in the system and for personal success in the local arena. This situation differs considerably from that of the central countries, where many very powerful centers of resistance to and struggle with the state exist and more complex alliances (reflecting both technocratic and class divisions) must be forged to expand the state. In this sense, then, expanding state dominance is easier to achieve in the periphery than in the center.

If we grant that the internal context allows for increasing state dominance in peripheral countries well integrated into the world system, we must still deal with the world stratification perspective's argument that external states and multinational corporations will prevent state expansion. This

---

[8] I do not imply that the USA and Canada are not important actors in the world system; rather, as national units they are relatively isolated from the system in the sense that most of their exchange (of all sorts) and development is internal rather than external and they are not penetrated so much by external ideologies and cultures.

point is discussed in the next section. Let me summarize this section with another proposition:

3. *State dominance directly depends on integration into the world system.*

Global Integration, Pluralization of the Center, and Bifurcation of the World System

I shift now to a higher level of analysis: properties of the world system as a whole that affect state dominance. The system as a whole undergoes changes that affect the development and roles of its subunit countries and the relations among them. Two properties of the system that are reciprocally related are relevant here: the degree of integration of the system, and the degree of pluralization of the system's center.

By 1900 almost the entire globe had been incorporated in some way in the world system and its complex division of labor. Since that time we have seen an enormous increase in the degree of integration of the system; the system's subunits (states, corporations, individuals, and so on) have become increasingly strongly linked together across geographical barriers and national boundaries and the degree of interdependence among these subunits has risen dramatically. Rates of exchange have multiplied manyfold in virtually every dimension we can identify (cf. Inkeles, 1975): Commodities, university students, tourists, publications, films, diplomats, scientists, and technical information circulate increasingly rapidly and extensively as time goes on.

An increasing proportion of the world's population has become tied into the world system, and the system affects people's lives in an increasing number of ways. In short, in the twentieth century we have witnessed a global integration process similar to national integration processes occurring in numerous countries for several centuries, with the creation of a world polity (cf. Meyer, Chapter 6 in this volume) as an even larger unit than the national polities forged by national states.

Global integration has three important implications for state dominance; two of these implications involve a heightening of factors discussed before that affect state dominance. First, global integration leads to a general increase in economic/technical development throughout the system. A more complex division of labor and fuller employment of the world's resources mean that the system as a whole can advance to a higher level of development. The periphery remains relatively less developed than the center, but the periphery is not stagnant. By the present decade, for example, we find that peripheral countries produce textiles and some basic metals and manufactured goods, and they are increasingly involved in such other non-primary economic activities as the assembly of high-technology commodities (electronic products) and tourism. Central countries continue to take the lead in research and development as well as the organization of new forms of economic activity; their technical systems have become extremely complex. Hence global integration heightens the process described by proposition 1: Everywhere in the world economic/technical development increases, and the state must become more dominant everywhere to manage the complexity and problems this development entails.

Second, global integration as a systemic process implies that subunits of the system become more highly integrated into the system. The ideologies and commodities of the world system penetrate countries more thoroughly, especially those peripheral countries that were locked into relative isolation from the world system by their colonial status—one striking example: Ethiopia, almost completely isolated until the 1930s and then integrated well enough into the world system only 40 years later that selfproclaimed "Marxist revolutionary forces" overthrew the ancient imperial order. As countries become better integrated into the system the ideology and organizational forms of statism become more powerful; in line with the third proposition, state dominance increases.

The third implication of global integration for state dominance depends on global integration's reciprocal relationship with the pluralization of the center of the world system. By the latter term I mean the degree to which power in the center of the system is dispersed among several central countries rather than monopolized by one country (cf. Bergesen and Schoenberg, pp. 231–277 in this volume). Chase-Dunn (1977) has shown that since the mid-nineteenth century, when data first became available to assess the issue, Britain's dominance of the world system in terms of her share of world output of various industrial commodities has continually declined. Meyer *et al.* (1975) shows that center dominance of the world system has similarly declined between 1950 and 1970, when the USA had replaced Britain as the major central country, with respect to a number of measures of economic and social development. That is, there is a secular trend toward increasing pluralization of the center throughout the past century, as I will show more directly.

Pluralization of the center is both cause and effect of the integration of the world system. On the one hand, increasing pluralization means that there is greater competition among central states and economic organizations. When a single central country strongly dominates the world system, as, for example, did Britain after the Napoleonic Wars, it is able to establish monopoly relations with most of the periphery and prevent other central powers from interfering with its operations. In Wallerstein's (1974) terms, the single dominant power tends toward establishing a world empire rather than a world system. But a world empire is relatively static and economically stagnant, for the forces of competition and struggle tend to be kept under control. With pluralization, competing centers are on a rough par with each other and establishing monopoly relations is much more difficult; the struggle to establish monopoly provokes higher levels of foreign investment and greater effort to extend the world system to new territories. That is, the forces that produce global integration become stronger when a single dominant center gives way to parity with other central countries.

On the other hand, the more rapidly global integration occurs, the more likely it is that pluralization of the center will occur. As more countries formerly external to the world system are brought into the system, the probability that one or more of them will be able to achieve a relatively high degree of autonomy and embark on a course of rapid economic/technical development outside central country control increases. That is what happened with Japan and is in process with China. As these two cases illustrate, it is only those countries that are never fully incorporated into dependent status that can even hope to challenge central dominance successfully. These "latecomers" to the development project have the significant advantage that they can use their knowledge of the history of development in the older central countries to avoid many of the pitfalls and mistakes that originally hampered development in them, and much more powerful and efficient techniques can be adopted wholesale for a "leap-frog" form of development.

Integration increases pluralization in the center not only by bringing a few eventually successful peripheral countries into the world system; it also tends to increase parity within the established center of the system. In integrating the system, central countries operate largely in ignorance; it is very difficult to predict which peripheral areas will finally be most useful in hastening central development, not least because the direction of development itself is hard to predict. Who can say where the resources that will be crucial for development and hence, world-system dominance two or three decades in the future will be found? Central countries thus are gambling with their investments and the payoffs are, to a considerable extent, randomly distributed. As with any random process, global integration payoffs tend to favor "regression toward the mean" among central powers in the long run; more dominant countries, having had big payoffs in the past, lose out to the less dominant countries. Thus relative parity occurs among the central countries.

Pluralization of the center, all other things being equal, operates to the advantage of the periphery rather than the central countries. Peripheral countries can play competing central countries off each other, bargaining for more advantageous (or less disadvantageous) terms of trade and political relationships than they must accept from a single dominant center. Central countries are more willing to make concessions to the periphery; while the center retains the upper hand, the hand squeezes somewhat less firmly.

Central countries have recognized this danger, and in periods of relative parity they have tried to cope with it by formalized agreements about center–periphery relations. Thus the partition of Africa occurred just at the time (1885) when Germany and the USA threatened to reach economic parity with Britain; the Treaty of Berlin reestablished monopolistic center–periphery relations, with each central country awarded an explicit set of African peripheries. The advantages of pluralization of the center were thereby denied to the periphery.

Compromises among central countries to maintain monopoly control of the periphery continued to be made until World War II (we can recall the Treaty of Versailles at the end of World War I and the Munich pact in 1938), so that the advantages of pluralization were never fully realized to that point. After World War II a decisive change occurred in center–periphery relations. The change is threefold. One, pluralization proceeded further than it ever had before (since 1850, the earliest point at which we can measure it); while only a quantitative change, this extreme pluralization has led to a great deal of competition for peripheral-country resources and great potential for peripheral bargaining power. Two, the dominant central country became the USA rather than Britain. For reasons I cannot develop here, the rise of the USA meant that formally monopolistic center–periphery relations (i.e., imperial–colonial relations) gave way to informal "free trade" relations, in much the same way that Britain promoted free trade in the early nineteenth century while pushing for Latin American independence from Spain (cf. Bergesen and Schoenberg, pp. 231–277 in this volume). However, the third and absolutely crucial change that occurred made it impossible for the USA, once established as the dominant central power, to establish monopoly informally through the customary mechanisms of military invasion and threat.

This third change in center–periphery relations is the radical bifurcation of the world system with the secession of the USSR and its satellites from the capitalist arena. Underlying this bifurcation is the development of nuclear weapons, which are in a very real sense "ultimate" weapons that have changed the role of warfare in the world system quite drastically because no one dares to use them. Possession of weapons too dreadful to employ by two competing centers in a split world system has emerged as the crucial condition of peripheral resurgence in recent decades. Now pluralization of the center takes two forms: there is not only heightened competition among central countries in the capitalist center, but there is a more basic conflict between the main centers of the world system's two halves.

We have seen considerable effort by the USA and the USSR to eradicate the maneuvering room afforded the periphery by this radical pluralization (détente, especially in the Nixon–Brezhnev years), but resistance from powerful subordinate centers (France, Japan, China) as well as the irresolvable historically founded antagonisms between the major powers have obviated any formal division of the globe among competing centers. The impasse between the USSR and China in the socialist sector only further strengthens the forces preventing central-country agreements to reestablish monopoly relations with the periphery.

Pluralization of the center, especially in this radical form, aids peripheral countries in terms of both economic/technical development and state dominance. Let me mention only the emergence of peripheral-country commodity cartels to illustrate the kind of maneuvering room the periphery (or at least its upper tier) has used economically. Politically the effects are much more dramatic. External resistance to state expansion is the major barrier the state-oriented elites in peripheral countries have faced; as it has weakened, because of the pluralization of the center and the bifurcation of the system, peripheral countries have begun to marshal greater resources to implement statist ideology. Hence state dominance has increased very rapidly in peripheral countries. As Figure 5.3 shows, the rate of increase of state dominance in the periphery between 1960 and 1970 was even higher than the rate for central countries. This high rate is even more striking when we recall that much of the periphery in this decade consisted of countries having achieved political independence only at the beginning of the decade. We reach, then, my final proposition:

4. *State Dominance Directly Depends on Pluralization of the Center of the World System.*

In sum, the global integration perspective explains state dominance through two arguments. In contrast to dependency theory and the world stratification perspective, I have argued that the degree of integration into the world system, rather than the degree of centrality in the system, boosts state dominance by implanting the ideology of statism and the organizational forms and techniques needed to implement the ideology; better integrated countries conform to statism more fully. Further, global integration increases the economic resources available to peripheral states to aid their expansion and, through the pluralization of the center that accompanies global integration, external sources of resistance to state expansion become much weaker. Coupled with a relatively exogenous technical fact, the development of nuclear weapons, pluralization has taken a radical bifurcated form that gives the periphery greater room for autonomous development than ever before. Hence we find that state dominance increases in both the center and the periphery, and there is considerably less difference between

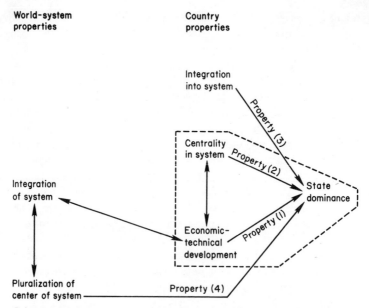

Figure 5.4. *The global integration model explaining state dominance. The portion enclosed by dashed line is the initial model given in Figure 5.2.*

these two sectors of the world system than either the internal development or world stratification perspectives can account for. Increasing state dominance is a universal phenomenon, and there is considerable convergence in the degree of state dominance throughout the world system.

Figure 5.4 presents a model incorporating all four propositions explaining state dominance. The portion inside the dotted line is the earlier model based on the first two propositions, showing how it fits in the more complete model.

Analysis of the Global Integration Model

Figure 5.3 shows that neither the internal development perspective nor the world stratification perspective can adequately account for state dominance in the twentieth century. Figure 5.3 is consistent with the global integration model but offers no direct evaluation of it—the task I take up in this section. I first discuss data reflecting the changes in the world system outlined above and then test the four propositions of the model.

Table 5.1 contains several indicators of the degree of integration of the world system and a pair of indicators of the pluralization of the center. I

Table 5.1
Properties of the World System, 1870–1970

	Years										
	1870	1880	1890	1900	1910	1920	1930	1938	1950	1960	1970
Number of states	47	50	51	52	56	66	68	67	82	113	142
Economic indicator[a,b]											
Total world trade 10^9)	25	39	48	58	79	73	92	73	114	191	373
Political indicators											
Treaties per decade (10^3)	1.3	2.6	2.5	2.3	3.6	4.0	6.4	—	15.0	18.7	—
Diplomatic exchange index (10^3)	1.1	1.3	1.5	1.7	2.2	2.2	3.1	3.8	—	11.1	13.3
Percentage of world trade[a] controlled by											
Top one country	28.2	24.3	23.3	21.5	18.3	22.5	12.8	18.9	18.7	14.8	13.5
Top four countries	62.6	61.1	58.8	57.4	52.7	54.6	42.9	50.6	42.8	38.5	36.4

(Expansion of the system — Number of states)
(Integration of the system — Total world trade)
(Pluralization of the center — Percentage of world trade controlled by)

Sources: Number of states, world trade variables, and diplomatic exchange index from Banks (1975); treaties coded from Martens (1875–1935); League of Nations (1927–1947), and Rohn (1974).

[a] Three-year averages.

[b] In constant 1947–1949 $US.

97

present this data for the last 100 years, not just since 1910, to give a more complete historical perspective on the development of the world system in the present century. Notice, first, that the expansion of the system as indicated by the number of states is quite considerable; from 47 states in 1870 the system expanded to 56 states in 1910 and, with rapid state-formation after World War II, to 142 states by 1970. By the latter date almost every territory in the world was incorporated into an independent state. While the increasing number of states may appear to indicate a disintegration of the system, the indicators of integration tell a different story. Total world trade increased by a factor of 15, from $25 billion to $373 billion (constant dollars). The number of treaties per decade among independent states increased from 1300 in 1866–1875 to 18,700 in 1956–1965 (latest decade available), and the sum of Singer and Small's (1966) index of diplomatic exchange increased from 1100 to 13,300—both increases of similar magnitude to the increase in world trade.

Thus in both the economic and political dimensions the rate of increase in the integration indicators is much higher than the increase in the number of states. The world system contains more states as time goes on; these states are linked together politically with increasing tightness; and economic ties among countries have greatly increased. It is reasonable to believe that integration in other dimensions (cultural exchange, tourism, students abroad, information exchange, etc.) has similarly increased.

Turning to the indicators of pluralization of the center, we see that they follow a pattern exactly inverse to that of the integration indicators. The percentages of world trade controlled by the top one and top four trading countries are inverse indicators of pluralization: The less the top country controls, the more pluralized is the center. The decline in control by the top country implies increasing parity among the top trading nations; for example, in 1870 the nearest competitor to Britain's 28.2% of world trade was France with 14.8%, followed by Germany with 10.2% and the USA with 9.5%; in 1970, the USA's 13.5% was more nearly matched by Germany with 10.2%, followed by France with 6.69% and Japan with 5.97%.

Notice, further, that the up-and-down cycles in integration and pluralization closely correspond. World War I arrested both integration and pluralization; so did the Depression in the 1930s. Periods of rapid integration in the system (e.g., 1920 to 1930, and 1950 to 1970) brought rapid pluralization of the center, so that by 1970 the center was more highly pluralized than ever before. The connection between integration and pluralization is very strong: The rank order correlation between total world trade and the percentage of world trade controlled by the top one country is −.92, and correlations among the other indicators of the two processes are of similar magnitude.

Table 5.1 provides initial support for the global integration perspective. The increase in state dominance shown in Figure 5.1 is accompanied by increasing integration of the world system and pluralization of the center of the system. In Table 5.2, I give the mean figures for an indicator of the degree of integration of countries into the world system, trade as a percentage of national income. This is the only conceptually adequate indicator available, and unfortunately it is available for few countries before 1950. As the table shows, the degree of integration into the system was nearly constant over the 1910–1970 period, with the only major fluctuation during the Depression. However, because this indicator is moderately correlated with economic/technical development and most of the cases before 1950 are more developed countries, fuller data would probably reveal some general increase in the indicator. Nevertheless, it seems unlikely that this indicator can account for much of the increase in state dominance in this century, though it may well account for a good deal of the variation in state dominance.

In Table 5.3, I present a direct evaluation of the four propositions explaining state dominance. The table contains cross-sectional multiple regression analyses of GR/NI for data taken at 10-year intervals between 1910 and 1970 (data are 3-year averages; 1938 was used rather than 1940 because the war interrupted most statistical series). Except for the indicator of economic and technical development, the independent variables used have already been discussed: Centrality in the world system is indicated by the percentage of world trade controlled by each country and integration into the system by trade as a percentage of national income.

The indicator of development, urbanization (proportion of the population in places of 20,000 or more inhabitants), is not, for well known reasons, the most adequate indicator conceptually. I use it for two reasons: It is available for more cases than other indicators, and analyses including it develop fewer problems with multicollinearity among the independent variables. It is moderately to strongly correlated with the two other possible in-

Table 5.2

Degree of Integration of Countries into the World System, 1910–1970

	Years						
	1910	1920	1930	1938	1950	1960	1970
Trade as percentage of national income[a]	54	56	49	25	48	45	54
Number of cases	23	23	25	28	58	93	108

Sources: Clark (1957), Banks (1975).

[a] Mean value; 3-year averages.

Table 5.3
Multiple Regression Analyses of State Dominance, 1910–1970[a]

	Years						
Independent variables	1910	1920	1930	1938	1950	1960	1970
Urbanization (development)	−.17	−.093	−.24	−.011	.21*	.17*	.12
	(.20)	(.18)	(.18)	(.32)	(.10)	(.053)	(.065)
	−.28	−.12	−.20	−.01	.27	.32	.19
Percentage of world trade	−.072	.48	1.21	−.057	.19	.81	.24
(centrality)	(.20)	(.41)	(.70)	(1.02)	(.53)	(.46)	(.67)
	−.05	.27	.27	−.01	.05	.18	.04
Trade–national income	.0066	.11*	.29*	.11	.16*	.12*	.12*
(integration into structure)	(.041)	(.040)	(.046)	(.28)	(.044)	(.038)	(.035)
	.04	.53	.78	.09	.45	.31	.30
R^2	.10	.32	.70	.01	.29	.26	.14
Number of cases	22	22	24	27	56	91	108

Sources: Urbanization from Banks (1975). For other variables, see previous tables.

[a] Dependent variable is government revenue as a proportion of national income. Entries are unstandardized slope, standard error in parentheses, and beta. All data are 3-year averages.

* $p < .05$

dicators available for my period, national income per capita and the percentage of the labor force not in agriculture (see the Appendix), and its behavior is, fortunately, extremely similar to that of these conceptually preferable indicators (see Boli-Bennett, 1976). None of the results presented in Tables 5.3 and 5.4 differ significantly when these other indicators are used.

Considering the first row of Table 5.3, we see that urbanization has inconsistent effects on GR/NI. After having weak negative effects for the first half of the period, after World War II urbanization has significant positive effects (cf. Rubinson, 1977)—but for 1970 the effect is insignificant. Hence proposition 1 is supported only for recent decades; internal development does not consistently increase state dominance. Note, however, that most of the cases until 1950 are the more developed countries, so that inadequate sampling might be supposed to underlie the weak negative effects through 1938. I have indirectly evaluated this hypothesis by doing separate regressions for the more and less developed halves of countries (split at the median urbanization rate for each time) for 1950–1970, and in these analyses urbanization continues to have positive effects on GR/NI for the more developed half of the countries for 1950 and 1960 but no effect in 1970. Thus the negative effects before 1950 for relatively highly developed countries do not carry through for the later times, and it seems reasonable to infer that the first proposition is not fully supported by analysis because of the negative effects until 1938.

Considering the second row of Table 5.3, the world stratification per-

Table 5.4
Aggregate Analyses of State Dominance, 1910–1970[a]

Equation 1		Equation 2	
Urbanization	.14*	Urbanization	.13*
	(.039)		(.038)
	.19		.18
Percentage of world trade	−.068	Percentage of world trade	.070
	(.21)		(.21)
	−.02		.02
Trade–national income	.13*	Trade–national income	.12*
	(.019)		(.018)
	.34		.32
Percentage of world trade	.0084*	Total world trade	.30*
by top one nation	(.0023)	(integration of system)	(.054)
(pluralization of center)	−.18		.28
R^2	.20	R^2	.24
Number of cases	350	Number of cases	350

Sources: See previous tables.

[a] Dependent variable is government revenue as a proportion of national income. Entries are unstandardized slope, standard error in parentheses, and beta. All data are 3-year averages.

* $p < .05$

spective is almost completely unsupported. For four of the seven times the effect of the percentage of world trade on GR/NI is nil; for the other three times it is in the right direction but it never reaches statistical significance. That is, centrality in the world system has only small effects on state dominance over my period. More central countries have only slightly more dominant states when we control for differences in development. This finding is replicated almost exactly when using other indicators of centrality; both the proportion of world diplomatic exchange and the proportion of world treaties behave like the percentage of world trade (Boli-Bennett, 1976). No matter how it is measured, centrality has very weak effects on state dominance.

The third row of the table evaluates one of the arguments from the global integration perspective. Here it is evident that proposition 3 receives strong support: The degree of integration into the world system consistently and significantly affects state dominance. Trade as a percentage of national income has significant effects on GR/NI at five of the seven times, and at every time but 1960 the effect is the largest positive effect in the equation (its beta coefficient is greatest). Hence, beyond the effects of internal development and centrality in the world system, the degree of integration into the system is a strong determinant of state dominance. While dependency theory may be correct with respect to external state power, so that central states are significantly more powerful in the external arena than are peripheral states, it does not receive support with respect to internal power. Here it is the degree of integration into the system and, hence, the degree of penetration of world system ideologies and organizational forms, that is better able to account for state dominance.

Table 5.3 evaluates only the first three propositions. In Table 5.4, I present aggregate analyses of the 1910–1970 period that permit a simple test of proposition 4, the claim that pluralization of the center increases state dominance. In each of these equations the same indicators of the variables are used, but data from all seven analysis times enter the equation simultaneously and an additional variable is added. In the first equation, on the left, the variable is the percentage of world trade controlled by the top trading country, the indicator of pluralization of the center. Every country at a given time receives the same score on this variable; for example, all countries in 1910 receive a value of 18.3%; all countries in 1970, a value of 13.5%. There are thus a total of 350 "cases" in this equation, each case representing one country-year.

The left half of Table 5.4 contains the following results. The effects of urbanization, the percentage of world trade controlled, and trade as a percentage of national income are basically as described for Table 5.3: Urbanization has a weak but significant effect on GR/NI, the percentage of world trade controlled has essentially no effect (though slightly negative here), and trade as a percentage of national income has a moderate effect. Internal development and integration into the system increase state dominance; centrality in the system is basically unrelated to state dominance.

The indicator of pluralization of the center of the world system has significant negative effects on GR/NI: The more world trade is controlled by a single country, the lower is state dominance. Translated into positive terms, the greater the pluralization of the center, the greater the dominance of the state. This result appeared indirectly in relating Figure 5.1, showing the general increase in state dominance, with Table 5.1, showing the general increase in pluralization of the center. Here we see that the result remains even after controlling for development, centrality, and integration into the system. It is at least in part the properties of the world system as a whole that account for state dominance; these properties do not inhere in the system's subunits but operate exogenously at a higher level of analysis while they strongly affect the internal development of country subunits in the system.

In the right half of Table 5.4, I substitute an indicator of the integration of the world system into the equation in place of the indicator of pluralization of the center. Here I test the direct effect of integration of the system, which it should be recalled is reciprocally related to the pluralization of the center. The new indicator, total world trade, has an even stronger positive effect (beta) on GR/NI than the indicator of pluralization of the center. We can conclude that integration of the structure as a world system property also has effects on state dominance beyond those of subunit country properties; controlling for development and the other subunit properties, integration of the system continues to have a significant effect.

These results are replicated quite faithfully when other indicators are used for the various theoretical concepts. Other indicators of pluralization of the center and integration of the system have significant effects; other indicators of centrality in the system never have significant positive effects; while integration into the system and development nearly always maintain their effects. In some analyses, development has larger effects than any of the other variables, but in most of these it is clearly an artifact of multicollinearity that drives some effects strongly positive and others strongly negative.

To summarize these results, then, it is clear that the internal development perspective is only weakly supported and the world stratification perspective is completely without support. Development and centrality cannot account well for state dominance, particularly (as Figure 5.3 suggests) for state dominance in the periphery. The two arguments from the global integration perspective developed here add considerably to explaining state dominance. Integration into the system and the pluralization of the system's center have significant effects on state dominance throughout the twentieth century, and their effects in the analyses are stronger than those of internal development or centrality in the system.

Conclusion

The relationship between state and society is a good deal more complicated than we have been accustomed to think. I have shown that the degree to which the state dominates society is affected by both internal economic/technical development and external factors having to do with the larger world system, in particular the degree to which countries are integrated into the system and the degree of integration of the system as a whole. Contrary to dependency theory, the place of a country in the world stratification structure is not related to state dominance. What we observe in the twentieth century is a universal increase in state dominance and a good deal more convergence in the degree of state dominance among different types of countries than either the internal development perspective or the world stratification perspective leads us to expect. The global integration perspective developed here, focusing on the reciprocal relationship between integration of the system and pluralization of the center of the system, helps considerably in explaining this observation.

Let me say a few words about the future. The arguments I have presented lead to the prediction of continuing increases in state dominance throughout the world because the causal forces identified here can be expected to become stronger in coming decades. As long as the world system continues to become more highly integrated and economic/technical development continues to occur throughout the system, state dominance should increase. How long the worldwide development process can continue is an important issue, however.

It may be that the era of rapid expansion and integration of the world system is almost over, fueled as it has been by unrealistic price structures for energy sources and production costs that omit many of the real costs of economic growth. If the widely anticipated "crunch" should finally come, internal development and global integration may well be arrested. Yet it does not seem idle to speculate that a severe dislocation of the world system would serve not to weaken states but, rather, to strengthen them: The technical and political imperatives for state control of society would become even more compelling. The present sociological situation seems to point to further absorption of society by the state—regardless of the particular direction of world system development—at least for the next several decades.

Acknowledgments

I owe much to John Meyer for help with development of the theoretical perspective presented here. Al Bergesen, John Meyer, and several anonymous reviewers deserve thanks for their criticisms and suggestions for improvement of an earlier draft.

Appendix

Correlations among Independent Variables, 1910–1970[a]

	Correlation coefficients						
Variable	1	2	3	4	5	6	7
Development							
1. Urbanization	1.0	.55	.68	.38	.40	.56	.08
2. National income per capita		1.0	.73	.48	.46	.46	.06
3. Percent labor force not in agriculture			1.0	.44	.37	.45	.20
Centrality in system							
4. Percent of world trade				1.0	.54	.39	−.08
5. Percent of world treaties					1.0	.76	−.14
6. Percent of world diplomatic exchange						1.0	−.16
Integration into system							
7. Trade–national income							1.0

Sources: Population data to calculate national income per capita, from Banks (1975); nonagricultural labor force from Clark (1957). For other variables see previous tables.

[a] Data for all analysis times. Number of cases ranges from 250 to 460.

References

Acton, H. B.
1957   *The Illusion of the Epoch.* Boston: Beacon.
Banks, Arthur S.
1975   *Cross-National Time-Series Data Archive.* Binghamton: Center for Comparative Political Research. SUNY.
Bell, Daniel
1973   *The Coming of Post-Industrial Society.* New York: Basic Books.
Bendix, Reinhard
1956   *Work and Authority in Industry.* New York: Wiley.
1964   *Nation-Building and Citizenship.* New York: Wiley.
Berger, Peter, Brigitte Berger, and Hansfried Kellner
1973   *The Homeless Mind.* New York: Random House.
Bergesen, Albert
1977   "Globology and global cycles: A preliminary look at the formalization and deformalization of the world as a whole from 1500 to 1977." University of Arizona: Dept. of Sociology, mimeo.
Blau, Peter M.
1970   "A formal theory of differentiation in organizations." *American Sociological Review* 35 (April):201–218.
Boli-Bennett, John
1976   *The Expansion of Nation-States, 1870–1970.* Unpublished doctoral dissertation. Stanford University: Dept. of Sociology.
1979   "The Ideology of Expanding State Authority in National Constitutions, 1870–1970." Ch. 13 in John W. Meyer and Michael T. Hannan (eds.), *National Development and the World System.* Chicago: University of Chicago Press.
Boulding, Kenneth
1964   *The Meaning of the Twentieth Century.* New York: Harper & Row.
Braun, Rudolf
1975   "Taxation, sociopolitical structure, and state-building: Great Britain and Brandenburg-Prussia." In Charles Tilly (ed.), *The Formation of National States in Western Europe.* Princeton: Princeton University Press.
Bukharin, Nikolai
1929   *Imperialism and World Economy.* New York: International.
Burnham, James
1941   *The Managerial Revolution.* Bloomington: Indiana University Press.
Chase-Dunn, Christopher
1976   "The effects of international economic dependence on development and inequality: A cross-national study." *American Sociological Review* 40:720–738.
1977   "Core-periphery relations: The effects of core competition." Pp. 159–76 in Barbara H. Kaplan (ed.), *Social Change in the Capitalist World Economy.* Beverly Hills, Calif.: Sage.
Chase-Dunn, Christopher, and Richard Rubinson
1979   "Cycles, trends, and new departures in world-system development." Ch. 16 in John W. Meyer and Michael T. Hannan (eds.), *National Development and the World System.* Chicago: University of Chicago Press.
Clark, Colin
1957   *The Conditions of Economic Progress.* 3rd ed. London: Macmillan.
Dahl, Robert
1961   *Who Governs?* New Haven: Yale University Press.

Deutsch, Karl W.
   1961   "Social mobilization and political development." *American Political Science Review* 55:493–514.
Djilas, Milovan
   1957   *The New Class: An Analysis of the Communist System.* New York: Praeger.
Domhoff, G. William
   1967   *Who Rules America?* Englewood Cliffs, N.J.: Prentice-Hall.
Eisenstadt, S. N.
   1963   *The Political System of Empires.* London: Collier-Macmillan.
Ellul, Jacques
   1954   *La technique, ou l'enjeu du siecle.* Paris: Armand Colin. (Translated as *The Technological Society.* New York: Knopf, 1964).
   1967   *Metamorphose du bourgeois.* Paris: Calmann-Levy.
   1973   *Les nouveaux possédés.* Paris: Fayard. (Translated as *The New Demons.* New York: Seabury, 1973.)
   1975   *Trahison de l'Occident.* Paris: Calmann-Levy. (Translated as *The Betrayal of the West.* New York: Seabury, 1978.)
   1977   *Le systeme technicien.* Paris: Calmann-Levy.
Frank, André Gunder
   1967   *Capitalism and Underdevelopment in Latin America.* New York: Monthly Review.
Galbraith, John Kenneth
   1973   *Economics and the Public Purpose.* Boston: Houghton-Mifflin.
Grapevine
   1977   "Will IBM program Jimmy Carter?" January. Palo Alto, Calif.
Inkeles, Alex
   1975   "The emerging social structure of the world." *World Politics* 27:467–495.
Inkeles, Alex, and Peter Rossi
   1956   "National comparisons of occupational prestige." American Journal of Sociology 61:329–39.
Kerr, Clark, J. T. Dunlop, F. Harbison, and C. A. Myers
   1960   *Industrialism and Industrial Man.* New York: Oxford Univ. Press.
League of Nations
   1927–   Treaty Series. Geneva: League of Nations.
   1947
Martens, G. F. de, and successors
   1875–   Nouveau Recueil Général de Traités. Gottingen: Dieterich. Leipzig: Th. Weicher,
   1935   Hans Buske.
Marx, Karl, and Frederick Engels
   1922   *Manifesto of the Communist Party.* New York: International. Original in 1848.
Meyer, John W., John Boli-Bennett, and Christopher Chase-Dunn
   1975   "Convergence and divergence in development." Annual Review of Sociology 1:223–246.
Moffett, John Thurber
   1971   *Bureaucratization and Social Control.* Doctoral dissertation. Columbia University: Dept. of Political Science.
Mueller, Claus
   1973   *The Politics of Communication.* New York: Oxford Univ. Press.
Parsons, Talcott
   1966   *Societies: Evolutionary and Comparative Perspectives.* Englewood Cliffs, N.J.: Prentice-Hall.

Pirenne, Henri
  1937 *Economic and Social History of Medieval Europe.* New York: Harcourt, Brace, and World.
Polanyi, Karl
  1944 *The Great Transformation.* Boston: Beacon.
Rohn, Peter H.
  1974 *World Treaty Index.* 5 vols. Santa Barbara: ABC-CLIO.
Rose, Arnold
  1967 *The Power Structure.* New York: Oxford University Press.
Rostow, W. W.
  1960 *The Stages of Economic Growth.* Cambridge: Cambridge University Press.
Rubinson, Richard
  1977 "Dependence, government revenue, and economic growth, 1955–1970: A cross-national analysis." *Studies in Comparative International Development* 12:3–28.
Rushing, William
  1967 "The effects of industry size and division of labor on administration." Admin Science Quarterly (Sept.):267–295.
Samuelson, Paul A.
  1964 *Economics.* New York: McGraw-Hill.
Singer, J. David, and Melvin Small
  1966 "The composition and status ordering of the international system: 1815–1940." *World Politics* 18:236–282.
Soboul, Albert
  1962 *Histoire de la révolution française.* Paris: Gallimard.
Touraine, Alain
  1971 *The Post-Industrial Society.* New York: Random House.
Wallerstein, Immanuel
  1974 *The Modern World-System.* New York: Academic Press.

The World Polity and the Authority of the Nation-State

In this chapter, we will discuss the world political system and the forms of value and social organization it has helped to create. This system is linked closely to the rise and expansion of the world commodity economy, but it also operates to restructure and alter this economy, and to transform social life. We will proceed, first, by discussing the problem that arises if the world is seen simply in exchange terms: it is then hard to explain the contemporary expansion in the power of peripheral nation-states, and their related rapid modernization. Second, some of the central structural world political rules supporting the nation-state system will be described and discussed—a task of some importance, since these structures are only weakly built into world organizational forms that are commonly recognized as essentially political. Third, the effects of the world polity on the reorganization of modern economies and societies—especially in the periphery—are considered. We will conclude with some observations on the structure of the modern world polity as a whole: its elites and its expanding legitimation.

Our central arguments are these. The nation-state system is given world-wide support and legitimacy, and is importantly exogenous to individual societies. This system confers great and increasing powers on states to control and organize societies politically around the values (modern notions of rationality and progress) established in the world political culture. These powers are ideological and political reflections of the organizational and ideological logics of the world economy: Seen economically, they in-

109

STUDIES OF THE
MODERN WORLD-SYSTEM

volve the resources of control over labor and technology (especially the "technologies" of social services), but also control over the organization and definition of consumption. Dependent and peripheral states are given considerable ability to pursue modernization around purposes and in sectors to which these resources apply. Thus the world polity creates "subeconomies" in national societies, which tend toward isomorphism with each other and with the rules of the wider system—surprisingly similar institutions of modernity (e.g., state forms, state services, educational systems) appear in all sorts of societies. All these involve rapid state growth.

A useful analogue here is the political system of Western feudalism, in which a wider unified culture embodied only weakly in a system-wide political organization supported and legitimized the rise of strong, but rather homogeneous, political subunits with great power over their populations. The analogy cannot be carried too far—Western feudalism legitimized roles and the assignment of individuals to them around purposes and assumptions distinct from modern ones—but the structural similarity is considerable.

The notion of a powerful world polity enables us to explain a number of features of the world system that are highly problematic for theories depicting the world simply as an economic exchange system: (*a*) the political stability of the state system; (*b*) the rapid social "modernization" of peripheral societies in the modern period; and (*c*) the worldwide shift to postindustrial, politically constructed, forms of value and social organization (roughly, the "tertiary" or service sectors of what is erroneously called the "economy"). We argue that the world polity is a highly institutionalized system, reified in world social life. Critics will, of course, argue that the reification is going on in our arguments, rather than in the real world.

Theoretically, this chapter is an attack on the fundamental problem of modern social scientific theory: the separation of ideas about exchange from those about the social construction of the units involved in exchange. The main contribution of contemporary phenomenological thought (e.g., Berger and Luckmann, 1967; Goffman, 1967) has been to see that all action simultaneously constructs exchanges and the political world within which these exchanges occur and are given meaning. We bring this understanding to bear on the world system. In doing so, we take advantage of the newly emerging social scientific sophistication about the modern world exchange system, created by the work of Wallerstein (see particularly 1974), Tilly (e.g., 1975), and others (including many variants of dependency theory). In this line of thought, such political elements of the world as the modern nation-state system are seen to arise from competition within and reactions to the expanding system of economic exchange. This is an important and useful insight, but misses an important aspect of the modern world system.

Pressures for rationalization and progress arise not only through the system of exchange among individuals and other social units: They arise through the institutional system as well. Progress is to be achieved, not only through production and exchange in markets, but also through rationalized collective action—through bureaucratic rationality, especially as organized in the state. One of Weber's two engines of "progress" in the modern world —the reorganization of institutional life around rationalized bureaucracy— has been treated as derivative and secondary in contemporary world systems discussions. It is developed in a separate literature: most notably in the work of Bendix (1964, 1968, 1978) on the formation of modern nations and states. A main purpose of this chapter is to bring this theme back into the analysis of the modern world system.

Thus, we argue for the proper integration of ideas about rationalized exchange with ideas about rationalized collective action; and argue against the tendency of social science to follow modern ideologies (of both the left and the right) in isolating the two.

Theoretical Issues

The current inclination to analyze society in terms of economic exchange has distorted the meaning of some central terms. The term *economy* has been broadened to include any sort of rationalized and monetarized value in society, so as to make plausible the assumption that all such value is ultimately regulated by exchange processes. And the term *polity* has been narrowed to include only those collective agreements that are organized in the only constructions routinely seen as political—more or less rationalized states. Since at the world level there is nothing that can be considered a state, the analysis of the wider world polity is impoverished. It is seen only as a few weak international organizations together with a number of coalitions among states.

Economy is here given more restricted meaning, as the system of creating and organizing social value through the extraction, production, exchange, and consumption of commodities. Conventionally, this includes various constructed social factors: labor, capital, land, organization, technology, and so on. These factors vary over time in their social definition and importance. Individual and subgroup choices create and organize commodity value through markets, but also through collective political action. In modern usages, the term economy has been distorted to include all sorts of social value: This is an important organizational and ideological process, but obscures analysis. In order to be clear, we sometimes use the term *commodity economy* to return to appropriate usage.

Polity is here defined as the system of creating value through the collective conferral of authority. The rules involved may be formed and located in collective cultural or religious processes, but are now often located in state action. Authority may create value through the economy: by (a) defining or consuming commodities; (b) defining appropriate technology and organization; or (c) by organizing factors of production. But authorities may create value directly: through the construction of goals and of invisible commodities, and the direct conferral of value on these ends, the means understood to produce them, and the social units involved.

Our term polity includes state action, as is conventional, but also other forms of collective action that might in the modern social scientific lexicon be dismissed as merely "cultural." Costs are involved in our usage, but the narrow conventional usage leads to the ignoring of broader political processes, which are especially important in the stateless world polity.

We introduce the definitions above especially to clarify the prevailing misunderstandings of the nature of the economy. Because modern polities are rationalized and monetarized, it has become common to think of huge sectors of society as "economic" when they have nothing directly to do with the commodity economy. In postindustrial societies, most occupational work is not related to economic commodities, most money is not received for such commodities, and most of what is called "consumption" does not consume such commodities. Further, most rationalized technology is not related to commodity production or exchange, and most organization is similarly unrelated to commodity production (Bell, 1973; Meyer and Rowan, 1977). It is a matter of interest that originally economic theories have become guiding myths in the world (West, East, and South). It is a disaster that these conceptions have been swallowed whole in the social sciences. Everything rationalized, monetarized, or analyzed in terms of any kind of scarcity, is seen in these terms. It is odd that the decline in the relative importance of commodity production and exchange in human society has been accompanied by a rise to transcendent authority of the myths of commodity production—odd, but part of the logic that spreads the modern state system.

The following theoretical perspective is employed throughout our discussion: (a) Economic systems, as they become stabilized, generate polities: accountings of value such that the exchanges make sense and are given legitimacy—in other words, systems of justice. Many dimensions of social construction are available here: First, value is assigned to the commodities or activities exchanged, often through markets that are socially structured. Second, more or less binding theories or myths, rules and accounts (Scott and Lyman, 1968; Blum and McHugh, 1971; Meyer and Rowan, 1977) are constructed locating the origins of the values entering exchange. These are partial functional theories of production and value—broadly, production functions. They may attribute exchange value to external sources, such as nature, other societies, the gods, the primordial individual, the family, and so on. They organize and attribute value to elements of the social system itself, defining various factors of production in different instances: land, wealth, technology, entrepreneurship, capital, labor, "human capital," skill, motivation, ability, and moral sentiments. In early modern society these social analyses are simple, but later they become quite complex; in all cases they tend to be located in authoritative political and economic ideologies. Third, as a consequence of these rationalizations of the production and exchange of value, but also directly to balance and justify exchanges, systems generate and attach value to various social units—individuals, collectivities, and society itself. Constructed social units are in part precipitates of the rationalization of exchange value; examples are corporations, factories, labor unions, or business associations. But others, which may be assigned productive value too, are primordial. They are assigned rights and obligations to have goals or purposes of a broader character—in short, to consume value. The two great constructed primordial social units of the modern world are the individual and the nation-state. The value assigned to these units justifies many exchanges which otherwise might be unjust.

The construction of social units in an exchange system is both an organizational and an ideological process. Given units arise organizationally and are legitimated by the organizational network: they are also legitimated ideologically and supported by the wider political culture. Both processes spread these units; the construction of new units of a legitimated form is much easier than the building of novel units (Meyer and Rowan, 1977).

(b) Reciprocally, polities, which are, in a sense, authoritative accounts of justice, construct and restrict exchanges. Many forms of exchange are made possible by the definition of individuals as fundamental units; others are limited by the delegitimation of ethnic primordiality or of slavery. In most of the modern literature, this process is emphasized less: It is generally thought that a main driving force of the modern world system was the spread of exchange around the world. We argue, however, that the social units formed in the world exchange system constitute a world polity defining and controlling and constructing exchange itself, and increasingly so.

The Problem: A World-Wide System of Structurally Similar Nation-States

We often describe the world system (following Wallerstein, 1974) as if it were primarily a free world economy operating in the absence of a controlling world state or empire; as if it permitted the forces of economic progress and exploitation to operate relatively freed from processes of political control or redistribution. This conception is modified by the definition of states as major actors under, and implementers of, the economic forces involved. States then enter the analysis as competing economic actors: central ones as capitalist; peripheral ones as proletarian or peasant. World politics is simply a direct reflection of world economic relations; a network of economic relations among competing nation-state subunits, along with a few other organizations. Suppose this were true. What world social arrangements would follow?

First, there would be great organizational instability. As with firms competing in the marketplace, all sorts of reorganizations would occur: the expansion of successful units and the incorporation or destruction of marginal ones, for instance. Among nation-states, the larger and more powerful would do better: Their boundaries would expand, and they would rapidly gain economic and other resources. Small or weak states would disappear or be absorbed. These results do not occur. Small states grow internally as fast as larger ones (Meyer *et al.*, 1979), and boundaries change very rarely. Regimes rise and fall, but states and state boundaries remain. Even in the organizationally weakest parts of the world, such as Africa, boundaries and state organizations show astonishing stability, which the development theories of 20 or 30 years ago did not predict.

Second, there would be a sharp and increasing economic division of labor in a world economy standing alone. Central areas would probably specialize in services; less central ones in industrial production; and peripheral ones in extra-active activity. There are indeed great international inequalities, and a considerable international division of labor, but the main observable changes are not in the direction of an increased division of labor at all. Instead, industrial production and service activity increase in both central and peripheral societies at rates that are broadly similar (Meyer *et al.*, 1975).

Third, political entities in the world would increasingly be subordinated to economic ones. Many states would be weakened, and transnational economic forces (e.g., multinational corporations) would become progressively stronger. But states do not weaken, even relative to the expanding world economy. Each year, government revenues in the world take an increasing proportion of the gross world product (Meyer *et al.*, 1975).

Fourth, political differentiation in the world would increase. Economically stronger states might become stronger in their societies, but economically peripheral states would become weaker and more pastoralized, relative to the expanding world economy. This does not occur. States in both rich and poor countries expand their proportion of the growing economic resources of their societies, and at similar rates (Meyer *et al.*, 1975).

Fifth, societies would adopt distinct institutions in accordance with their "class" positions in the system. Central societies would modernize; peripheral ones would become absolutely or relatively pastoralized. But this is strikingly contravened by the evidence: Both rich and poor societies evolve similar institutional arrangements, in important respects. Education expands everywhere (Meyer *et al.*, 1977). So does urbanization (Davis, 1969). So do all sorts of state services and communications systems.

The theoretical problem, at the world level, is simple.[1] We need a theory that will explain how it is that in the face of the differentiating power of the world economy, the state system expands—organizing more and more social value in the state, and around the ends of postindustrialism: service sectors, rather than simply structures of commodity production and exchange. We need this theory, most strikingly, to explain the rapid state expansion and structural modernization of the economically dependent periphery of the world-system. In the face of enormous and continuing world economic inequalities, strong and stable states (though not regimes) rise in the periphery, elaborating state bureaucracies and the services of postindustrial society. Many developmental theories could explain these phenomena in central societies. Few theories had it that social and political modernization would, for better or worse, so completely outstrip the growth in economic production in peripheral societies.

It should be clear that we are not discussing an overall trend to world equality. The proportion of world gross product controlled by the most peripheral societies does not increase (Meyer *et al.*, 1975), though it does not decline, as most simple economic dependency theories would have it. But in other respects isomorphism is striking: Peripheral societies shift to modern forms of industrial and service economic activity; to modern state organizations; to modern educational systems; to modern welfare and military systems; in short to all the institutional apparatus of modern social organization. And these changes occur most rapidly in the present world nation-state system—not in the previous colonial systems in which it might have been

[1] Interestingly, the failures of theories portraying the world system as simply an economy parallel quite precisely the failures of the same theories to account for the evolution of industrial societies. The expectation that the industrial society would be completely dominated by its economic organization was contravened by the flowering of all the institutions of individualism in religious, associational, political, and familial life. The expectation that industrial society would be vertically and horizontally fragmented was contravened by the emergence of great social and cultural homogeneity. And the expectation that industrial societies would generate mass proletarianization in its simplest forms, with mass impoverishment, was contravened by the evolution of huge middle classes—proletarianized, in many ways, but organized in a complex and differentiated stratification and institutional system. Similarly, in the world system, the strength of the state, even in the periphery, the lack of evidence of simple peripheralization, and the emergence of substantial levels of structural homogeneity around modern institutional forms in so many societies, come as a surprise to narrowly economic theories.

expected that clear organizational arrangements existed to rapidly transmit modern social structure.

Several lines of thought on the problem of the expansion and domination of the modernizing state system have been advanced. First, attempts are made to deny the fundamental significance of the problem—to see the phenomena involved as temporary or unstable or meaningless. The rapid industrialization of the periphery is discussed as somehow inferior—"dependent industrialization," it is called. The expansion of the tertiary sector in peripheral economies is discussed as a kind of historic mistake made by new nations aping old ones: on the right as premature socialism, on the left as "overurbanization" or the "bloated tertiary sector." The expansion of peripheral states is seen as somehow taking place at the behest of central powers, though there is no evidence of this (Rubinson, 1977). By and large, these lines of discussion ignore the facts, or decry them, rather than offer explanations.

Second, theories of the system as a network of competing and exchanging units are repaired to explain the expansion of the state system. To rescue pure network theories from this problem, exotic conceptions of the world system as very delicately balanced are developed, in an attempt to treat each local stability (i.e., instance of stable state formation in the periphery) as resulting from a network balance of power. The classic ideas of pluralist political theory are used to explain how it is that a fragile stability is achieved. But given rapidly changing interests and alliances in the network, and given the empirical stability of the state system, these lines of thought are not adequate. A direct application of network arguments will not explain how it is that American political leaders end up agreeing to pretend that Panama, for instance, is a nation-state, and as such is entitled to control a huge American capital investment. Clearly, the agreement that Panama is a nation-state takes on a legitimacy that transcends the local balance of particular interests. Third and fourth parties with no direct interest in the matter sustain the agreement as rule-like. The origins and maintenance of this rule require extended discussion; its existence does not.

Third, neoclassical theories of economic development are used to explain some competitive advantages of peripheries. But they do not explain the expansion and stability of peripheral states, or the elaborate expansions of peripheral tertiary sectors (e.g., education, state bureaucracy), which by economic lines of reasoning are out of place.

Fourth, arguments are advanced that the *culture* of the modern system spreads rapidly, and lies at the base of rapid peripheral modernization (cf., Inkeles and Smith, 1974). The penetration of modern culture, in this line of thought, may generate "revolutions of rising expectations" in peripheries. These ideas make some sense. But they do not clearly explain what structural features of the modern world make modern cultural ideology a special candidate for diffusion in the present period. Nor do they explain how it is that peripheral states acquire the stability and strength, in very short periods, to mobilize society along modern lines. It is very clear that few peripheral societies in the modern world have the internal societal resources and structural coherence to generate, fund, and sustain strong and legitimated states, whatever the cultural commitments of their populations. No resources internal to most African societies, for instance, would generate by internal functional processes the organizational power and stability built into the system of African states in the last generation.

Explanations of the world-wide state system that stress cultural factors are on the right track. The important element they miss is the awareness that modern world culture is more than a simple set of ideals or values diffusing and operating separately in individual sentiments in each society. The power of modern culture—like that of medieval Christendom—lies in the fact that it is a shared and binding set of rules exogenous to any given society, and located not only in individual or elite sentiments, but also in many world institutions (interstate relations, lending agencies, world cultural elite definitions and organization, transnational bodies, and so on). The United Nations, though a weak body organizationally, symbolically represents many of the rules of the modern world polity. (See, for example, Section 51 of the United Nations Charter, which defines some very distinctive rights for modern nation-states.) It symbolizes the rules of a political system in which nation-states are constitutive citizens.

The operating set of rules stresses, centrally, the primacy and legitimacy of nation-states as organizational forms, and the obligations of these organizations to rationally pursue modern "progress" on behalf of their populations. All this is more than a set of attitudes: it can best be seen as a world polity, forming and supporting the nation-state system in the most unlikely parts of the world, and carrying the social institutions of modernity with it.

The World Political Rules Legitimating Nation-States

The rules defining the nation-state system as legitimate are clearly located and shared outside the boundaries of any given nation-state. These rules have two aspects: They define the structural form of the nation-state as the most highly legitimated form of corporate social authority, and they define the purposes to which this organizational form is to be devoted and in terms of which it is legitimated. We separately describe the appropriate organizational forms, and then the social content, jurisdiction, or purposes properly located in this organizational form.

Structural Forms

States are given legitimated controls over:

Territory   Nation-state dominance of territory is legitimated. Territory not included as an intrinsic part of a recognized nation-state represents a "social problem" in the system. (*a*) Colonies, or other formalized dependencies, are seen as illegitimate: e.g., Namibia, Angola. Even the dependency of Puerto Rico on the United States, or the Eastern European countries on the Soviet Union, are of marginal legitimacy, though given the dominating powers involved, protest is mostly rhetorical. It is often proper for states to offer arms, funds, and other support of independence movements in colonies. (*b*) The lack of clear nation-state control over the seabed, Antarctica, the air, and outer space represent social problems, and much social and legal repair work is done. (*c*) Other territory not clearly given an unambiguous nation-state location is also seen as problematic: e.g., parts of Palestine, Hong Kong, Gibraltar, foreign bases in any country, Bantustans, Indian reserves, or Northern Ireland. Issues about such territory become of concern generally through the system. (*d*) Nation-state control over properly incorporated territory is highly legitimated. Efforts to break up a nation-state or to alter established boundaries are illegitimate, and many forces in the system assemble to resist them. The Biafran attempt to break up Nigeria was resisted by a great preponderance of external forces, despite a great deal of substantive sympathy for the Biafrans; so also with attempts on Ethiopia by Somalia and the Eritreans.

So all through Africa—the arbitrary boundaries formed during the colonial period, everywhere cutting across ethnic boundaries—remain and attain great external legitimation despite the utter internal weakness of most of the states involved. World forces assemble to maintain them: Cuban troops and Russian arms in Angola and Ethiopia, French troops and aid in Chad and Zaire, and so on. Even in the case of territorially anomalous Pakistan, the separation of Bangladesh was resisted by many external forces (the U.S. among them). Only in the case of direct great-power conflicts or interventions are state boundaries broken, as in Korea, Vietnam, Germany, or Eastern Europe after World War II.

The system-maintained territorial legitimacy of the nation-state is overwhelming: Nation-states almost never break up, and almost never really unite; boundaries rarely change, despite all the flows and changes of interests and power in the system. This contrasts sharply with systems of competing organizations, such as firms in a market.

Population Nation-state dominance over populations, and the incorporation of populations in nation-states, is legitimated by the world polity. States that are not complete nation-states—which do not directly incorporate populations in citizen membership are of dubious legitimacy, and it is often proper to attack them: e.g., South Africa, Rhodesia, Taiwan, Israel. But once a population is incorporated into complete citizenship, a nation-state is given almost complete authority to subordinate the population: It can expropriate, kill, and starve, with relatively little fear of external intervention. Such interventions are not legitimated: e.g., Uganda, Cambodia, pre-World War II Germany, post-World War I Russia.

Any attempt by a population to resist nation-state incorporation and control is likely to be externally illegitimated, as in Quebec, Biafra, Kurdistan, Eritrea, or the Basque country. External attempts to support such efforts are likely to be criticized (the French in Quebec) and covert (the CIA in Kurdistan and elsewhere; the Libyans in Chad). The preponderance of world forces supports the nation-state against its dissident members.

Further, economic movements of populations from one nation-state to another are legitimately restricted by states. This further enhances control over populations. Movements of higher status people are stigmatized as "brain drains," and questions of loyalty are raised, though such movements were common in previous centuries. Economic movements of ordinary people, as of southern European workers to northern countries, are treated as reflecting badly on both types of countries; in any event, such workers are not often incorporated as regular members. States that restrict such movements, and thus restrict the economic opportunities available to their populations, are treated as on firm ground. The exceptions here are population movements in the course of nation-state formation or redefinition—these movements occur more on political than economic grounds, as with Jews and Germans in Eastern Europe, Chinese in Southeast Asia, or the huge population movements associated with the shifts in Polish boundaries after World War II (Tilly, 1976).

It often seems to be the case that a nation-state gains more external respect and legitimacy by the coercive incorporation of dissidents than by allowing them to leave. The claims to authority of the state to ultimately control its population can in the extreme be established by killing groups of them—a form of nation-building not uncommon in our century.

The Means of Violence Nation-states are given legitimate monopolies over the important means of violence. It is proper to lend, sell, and give arms to states, but improper to do so to other groups and organizations (when this is done, it is ordinarily managed covertly). Private groups involved in arms trades are stigmatized as "arms merchants" and efforts at control are attempted. But states may, with little question, build up very high levels of arms. This is true even of the extreme instance of nuclear weaponry. More and more states acquire such weapons, and the process is generally seen as legitimate, and is even aided. On the other hand, great efforts are made to keep such weapons out of the hands of organizations that are not states.

The Delegitimation of Other Organizational Forms   The nation-state system is further supported through the weakening of alternative organizational forms, and their claims to control over population, territory, and the means of violence. The efforts of groups organized as ethnic or religious are seen as reactionary; it is generally illegitimate to support them. Economic associations are kept from maintaining private armies, their territory and property are subject to state expropriation, and their attempts to control their populations are stigmatized as slavery or serfdom—though states routinely exercise such controls with little question. A worker may properly be kept from crossing state boundaries, and may even be kept from crossing firm boundaries by the state, but not by the firm.

Cultural Content of the World Polity

Worldwide meanings and justifications, not only organizational forms, define the world political supports for the nation-state system. These meanings can most easily be found by inspecting the standard definitions of modernity (see Inkeles and Smith, 1974, for the best developed scheme). But it must be understood that we are not here considering these rules as collections of individual attitudes. Beyond this, they are world definitions of the justifications, perspectives, purposes, and policies properly to be pursued by nation-state organizations. The state, above all, is to be a modern rational organization, not a primordial entity. It is to pursue progress rationally on behalf of the nation with progress understood to be measured by world economic and social standards (roughly, GNP/capita, plus some nonmonetarized status elements), and with the nation understood as partly primordial, but increasingly to be constructed in the *future* through the state directed attainment of progress.

The means to be brought under state jurisdiction and organized toward the ends of progress have elaborated over time as the state system has evolved. In earlier centuries, various military powers and a few simple mercantilist controls were involved (see the papers in Tilly, 1975). In the last century, the world cultural definitions of proper state efforts have expanded enormously, perhaps with the increasing complexity of the world economic system, but certainly in accord with the increasingly elaborated ideological definitions of the nature and sources of progress. These basic definitions have now expanded to the point of establishing the proper state as essentially socialist in one or another form, incorporating the economy in its structure and assuming a commanding role.

But this system of justifications has expanded even beyond the focus on economic production of classic socialism. All sorts of sources of social value and progress come to be defined in rationalistic ways, and incorporated in the agenda and structure of the state. This is the rise, in world political culture, of the myths of "post-industrial society" (Bell, 1963; Ellul, 1964): rationalized depictions of progress and social control as involving all the components of the social system; or production function ideologies so broad as to almost completely transcend a narrow focus on economic production. The languages of economics are still used, but they are extended beyond any classic meaning to include every element in society as part of a general ideology of progress. Thus, the huge tertiary sectors of the "economy" arise and are justified by myths of their contribution as services to the economy and to economic progress. Payments to God and motherhood are justified, not as consumption, but as productive investments in human capital (apple pie has, of course, long since been commodified). Old activities are redefined and new ones constructed around these definitions. And in each case, the new definitions have the activities contributing to progress (read GNP/capita). Friendly advice and the confessional become psychotherapy, and the GNP rises. Mothering is rationalized in schooling, community recreation, medical and day care, and the GNP rises.

Boli-Bennett (1976, 1979a, 1979b) provides evidence on nation-state ideology that is directly relevant here. He studies the extant national constitutions in 1870, 1890, 1910, 1930, 1950, and 1970. All constitutions are coded in detail on the extensiveness of claimed state authority over many sectors of social and economic life, and also on the elaboration of the formal rights and duties of citizenship. Over the century of his study, great increases on these variables occur: States acquire constitutional authority and responsibility over many aspects such as economic life, family organization, and education. And they greatly expand the formal rights and duties of citizenship. Furthermore, new states entering the system in a given period claim the sets of powers prevailing in the system at the time: The prevailing world ideology of the state becomes the basis for new states—they do not start at the beginning. Still further, Boli-Bennett shows that *societal* development has little to do with these issues; in fact, peripheral states are likely to claim more constitutional powers than central ones, in any period. This is the important point: The state system is imbedded in and supported by a wider world polity, and is not simply a product of local factors operating in unison. The abstract authority claimed by any given nation-state, especially in the periphery, is much more a reflection of the state of the world system as it evolves over time than of basic societal complexity or development.

Mechanisms of Transmission

We have sketched out some of the rules of the contemporary world polity, arguing that they reflect more a genuine polity than simply a set of ideas or individual and subgroup values that happen to have diffused around the world. For this argument to be sustained, the case must be made that these rules are enforced as rules by parties outside any given social relation or national society. This is a major task, and only some brief notes can be made here.

First, the support of the other members of the state system is much more likely to go to organizations that take on the appropriate nation-state forms and responsibilities. Flows of economic aid, of arms, of support in international crises, follow these lines: They help the state against its external enemies, against alternative organizational forms (like ethnic organizations), and against the claims made by subgroups in its own society. It is easier to aid the Israelis than the Palestinians (despite much world sentiment in the opposite direction); to support the South Vietnamese when organized as a nation-state than when organized as a colony; easier and more legitimate to support a party when it controls a state (or makes such claims) than when it is simply a party. Further, it is easier to justify aiding a state that is making claims to be directing national progress—such aid is seen as transcending immediate network or coalition interests, and thus as lying beyond bribery or the maintenance of military coalitions.

Second, these relations of support among states are themselves supported by other states as third parties. The state system in part consists of the power of the shared public opinion of states, like many decentralized political systems. States tend to support the legitimacy of proper relations between other states. Disadvantages of a long-run kind are incurred by violations.

Third, the rules of transnational political bodies, such as the United Nations, symbolize and add force to the system. The same is true of transnational financial organizations, such as the World Bank or the IMF. These bodies support in very tangible ways, not only the state system as an organizational structure, but also its substantive purposes: Approved national development plans, for instance, are vital devices with which to obtain loans.

Fourth, even "private" transnational associations find it easier to deal with states—and often states rationalized around the goals of progress, at that—than with other kinds of bodies. The agreements they make are more stable and certain, and more likely to be supported by third and fourth parties.

Fifth, the organization of all this in a kind of world prestige system should be noted. World standards are invested in the depictions of the world communications system and built up in the dominant intellectual ideologies. Much of this simply reflects the economic standing of a given country, to be sure, but there is a good deal more, too. Having a fashionably elaborated state structure is an important asset. For one thing, it enables a rational account to be given of how progress is being achieved. For another, a possession of the approved structure provides internal organizational elements that parallel and link up with similar elements in other countries and in the system as a whole. A state organization parallel to the others in the system maximizes external linkages and supports. For many practical purposes— for instance getting loans—it is more important to have a national economic plan formulated so as to be interpretable by outside planners than to have one maximally attuned to local considerations.

Finally, all these exogenous forces are also represented in available elite ideologies internal to each country. World perspectives become the devices used by internal elites in deciding when and why and how to attack the established state. As external agreements rise that a given state or regime is inadequate, alternative elites formulate their plans, arrange their alliances, organize their ideological claims, and so on. Thus it is that in the modern period all sorts of unlikely national elites—the military, for instance—become the carriers of world standards of modernity. Generals who wish to take power learn the new grounds on which this can legitimately be done. And generals who have given little thought to the matter are called into action by problems which enter the world-defined agenda as crises.

Rational Strategy in Peripheral Societies

We have taken a systemic perspective, but shift now to consider effective action from the point of view of peripheral actors. These actors conduct themselves in a world system that contains: (*a*) a growing world economy providing much value with which to reward membership, but only on terms involving high dependence; and (*b*) a world polity defining progress and legitimating increasingly rationalized nation-states as central means for obtaining it. Some principles of action follow:

1. Peripheral actors increasingly organize as nation-states. The system selects out this organizational form from competing ones. Rational peripheral actors will learn to make the most effective claims: ethnic and religious ones, for instance, may help mobilize the internal population, but lack external legitimacy. In the long-run competition, those elites organizing as modern nation-state leaders win out.

2. The nation-state must be organized to control and incorporate the sources of value defined by the social organization and ideology of the sys-

tem as a whole. As the system evolves, these controls must be intensified, and social life is broadly controlled. More and more government is demanded by the system, and responsibility must be at least claimed (Huntington, 1968).

3. Over time, and as we move toward the periphery of the system, the externally legitimated state is increasingly at odds with ongoing peripheral social organization and dependency: The inconsistency, hypocrisy and ritualism involved is one of the most obvious properties of the modern world (Riggs, 1964).

Failure often results: It can involve the collapse even of formal independence. Or ritualism can result, with the maintenance of the normative fictions of state responsibility with no implementation—this often involves corrupt and passive praetorian regimes (Huntington, 1968) that coercively maintain the situation. This outcome is common in the extreme periphery. Alternatively delegitimation is accepted, coming to normative terms with the facts of dependence. This is stigmatized around the world as reactionary, but may involve temporary economic success. It requires strong coercive power, and often external military support. Such states may succeed economically, but fail to sustain legitimacy and reputation—Taiwan, Hong Kong, Singapore, Cyprus, Panama, South Africa, Rhodesia, Spain, Portugal, and South Korea are examples.

The politically successful strategy here is mobilization around the goal of progress (Apter, 1965). The state and its purposes are ideologically located with respect to the future. Individuals and society in the present are delegitimated as reactionary—to be molded by the plans and projects of the state. This strategy, with some Stalinist properties, requires great state power and strong state boundaries and controls. It also requires a myth of the regime other than that of present societal responsiveness. Communist parties, or increasingly military elites, take this role. The official separation of state and society is involved: Society becomes the object, not the source, of state authority and action. States of this kind have some common properties: Regimes are unitary, not pluralistic (Thomas *et al.*, 1979); state bureaucracies expand rapidly; flows of value in the wider system are brought under control; and sacrifices in present value are justified by claimed gains in future value.

Socialisms—though of strange kinds, as we note later—come to be dominant in the modern periphery. They defend against dependence, and they construct a future by incorporating the modern sources of value.

Resources of the Peripheral State

The external supports of the world nation-state system give each peripheral state a great deal of control, enabling it to become differentiated

from the society over which it assumes dominance. These external supports
—aid, military support, protection, legitimation—have greatly increased.
With the elaboration of the world polity, internal supports rise too: Elites
(military, political, intellectual) and sectors of the population subscribe to
the goal of competitive progress in the world.

But the rules of the world political system confer much more concrete
resources than these. We have been misled in this by imagining that the rationalized world is really a world commodity economy. Consider the types
of value available and legitimated in the modern system—the fashionable
factors of production. It turns out that increasingly, many of these are local
—not under the direct controls of exchange in the world commodity economy:

1. *Capital* is indeed scarce, organized in terms of world prices, and
controlled in centers. Peripheral countries, if they depend on capital, are dependent and grow slowly (Chase-Dunn, 1975). Some possibilities for the
forced local mobilization of capital can be found, however.

2. Many necessary *commodities,* too, must be obtained externally
from central societies. Here again there is a world economy: high prices—
world prices—carry the social and political costs of central societies values.
Capital and commodity utilization, in the effective peripheral strategy, must
be minimized.

3. *Land,* however, is controlled by local states. Much expropriation,
even, is possible and legitimated. The value of land falls under state control,
in some part.

4. *Technology* and the technical division of labor have never been
brought under effective collective control in the system primarily because of
the absence of a world empire. Technical gains have never been stably accounted in the system. Technology has been heavily valued, but this value
has been assigned in varying ways, depending on ideological considerations:
sometimes to individual creative action, sometimes to state action, later to
capital, and in the current period to the virtues of a differentiated and in-
structed labor force. More important, organizationally it has been structured frequently as a collective good, available to peripheral societies at relatively low prices. Technology is readily available, sometimes through
licensing arrangements, but much more often through the social creation of
the relevant technicians in the educational system and elsewhere. The costs
here are labor costs, and are very low in the periphery as we note later. In
any event, peripheral societies pay much lower relative prices for technical
development than for capital and commodities.

5. The world system guarantees the state a *labor force,* and defines an
enormous amount of technical (or capital, or labor, depending on the particular ideology involved) value as located in this labor force if it is properly
organized (e.g., human capital). The state is given the feudal power to re-

strict labor flows across boundaries—otherwise workers would flow to central societies as a few do now, legally or illegally. And the political culture locates much value in labor. This means that the cumulative thrust of world inequality shows up overwhelmingly in wage differentials among countries. World commodity and capital prices thus extract resources from peripheral countries, inasmuch as exchange occurs, and indeed thus derive value from the low wage rates of peripheral societies (Amin, 1974). But insofar as value is generated locally, these low wage rates confer an enormous resource on peripheral states—one that counteracts their dependence on those factors organized in terms of world prices.

The world polity thus confers the opportunity for "progress" on the periphery, and constructs a rational strategy for pursuing this progress. It is rational to reorganize the population around modern labor-intensive technical activity, and to minimize the utilization of external capital and commodities.

6. *Politically defined production,* a further constraint (and opportunity), exists: Reorganizing populations is difficult, and technology is complex. Failures are likely. But this is the case only with technical commodities: One can try to organize people around the assembly of transistor radios and fail to produce them. Social services do not have this property—the value of an elementary school graduate, a state service, or a military unit is politically and institutionally defined by the local nation-state itself, not the world market. The power given to the nation-state by the world system to institutionalize the complete ideology of modernity in its structure is the power to define rationalized value, within the constraints of abstract world cultural definitions, as having been produced. The state can organize the "production" of technically invisible services, and can define these services as having been produced. And by all the world standards of progress and national accounting (GNP), success is attained.

Thus, the rational strategy for peripheral growth emphasizes the labor-intensive production of technically validated social services: in other words, the quick development of postindustrial society even in contexts with little industrial development.

7. Consider *state primordiality: Politically defined consumption.* What if the people in peripheral society do not choose to value the state-produced invisible services? What if they claim the emperor has no clothes? Our problem is that we have considered as resources only the state's legitimated capacity to control factors of "production." This is inadequate. Just as modern society and exchange precipitated the authorized individual as a primordial unit capable of expanded consumption choices, so the world system constitutes its citizen nation-states. Within the bounds of world-defined value, the state is endowed with the right and power to define, control, and

coerce consumption; and thus to construct internal social value. This development is not yet complete; state coerced consumption must still be justified in part as an investment in production—that is, in the long-run future developments of society. This maintains a general submission to the standards of world political culture.

Thus, a modern individual can value decorations on cars, a face-lift, or a variety of invisible joys—he can even pay for the pleasures of resourcelessness in the wilderness. All these validated choices enter the collective value system through the market economy. So the modern state can define a whole host of services as valuable or essential, and "distort" both production and consumption of them, through its own choices. This can be done directly through the taxation of subunits and through explicit state expenditure. Or it can be done through the compulsion of subunit choices (e.g., requiring individuals and communities to opt for education).

Thus, in a host of service areas, the state gains the power to produce value, to define the value that has been produced, and to define the value as having been used or consumed: for example, producing, defining, and consuming elementary school graduates, university-trained sociologists, government services, or military services. The GNP rises—and modernity is obtained by world standards. All these services are rationalized and monetarized, and defined in the new usage as somehow "economic."

Through its capacity to define consumption (or production for the very long distant future, which is almost the same thing) the modern state, perhaps even more than the modern individual, is given legitimated primordial status in the world polity. If an internal economy arises in the individual, a family, a village, a tribe, a commune, or an ethnic group, it is treated as reactionary, and of no collective value—inasmuch as exchanges are withdrawn from the national and world systems, national and world gross products fall. But if the state engages in the same activities, rationalizing services and creating new ones, progress is, by definition, attained. The modern state can even account as accruing to value, for instance, expenditures for the extermination of parts of its population. GNP per capita will rise even more rapidly than GNP.

Of course, socially constructing and sustaining definitions of invisible commodities requires much political work. It is much easier when the world polity provides strong supports. Education, for instance, is ideal. It is a world-legitimated consumption good, but is also a world-legitimated investment: All sorts of ideologies define it as an important factor of production (e.g., Harbison and Myers, 1963). Peripheral countries can import central professional economists and manpower planners who will help legitimate it, and even make possible external loans and aid for its development. Its production is labor-intensive; furthermore, the value of the professional labor, defined as relevant to educational production, is itself socially defined—supported by the world polity but scaled in terms of local prices. Education thus expands greatly in peripheral societies, but many other services do too.

Problems

The strategy outlined here creates difficulties that require control and adaptation. In its extreme form, it involves the construction of a whole mandarin system in which state functionaries provide social services for each other. Problems arise, requiring the further expansion of the state and its further separation from society; when this is not done, inflation results.

The difficulty lies in the fact that individual, subgroup, and state expenditures—using money deriving value from the constructed services—are sometimes directed to commodities that have world market prices. But the expanded local tertiary sector does not expand production of these commodities or of any commodities that can be exchanged for them. Money, thus, comes to be inflated in peripheral societies, when defined in terms of world commodity prices.

To control this, controls on money—or better on commodity consumption—are required. Tariffs, import restrictions, prohibitions of consumption, and so on, are necessary. From the point of view of the commodity economy, the whole state system is a gigantic set of sumptuary laws—a refeudalization of the world economy. If complete control is impossible, commodity import substitution is useful. From the point of view of maximizing progress (GNP), this is less desirable than pure postindustrial mandarinism, but it is not as expensive as purchasing commodities from the center. Technology is cheap and labor is cheaper. Some success can be obtained.

There is a special problem here with food: To obtain world commodities, land is directed to the production of world agricultural commodities—coffee, tea, sugar, cotton, cocoa, poppies, bananas, rubber, marijuana, etc. This diverts land from traditional food production, and given the unfortunate inelasticity in human demand for food, the possibility of some starvation arises; only to a limited extent can progress in education and state services be substituted for food. One solution is to distribute food to those groups central in the emergent modern state-centered stratification system —those groups maximally involved in the new state-constructed value. This involves the repression and sometimes starvation of rural populations (Lauwagie, 1978). As is often noted, stratification in the modern periphery involves the urban–rural distinction. The sources of this in the modern nation-state are less often noted.

In managing all these problems, advantages lie with the one-party or military state, stigmatizing social demand as illegitimate, reactionary, self-ish, and undisciplined. Thus the peripheral states expand so rapidly, not only through isomorphism with the organizational structure and ideology of the center, but out of the requirements for social control reactively imposed on them by the world system. This does not, of course, explain how they can obtain this control. Clearly the wider state system, with its organizational network and ideology, helps here.

Some Organizational Features on the World Polity as a Whole

The modern system is in contrast with a simple world capitalist structure, built around commodity production and exchange in an expanded division of labor controlled by capital—a system organized around relatively free markets in capital, commodities, and labor. We have described a world in which commodity production becomes less important, in which political controls take precedence over, and replace, capital; in which labor markets are closed; in which exchange (international, at least) is politically regulated; and in which the units of exchange begin to lose common social meaning.

Polanyi's Great Transformation (1944) was the differentiation of economic life from local social and political life, and its integration (along with that of the individual and group identities that enter into it) with long-distance markets. He saw the nineteenth and twentieth centuries as producing the slow assumption of social and political control over the new economic system. Schumpeter (1950) saw the same process, though with less optimism. So did Marx and Weber. In our own period, Ellul (1964), Bendix (1964, 1968, 1978), and Bell (1973), follow up the Weberian discussion with very different assessments.

Our point here, following these earlier discussions, is that with the modern world polity, a Great Untransformation occurs. International markets and controls are separated from national ones. States, operating with their general world charter, assume the powers to define and control value, and do so in terms that are increasingly distant from any world price arrangements. Thus, the world polity with its legitimated nation-state system assaults many of the properties of the integrated world economy that helped create it. Though it has no center, a great deal of control over the production and exchange of value is obtained.

So far as its wider structure goes, the critical legitimating rules of the world polity can be summarized as follows: Those elements and values of the world polity whose local prices and values are defined, controlled, and mediated by the nation-state system, are most highly legitimated. But those organizational elements which operate through the international exchange system are delegitimated. This basic distinction defines a fundamental fact about the legitimation of the various elites and functionaries of the world political and economic systems.

Feudal Functionaries

THE DELEGITIMATION OF THE INTERNATIONAL CAPITALISTS

The long-distance traders—in particular the multi-national corporations that embody this process—are delegitimated, and states attempt direct controls over them. As it were, they are the Jews of the modern world polity; they are perceived as necessary, powerful, wealthy, but stigmatized in important ways as illicit pariahs. Attempts are made to ghettoize them and to restrict their bases of operation, control them, and separate their structures and values from the local population. They are seen as lying outside the collective interest, as exploitative and selfish; elaborate literatures describe their special and illegitimate powers in the system. They lie outside society yet are linked to, and partly controlled by, states (as Huntington, 1973, notes, their power is not inconsistent with the state system at all). In periods of trouble, difficulties can be attributed to them and expropriatory programs attempted: Occasionally their agents can even be imprisoned, kidnapped, or killed, with at least some legitimacy (e.g., Uruguay, Argentina, and elsewhere). Empirical research could easily establish the greater legitimacy of the assassination of one of these agents than of a member of a more legitimated elite of the system.

Note how distinctively these organizations are treated. States and regimes form all sorts of relations with each other; they bribe each other routinely, and employ all the standard political manipulations. It is all more or less acceptable, however unattractive. But when a multinational corporation plays the same game of bribing and manipulating states and regimes (for instance, to make sales), it is seen as the height of illegitimacy. The acceptable forms of corruption are monopolized by the state system: A regime can bribe another regime for a UN vote or to sell commodities while a firm cannot properly do so.

STATE FUNCTIONARIES AS ORGANIZATIONAL ELITES IN THE SYSTEM

Clearly the elites of each state are privileged functionaries in the wider system, as with any feudal nobility. Even the weak elites of such central institutions as the UN have a distinctive status as symbolizing the collective polity. Separate legal arrangements define the status of these people as they move about. Their troubles receive world-wide attention; when one rises or falls a great drama is created. One could empirically study the world attention given to the rise or fall of such elite members compared with other elites in the system.

World-wide charisma is attached to these functionaries—much more than to other elites in the system (the past charisma of the great international capitalists has been turned to deviance). A state leader is seen as much more potent than an important business leader, and becomes increasingly so over time. Some of this charisma, as with any feudal system, is linked to privileged access to special weaponry (especially, in the modern instance of nuclear weapons).

THE ELITES OF THE WORLD POLITICAL CULTURE

Like any decentralized polity, the world polity is held together by something of a common culture, and by a clergy that embodies this common culture and its authority, without operating either through the formally legitimated hierarchies of bureaucracy or through the exchange system. Broadly, in the modern world, these are the modernizing intellectuals. These people carry with them the great values—but not the delegitimated exchange values and prices—of the modern world, especially science, technology, and the more universal professions. They are highly legitimated by the nation states in the system because they bring the supports of progress (enhancing, by and large, state power) without many costs by way of exchange dependence. Thus the intellectuals, especially those linked to myths of technique, have a distinctive world standing and act with special privilege. Their culture and international links are not nearly so suspect as those, for instance, of the capitalists. They are members both of their own societies and of a world elite and are protected both by their wider cultural status and by the legitimated international organizational networks in which they participate (i.e., their Church and Orders).

A state that takes one of these persons is much more likely to run into difficulty and protest than is occasioned by the taking of a member of some more local elite. World protest is much more common; the state's legitimacy is brought, to some extent, into question. This is true, not only of scientific and technical elites, but to some extent of all representatives of the mysteries of the common culture. Experiments with hypothetical situations can show it: How much more protest will be occasioned by the taking of a trombonist from the national orchestra than, say, by that of a local lawyer (the law, by and large, is particular to individual states)? The trombonist carries value from the whole world system—world human capital, as it were, is being lost. In addition, of course, the legitimated trombonist network may be activated in protest.

A Note on the Reconstruction of the Individual

The rise of the nation-state system subordinates not only the world exchange system, but also the status of the individual. As production and exchange come to be rationalized around state purposes, and as these purposes come increasingly to comprehend the long-distant future, states achieve more and more primordiality (in a sense, as ultimate consumers). The authority of the individual, acting in exchange as a legitimated agent of himself, is weakened. Increasingly, individual rights are not primary, but are derived from individual membership in the state (Bendix, 1964; Boli-Bennett, 1979b). The individual loses validity as an autonomous actor in the system, but does not necessarily lose value. The modern state accounting has the individual as manpower for societal purpose. Like other objects of value, he may receive even more protection than in classic individualisms.

Of course, the battle to delegitimate the individual and the myths of free action and exchange occasioned some violence. The twentieth century has seen sustained wars of the state system against the individual, with mass extermination extending (as with other state powers) from marginal centers (Germany) and near-peripheries (the USSR, Turkey) to the furthest marginal peripheries (Cambodia and elsewhere). Now, the state system has triumphed; states are sufficiently supported, validated, and justified by the external culture and political network that the great period of witchhunts (Bergesen, 1977) may be almost over.

But the individual retains a shadow primordiality; the wider culture is built on myths of ultimate individual progress and welfare. In earlier feudalism, the primordial value of the individual was located in an Augustinian other world. In our world, something of the same phenomenon occurs: the individual acquires a kind of sentimental status—the peasant of the modern world, to be protected by the state in conformity with a new kind of natural law.

COSMOLOGICAL CHANGES

With the increased legitimation of the world polity, and the decreased legitimation of the world exchange economy, come alterations in the broader depictions of reality. There is a decline in the conception of the world around human society as an impersonal, natural, lawful, and essentially infinite system, within which individual and subgroups' exchanges and production can indefinitely expand. Fueled especially by the cultural labors of the elites of the world polity, there is a rise in the depiction of the natural order as infused with meanings that impose or require limitations on human society. Many of these meanings are given some kind of technical or scientific basis, while a few attribute to the natural world something like intentionality. Almost all have the long run import of strengthening the social control of the world polity, by elaborating new forms of natural law justification for world-level rules.

First, there is an elaboration of cultural doctrines about the "collective other" of human social life—the natural and moral universe confronted by humans collectively. Scientific ideas about the structure, origins, and future of the universe receive more attention, for instance. But attributed intentionality builds up around these concerns too. Serious scientists discuss the prospects for finding other life in the universe, and obtain large state fundings to try to communicate with this putative life. Expensive messages are sent out to the universe. On a more popular level, interest and faith in visitations by other intelligent beings in the universe is high: All these concerns are secularized, as visitations are understood to occur in the natural universe, not in a spiritual one.

It can be noted, however, that there has also been a rise in agreement that humans face a common transcendental other. The gods of the various world religions become increasingly unified, and religious techniques and ideas flow from one to another society. In a secularized world, these changes seem relatively unimportant. It seems more rational to pay engineers to send electronic statements of the Pythagorean Theorem out into the universe than to work out the unification of Jehovah and Allah.

Second, the world outside human society is depicted as posing collective problems. Self-interest is delegitimated as a source of progress; and various "discoveries" symbolize its conflicts with common human collective interests. Thus, it comes to be supposed that continued simple exchange relations will generate chemicals that pollute the air or the oceans or that destroy a vital protective ozone layer in the upper atmosphere—or something will destroy or alter the radiation belts that surround the earth, or too much carbon dioxide will create a "greenhouse" effect that will make the earth less livable, or the limitations that unified and expanded human life places on the prospects for other species (in both number and diversity) are rediscovered. We want to save the whales, and even find reasons to preserve the bacteria that create smallpox. All these depictions, of course, increase the prospects for collective action in the world polity and hence the strength of that polity itself.

Third, re-emergent conceptions describe unregulated human exchange or competition as creating fundamental conflicts and inconsistencies, and thus as requiring collective world control. A central image here is the need to control nuclear weapons, and the modern delegitimation of war as an instrument of national policy. One of the central justifications of the world polity—and thus, ironically, of the nation-state system it supports—has been the fear of war and, correspondingly, of disorder. As each state takes its place in the system, and acquires the organizational capacity to subordinate its population, we perceive peace.

Further, the world economy's exchange relations are seen as directly threatening and conflictful. Rather than being defined as a system of expanding production only, the world economy is seen as a system of distribution and (given norms of equality) as highly inequitable. With an increasingly integrated concept of the world economy, that is, the great economic inequalities among nations come to be seen as inequities requiring social control. So, we less often describe national development as autonomous (i.e., bars on a graph) and increasingly depict it as a division of common resources (i.e., sectors of a pie). These changed definitions of world exchange as inequitably dividing up a relative fixed set of commodities are engines of further mobilization of world political rules on behalf of equity. They are also, of course, legitimators of national mobilization in nation-state subunits.

Conclusions

We have described the world polity as a system of rules legitimating the extension and expansion of authority of rationalized nation-states to control and act on behalf of their populations. We see these worldwide rules as helping to account for the dominance and rapid "modernization" of states and societies in the economic peripheries of the world, or as rapidly extending world "citizenship" to even very weak national societies. We have further argued that world political rules counteract powerfully some of the forces of exchange dependence built into the world economy. These rules give peripheral states many resources with which to act for progress: (*a*), the power and external supports to mobilize for progress even against the preferences of local populations; (*b*), the resource of legitimate control over labor supply at very low wage rates (arising from the blockage of labor markets at national boundaries); (*c*), the use of many available technologies at low cost; (*d*), the legitimation of many social service technologies that can be implemented and will produce benefits *by state definition;* and (*e*), the right and power to control consumption (or investment for very long-run purposes, which is almost the same thing), diverting it to state-produced and defined modern values.

Under all these forces, industrialization and especially postindustrial activities have spread around the world more rapidly than would have been predicted by simple exchange theories. These developments have many peculiar qualities, and especially make world inequalities seem glaring. But this in itself is a source of further mobilization in the world polity. The definition of world inequalities as inequitable is used to justify some of the most extreme forms of coercion and control by states over their populations.

In all this discussion, we have made only scattered comments on the logic of the origins of the world as a polity. Clearly, many lines of thought beyond our discussion are relevant here: e.g., network or coalition arguments about the conditions under which peripheries gained autonomy (Ness and Ness, 1972; see chapter 10 of this volume by Bergesen and Schoenberg). However, it also seems to be the case that the process is a kind of dialectical reaction to the rise, and institutional codification, of the world economy. Exchange generates power; the analysis and institutionalization of exchange generates authority. The norms of justice created in the world exchange system also legitimate the rise of the peripheral state. The evolving ideologies— or accounts of progress, or myths of production—of central societies provide legitimacy for the peculiar forms of progress pursued in peripheries.

Acknowledgments

This chapter has benefited from many discussions with colleagues—particularly Christopher Chase-Dunn and John Boli-Bennett. At several points, ideas and data from papers written with these colleagues are incorporated: especially Meyer *et al.,* 1975; and Chase-Dunn *et al.,* 1974. See also Meyer and Hannan (1979, Chapter 17). I have also been helped by extended comments on an earlier draft of the paper from Albert Bergesen, Paul Hirsch, Jacques Delacroix, Francisco Ramirez, Richard Rubinson, Arthur Stinchcombe, Charles Tilly, and George Thomas. These colleagues are, of course, not responsible for the arguments presented here—in a number of cases they provided assistance despite major disagreements with these arguments.

References

Amin, Samir
    1974   *Accumulation on a World Scale* (Vol. 1). New York: Monthly Review Press.
Apter, David E.
    1965   *The Politics of Modernization.* Chicago: University of Chicago Press.
Bell, Daniel
    1973   *The Coming of Post-Industrial Society.* New York: Basic Books.
Bendix, Reinhard
    1964   *Nation-Building and Citizenship.* New York: Wiley.
    1968   State and Society: a Reader in Comparative Political Sociology. Boston: Little, Brown.
    1978   *Kings or People: Power and the Mandate to Rule.* Berkeley, California: University of California Press.
Berger, Peter, and Thomas Luckmann
    1967   *The Social Construction of Reality.* New York: Doubleday.

Bergesen, Albert J.
  1977   "Political witch-hunts: The sacred and the subversive in cross-national perspective." *American Sociological Review* 42 (April):220–233.
Bergesen, Albert and R. Schoenberg
  1980   "Long Waves of Colonial Expansion and Contraction, 1415–1969." In A. Bergesen (ed.), *Studies of the Modern World System*. New York: Academic Press.
Blum, Alan F., and Peter McHugh
  1971   "The social ascription of motives." *American Sociological Review* 36 (December):98–109.
Boli-Bennett, John
  1976   The Expansion of the State, 1870–1970. Unpublished doctoral dissertation. Stanford University, Department of Sociology.
  1979a   "The ideology of expanding state authority in national constitutions, 1870–1970." In J. Meyer and M. Hannan, *National Development and the World System*. Chicago: University of Chicago Press.
  1979b   "Human rights or state expansion? Cross-national definitions of constitutional rights, 1870–1970." To appear in a collection edited by J. Scarritt and V. Nanda. Boulder, Colorado: Westview Press.
Chase-Dunn, Christopher
  1975   "The effects of international economic dependence on development and inequality: A cross-national study." *American Sociological Review* 40:720–738.
Chase-Dunn, Christopher, John Boli-Bennett, and John W. Meyer
  1974   "Some effects of the contemporary world structure on nation-states and other subunits." Paper presented at the Annual Meetings of the Pacific Sociological Association, San Jose, California, (March).
Davis, Kingsley
  1969   *World Urbanization* 1950–1970. Berkeley, California: University of California Population Monograph Series Number 4.
Ellul, Jacques
  1964   *The Technological Society*. New York: Knopf.
Goffman, Erving
  1967   *Interaction Ritual*. Garden City, New York: Anchor Books.
Harbison, Frederick H., and Charles A. Myers
  1964   *Education, Manpower and Economic Growth*. New York: McGraw-Hill.
Huntington, Samuel P.
  1968   *Political Order in Changing Societies*. New Haven: Yale University Press, 1968.
  1973   "Transnational organizations in world politics." *World Politics* 25, 333–368.
Inkeles, Alex, and David H. Smith
  1974   *Becoming Modern*. Cambridge, Mass.: Harvard University Press.
Lauwagie, Beverly N.
  1978   "The social dynamics of hunger: Food production in the world economy." Unpublished paper, Dept. of Sociology, Stanford University.
Meyer, John W., Francisco O. Ramirez, Richard Rubinson, and John Boli-Bennett
  1977   "The world educational revolution, 1950–1970. *Sociology of Education,* 50 (October):242–258.
Meyer, John W., and Brian Rowan
  1977   "Institutionalized organizations: Formal structure as myth and ceremony." *American Journal of Sociology* 83 (Sept.):340–363.
Meyer, John W., Michael T. Hannan, Richard Rubinson, and George M. Thomas
  1979   "National economic development in the contemporary world system." In John

Meyer and Michael Hannan (eds.), *National Development and the World System.* Chicago: University of Chicago Press.

Meyer, John W., and Michael T. Hannan
1979   *National Development and the World System.* Chicago: University of Chicago Press.

Meyer, John W., John Boli-Bennett, and Christopher Chase-Dunn
1975   "Convergence and divergence in development." *Annual Review of Sociology* I:223 –246.

Ness, G. D., and J. R. Ness
1972   "Metropolitan power and demise of overseas colonial empires." Presented at the Annual Meetings of the American Sociological Association, August.

Polanyi, Karl
1944   *The Great Transformation.* New York: Rinehart & Company.

Riggs, Fred W.
1964   *Administration in Developing Societies: The Theory of Prismatic Society.* Boston: Houghton Mifflin.

Rubinson, Richard
1977   "Dependence, government revenue, and economic growth." *Studies in Comparative International Development* 12 (Summer): 3–28.

Schumpeter, J. A.
1950   *Capitalism, Socialism and Democracy.* New York: Harper and Row.

Scott, Marvin B., and Stanford M. Lyman
1968   "Accounts." *American Sociological Review* 33 (February): 46–62.

Thomas, George M., Francisco O. Ramirez, John W. Meyer, and Jeanne Gobalet
1979   "Maintaining national boundaries in the world system: The rise of centralist regimes." In John Meyer and Michael Hannan (eds.), *National Development and the World System.* Chicago: University of Chicago Press.

Tilly, Charles, ed.
1975   *The Formation of National States in Western Europe.* Princeton, New Jersey: Princeton University Press.

Tilly, Charles
1976   "Migration in modern European history." Working Paper #145. Center for Research on Social Organization, University of Michigan. (October).

Wallerstein, Immanuel
1974   *The Modern World-System.* New York: Academic Press.

Chapter 7

George M. Thomas
John W. Meyer

Regime Changes and State Power in an Intensifying World-State-System

In this chapter, we consider the problems in the linkage between states and regimes in peripheral societies created by the modern world-state-system. We mean by "states" the collective agencies—for the most part now bureaucratized—that assume authority and jurisdiction over society and many of its domains (Swanson, 1971). By "regimes" we mean the social interests (parties, other organizations, and elites) that define the collective interests of society and command state policies.

We argue first that the world is organized in a state system that defines, legitimates, and supports state forms in societies—sometimes, indeed, imposing them on societies. In the weak, dependent, and new peripheral nations, states are mostly exogenous in origin, designed by both internal and external forces around standard world models and criteria of legitimacy rather than in terms of some organic relation to the societies over which they take authority.

Second, we argue that the exogenous character of the peripheral state creates problems of legitimacy and stability for the regimes that link state and society. These problems are greater where the peripheral state organization is strong and its claims to authority great, not where it is weak. Thus, the stronger the state in the peripheral society, the greater the conflict over the nature of the regime. This runs against a functional line of reasoning that might suppose that strong states support stable regimes. We argue further that in linking state and society, new regimes tend to increase the power

STUDIES OF THE
MODERN WORLD-SYSTEM

ISBN 0-12-090550-7

and authority of the state. Thus, regime turbulence in peripheral societies—given the larger context—creates not weaker states but stronger ones.

Finally, we present some quantitative empirical analyses of the interrelations between state strength and regime stability in peripheral societies. The data suggest that in the periphery of the modern world-state-system the relations between these properties are quite different from those we might expect in a world in which states evolved less from a larger system than from societies themselves.

The Expansion of the State System

The system of nation-states is now essentially world-wide. Almost all the world's territory is divided up among a set of legitimated states that have high levels of broad jurisdiction over social life. Some territories and populations are not yet incorporated, and some states have not yet acquired complete legitimacy in the system as a whole. But in the main, the system is firmly in place, with surprisingly few boundary conflicts or movements; the fact that unincorporated territories are seen as major social problems and receive much attention, underscores the world-wide agreement on the organizational form of the state system.

There is also surprising agreement on the state's jurisdictional content. Within the world-system, states are given the right and responsibility to control their populations, including labor flows across boundaries; to pursue social and economic progress; to press for modern developments such as education and welfare; to attempt to organize and control internal inequalities; to structure and impose a dominant national culture; and to suppress internal dissidents who resist all these efforts. Conflicts between first, second, and third worlds should not blind us to the facts that in all three worlds the state is the main legitimate mechanism for the pursuit of progress, and that progress is defined in remarkably similar ways. The political factions of the world-system differ on many issues, but they agree that the main organs that must be adapted to their goals are nation-states.

Evidence for these arguments is strong. Whatever may be going on with other organizations, such as multinational firms, the organizations that each year command increasing proportions of world or national gross products are nation-states (Meyer *et al.*, 1975). This happens in both rich and poor, or central and peripheral, societies. Similarly, the proportion of the world's labor force employed by states rises—again in both central and peripheral societies. The expansion of state-linked institutions, such as education, formalized welfare systems, armies, government bureaucracies, national planning systems, and national cultural institutions, has been striking. More abstractly, the ideological support for expanded states with expanded social jurisdictions has increased greatly. Boli-Bennett coded the constitutions of the national societies of the world since 1870 on measures of the extent of legitimized state authority (1979). There are extraordinary increases in the extent of state jurisdiction and authority over the period. The increases clearly reflect world-wide standards and characterize both rich and poor countries. If anything, peripheral states have higher formal authority and responsibility (though not organizational resources) than central ones.

Along with the world-wide agreement on the universal, expanded, and legitimized state, there is much political and economic conflict in the world-system. However, this conflict centers on the regimes that link these states to their societies and to other states in the world-system, and not on the existence or authority of states. There is world-wide agreement on the existence of an expanded Chilean state; the conflict has been over the regime and the internal policies and external relations that will govern this state. So, with the breakdown of the colonial system in Angola, there was world-wide agreement that there must be an Angolan state (presumably with the same panoply of powers that exists everywhere else), but sharp internal and external conflict over its controlling regime. The expansion of the state system, and its character as exogenous to the particular societies over which it assumes command, create many regime conflicts and much turbulence.[1]

Present theories account for these observations inadequately. Some are applicable only to an earlier world in which states emerged from societies (Fried, 1960, calls these "pristine states"). We cannot take seriously the view that modern strong states arise mainly out of interstate competition, whether economic or political or military. In earlier European history one of the driving forces for state expansion, and a determinant of state survival, was military competition. (See the papers in Tilly, 1975, and to some extent the discussion of the French, Russian, and Chinese revolutions in Skocpol, 1979.) Now, and even in the nineteenth century, many states are created and survive that cannot make their way in military competition. Weak states survive on the legitimation agreements that make up the state system; their initial emergence from the colonial epoch often had this character. Many of these states would not even be able to prevent internal fragmentation without much external legitimacy, aid, and support.

Other theories have it that earlier states formed out of the elites generated by the world economic system (Wallerstein, 1974). Strong states formed in economic core areas and weak ones (if independent states at all)

---

[1] The nature of the regime is also circumscribed by the larger world-state-system. There is room for many different regimes, but all must maintain the world model of the state to retain legitimacy. For example, Amin's regime in Uganda did not completely lose legitimacy until it invaded a neighboring state, a major violation of the world rules defining sovereignty.

in the periphery. Economic roles in the world-system still substantially affect state power (Rubinson, 1978), but a world division of labor cannot easily explain the present dominance of relatively strong states in all sorts of societies.

A useful theory must stress the causal importance of the world-system as a whole in creating and sustaining this system of national states. For instance, we suggest three lines of thought that emphasize the relevance of a world polity:

1. An expanded world culture defines progress and equality as goals but provides no world state through which they may be attained. This legitimates state action—even, or especially, in impoverished peripheries—as the means to achieve progress (Meyer, Chapter 6 of this volume). Internal and external groups come to see the state as a central device to attain progress and justice.
2. The state system itself has become an institutionalized polity in the world, and becomes a coalition in which all members support each other, analogous to other state-less polities in history.
3. Institutionalized conflicts among core powers give, by political processes, some momentum and autonomy to peripheral states (Ness and Ness, 1972).

These arguments are complementary; all of them suggest how states become highly legitimated actors in the system. The state becomes the device to attain growth, pursue internal equality, defend and advance society in the raw economic competition of the world, and so on. The social and economic integration of the world creates an agenda, or an account, of legitimate actions in the common stratification and value systems, and the state becomes the organization by which these actions can occur.

Once the state is fixed as the legitimate collective actor, its expansion need not be driven by specific elite interests. It may fulfill particular interests of dominant groups such as world capitalist forces; but the system has now become hegemonic. It is external to particular local interest patterns and organizations in dependent societies, and it is authoritative apart from particular economic or social interests. Groups internal and external to particular societies come to see the expanded state as a solution to their demands. The key conclusion is that *the expanded strong state arises in most of the modern world from forces external to the society it manages, and is sustained by such forces. Internal groups that support it derive their coherence less from the natural play of forces within society than from the operation and legitimating rules of the system as a whole.*

Thus the peripheral state obtains external support in two ways. External groups, especially other states in the system, directly provide legitimacy, aid, and military support with which the state can command its population. This network is legitimated in the world political culture. But the wider system sustains the state by its indirect influence on internal groups as well. As they are reconstituted in the modern world-system, diverse groups within the peripheral society come to see the creation and expansion of the state as an answer to their claims, less because of internal social evolution than because of the external legitimation of the state as the central instrument of progress.

Two aspects of the expansion of the modern peripheral state may be distinguished. First, the state grows organizationally, in terms of its taxing power and its bureaucratic control. An indicator of this is the proportion of the gross national product that is taken by the state (see Meyer *et al.*, 1975). This rises steadily in the periphery. The second aspect is the expansion of formal authority of the peripheral state: the number of social domains over which it assumes jurisdiction and the extent of its authority in each domain. One indicator of this is the extent of state power as legitimized in the national constitution (Boli-Bennett, 1979). This has been rising steadily in the periphery as well as in the core. The two aspects of state expansion are not as highly related as it might seem; the difference between them will be of some importance in our later discussion.

The Problem of the State Regime

Even pristine states are not built solely out of the evolution of internal forces. Although nation-building movements helped construct stable states by building societal interests into the regimes (often violently), many of these movements even in early European history gained their impetus from the initial penetration of society by a centralizing authority (cf. Polanyi, 1944). The state makes demands on and attempts to bureaucratically control individuals and subgroups, politicizing social life and constructing rules of universalism. The state thereby makes itself a central arena of social conflict. As the fixed larger context for conflicts, the state itself is usually not delegitimated, but early in the process there are no adequately defined and legitimated organizational and symbolic forms that link diverse constituent interests to the state bureaucracy. Dissident groups do not question the existence of the state or its universalism as much as they attempt to specify what these elements might mean, thereby constructing a more fully political nation. Each group has its own version of the nation and the state, and competition ensues over the nature of the regime in control.

These factors, to some extent present in Western development, are especially relevant to the modern world for two reasons: (*a*) the state system is much more highly institutionalized within the world polity (see Meyer, Chapter 6); and (*b*) within this system the state's powers and authority, and the degree to which it penetrates society, have greatly increased (see Boli-Bennett, Chapter 5). The strong and authoritative externally-sanctioned state makes the lack of integrating national symbols and loyalties a greater problem than in an earlier world. Established by fiat within the world polity, new states in the modern world do not have the advantage of long-term nation-building movements that construct a political society. More important, modern nation-building movements have much more to legitimate in a greatly expanded state system.

Much turbulence results. Lacking legitimating structures, any particular regime is likely to have too little support to remain in power. Given the irresistible presence of the state, "dissident" groups, with their own ideologies, little loyalty to established society, and their own external coalitions, form conflicting social movements. Some groups fight out particular economic and social interests within the state arena; others, usually factions around the state itself, attempt to deal more explicitly with the problems of state and society.[2]

Those groups that attempt to secede and create a new state (for instance, Biafra), or create a non-state organization (the early movement of the Kurds), violate rules of the larger state system: The breakdown of the state is viewed both internally and externally as a collapse into traditionalism and dependence. Such groups gain little external support, ending almost always in defeat or cooptation (cf. Ellul, 1978). Most dissident groups do not assault the state, but attack the regime in control.

Thus, part of the regime problem in the modern peripheral state lies in the ineffective linkage between a strong authoritative state and society. As a general assertion, *peripheral state expansion of central bureaucratic controls and demands, creates a problem of regime power and legitimation, and leaves regimes unstable and turbulent.*

A second aspect of the problem of peripheral regimes result from the fact that although state organization and control over resources expand in the modern world, the state authority and responsibility derived from the standard world polity models increase even more. The peripheral state is to

---

[2] There is a great vacuum here, and peripheral regimes tend to be unstable. Note how different this might be if the all-encompassing state were not the model—if the functions assigned to the state were few and its jurisdiction limited. As Lipset notes (1963), the American state was formed in a period and area involving little such pressure: It was a very weak state, by modern standards, but, correspondingly, the fragmented American regime was able to survive for a long time. Latin American states were formed later, with much stronger concepts of what the state was to be: The regime problem has been endemic for them. And new modern states in Africa and Asia formed in a world in which the state is to be very strong indeed; regime problems have been frequent.

manage broad aspects of life: It is responsible for rapid economic progress, reducing inequality, defending economy and society against external dependence, producing many types of social progress (education, health, welfare, justice), and so on. On the one hand, this legitimates claims for these rights and services by citizens and various groups within society. On the other hand, the lack of organizational resources ensures that such claims cannot be met. The gap between claims and reality is very great (Riggs, 1964; Huntington, 1968). The gap is not only a social psychological creation of the modern system (a revolution of rising expectations, relative deprivation, or discontent created by high aspirations), but it is also a structural fact that the peripheral state—with the same world-culturally-defined obligations as an advanced one, but with fewer social and organizational resources—legitimates social claims that cannot be met, makes national plans that cannot be implemented, and defines forms of national and international justice that cannot be sustained. The gap is not only between expectations and reality but also between the state organization and its legitimating environment (Meyer and Rowan, 1977).[3]

The result, again, is conflict over the regime. Because the state system dominates the world polity and defines state action as the legitimate way to command the culture and obtain progress, dissident groups attempt to right the situation, not by attacking the state but by attempting to overthrow the regime in power. They call for a new regime, not usually a new state, and for a stronger, not a weaker, ideology. The old regime is attacked as being dependent, weak, and out of contact with the real interests of the state and nation. Much potential charisma is stored here, and is available to a wide variety of claimants—generals, intellectuals, and even religious leaders. Thus, *the ideological expansion of the peripheral state's authority and responsibility, combined with resource and organizational constraints, produces regime turbulence and instability* (see Huntington, 1968).

Both of the previous assertions would be surprising if made about a world in which the state and its ideology arose through endogenous forces. They make sense because in the modern world the peripheral state and its ideological supports come not from internal societal evolution but from the environment.

Attempts to correct the problem of the regime in the modern peripheral state often take the form of nation-building movements. But these are quite different from those in European and Anglo-American history (at least as

---

[3] Given the institutional, external nature of the state model, it is questionable whether any state, even those within developed countries, can meet such environmental demands. The "crisis of authority" currently being descried in the West may simply be the manifestation of such environmental demands forcing the expansion of the state in countries built on an earlier, weak-state model.

the latter are conventionally described). In the first place, they are put forward by factions around the state itself, imposing definitions of nationality and citizenship on society from the top downward. In reorganizing political society and linking society and regime to the state and its ideology, state factions use the external legitimacy and power of the state not only to articulate and impose a corporate national interest but also to suppress and delegitimate diverse constituent groups and interests within the society. Centralized regimes arise (Thomas *et al.,* 1979), organized around state purposes and future national progress, cutting off some links with society, and delegitimating many subgroups of present national society as selfish, corrupt, and archaic. Representation and parties are suppressed, and potentially dissident groups controlled coercively. All this is possible because the modern state has exogenous sources of resources and legitimacy: The supports of other states, the world permission to control its population in its own way, aid, arms, and the control of the resources of international trade. Centralized regimes (the military regime, or the one-party state) attempt to sustain themselves by delegitimating societal opposition. In the long run this might result in greater stability.

Modern nation-building also leads to stronger state organizations as regimes are replaced in internal political and military competition, stronger regimes are built; sometimes they are ones with broad national support, but often they are regimes that find the resources to organizationally expand the state and slowly assume centralized control. Regime turbulence, in the modern world with the availability of the stronger state, is a competitive process and a mobilizing one by which social coalitions are created that can maintain linkages with society and begin to fulfill the expanded modern world-given charter. The result is a greatly expanded state-regime nexus.[4] The competitive and search process involved is described carefully in Skocpol's (1979) study of the French, Russian, and Chinese revolutions. This study depicts the main evolutionary process going on in these revolutions as an organizational one—not the implementation of a revolutionary ideology, but the construction and discovery of ways in which to expand the authority and power of the state enough to control society. Skocpol sees external pressures as a vital part of this process, but calls attention to them mainly as sources of threat through military competition. In the modern world, these external sources also provide valuable supports to a centralizing regime—aid, trade, arms, models, and legitimacy.

---

[4] This process is independent of the particular ideology of the regime. Whether it is rightist or leftist may make some difference in the style of mobilization, but because all factions take the state as the central actor, the expansion of the state is ensured. This is true even if a faction might be committed to such "libertarian" ideals as individual "human rights" as against the state (see Boli-Bennett, 1978).

Thus, regime instability in the modern periphery, combined with the availability of the strong state organization as a solution, tends not to break down the state (as might be expected if states and societies were functional closed systems), but to expand it: *Regime instability in the periphery tends to generate stronger state organizations.*

Summary of Hypotheses

Thus, we have two general arguments to explore empirically. First, we argue that the expanded peripheral state, in the new nations at least, tends to create regime instability. Expanded state organizations create regime legitimacy problems, and expanded ideologies of state responsibility and authority tend also to delegitimate regimes by building in failure and the ineffective assumption of jurisdiction. We will explore these ideas in a very direct way in what follows by examining empirically whether regime instability in the new nations is *positively* affected by the *organizationally* and *ideologically* expanded state. Most theories, which would see the state as an internal functional construction, would anticipate negative effects (as disorganized states rather than strong ones generate regime turnover), and we suppose such effects might occur in the older countries. Our argument rests on finding surprising positive effects of both organizationally and ideologically stronger states on regime instability in the new countries.

Second, we argue that the regime instability generated in peripheral societies tends to lead, through competitive and evolutionary processes, to expanded state organizational structures, and we argue that peripheral state power is positively (not negatively, as might be supposed) affected by regime instability. Again, we expect an empirical result in peripheral countries that would not be expected in a system in which states resulted from internal processes.

We examine these two broad hypotheses with some exploratory longitudinal quantitative data on national societies since World War II.[5]

---

[5] We have addressed a third crucial issue elsewhere (Thomas *et al.*, 1979): Do the forces involved produce a solution through regime centralization and the delegitimation of diverse interests in society? Effective modern centralization can undercut the competitive pressures involved, and the developing world now shows many examples of centralized regimes that expand the state and its legitimating claims more slowly than was earlier the case. Regime centralization may slow the rate of state expansion. Communist regimes are obvious negative cases, but most centralized regimes do not take an extreme socialist posture. Most of them take a conservative posture toward the expansion of the state bureaucracy and the breadth of its ideology.

Empirical Analyses

Problem 1

The first empirical question is whether, in new peripheral nations, expanded states have higher rates of regime turnover than less expanded ones. We define regime turnover as change in the *form* of regime, using the following categories: zero-party states, one-party states, multi- or two-party states, and military regimes. Ideally, we might prefer to have data on any major regime change, including changes that occur within such broad categories as military or one-party regimes. The foregoing theoretical arguments should apply to any regime change. But the present exploratory analyses only examine changes in the overall form of the regime, not more detailed data. This can be defended on the grounds that regime form changes are more likely than regime changes within a given form to represent extremes of delegitimation and turbulence. The more elaborate analyses, however, represent an area of useful further research.

Data are taken from Banks (1976) for each year. We begin with 1950 and count regime form changes through 1975. Analyses are presented for the whole sample of countries for which data are available, then for the subgroup of countries independent before 1945, and finally for those countries gaining independence after 1944. The new nations represent the special focus of the analysis, as their states are most exogenous in origin and their histories of regime construction and nation building are least complete. In all models and subsamples, only independent countries are included.

We also look at parallel models in which the dependent variable is movement to a more centralized regime. These analyses include only those countries starting with a multi- or two-party regime. These analyses show whether there are special effects of state power on regime centralization, particularly in the periphery.

For independent and control variables, we employ the following measures:

1. Government Revenue as a Percentage of Gross National Product is a measure used as an indicator of the state's organizational and resource expansion (Rubinson, 1978). Data are taken from the International Monetary Fund (1972) and Banks (1971). Our hypothesis is that government revenue will affect positively the rate of regime turnover in the new countries.

2. An Index of the Constitutional Authority of the State is taken from Boli-Bennett (Chapter 6, and 1979). This index describes the extent of authority in various social domains claimed by the state as of its 1950 constitution. Therefore, countries independent after 1950 are excluded from the

analyses in which this variable appears, and it cannot be used for the critical new nation subsample in which we expect its destabilizing effects to be greatest. Even though this crucial test cannot be made, we report that variable's effects for the whole sample, to see if further exploration is justified.

3. Gross National Product Per Capita in 1964 U.S. dollars, is used as a control, since economically developed countries are known to have lower rates of regime change (Hannan and Carroll, 1979; Thomas *et al.,* 1979). The logarithm of this variable is used because it is highly skewed. Data are taken from the International Bank for Reconstruction and Development World Tables.

4. Ethnic Diversity is also used as a control. It is measured by ethnolinguistic fractionalization (Taylor and Hudson, 1971): high scores indicate greater diversity. Diversity is generally supposed to indicate greater potential nation-building and regime conflicts (Hannan and Carroll, 1979).

The analyses used are roughly analogous to multiple regression, but take a somewhat different statistical form, appropriate to these data. They employ the event history method, which uses data on events over time (in this case, any regime form change) to make a maximum likelihood estimate of the instantaneous rate of change and estimates of the effects of various independent variables on this rate of change (see Tuma, 1979, for a detailed discussion; and Hannan and Carroll, 1979, for an example parallel to our own analysis). The estimated rate of change is logged because it is highly skewed. Thus, the coefficients in Table 7.1 are estimates of the effects of our independent variables on the likelihood of regime form change in our data.[6] The basic model used is shown in Equation (A), where $r_j(t)$ is the instantaneous rate (the hazard function) of regime turnover, and (t') is the first year of a spell.

(A) $\ln r_j(t) = b_1$ Gov Rev/GNP (t') + b_2 Ethn Div (t')
$$+ b_3 \log \text{GNP/Cap } (t') + a + e$$

Results

Table 7.1 presents the estimates of the unstandardized effects of the independent variables on the rate of regime form change, and thus of the causal effects of these variables. The table reports the findings first where the dependent variable is any regime form change (Equations 1 through 5) and

[6] Cases within an event-history analysis are actually "spells." If a country becomes independent in 1955 and there is a regime change in 1960, that country from 1955 to 1960 is one spell. If there is another change in 1964, that country from 1960 to 1964 constitutes a second spell. All independent variables are entered at the start of each spell, except where there is no data for that year, in which case a measurement at an earlier point in time is used as an approximation.

Table 7.1

Factors Affecting Rates of Regime Form Change: Event-History Analyses of the Instantaneous Rate of Change, 1950–1975[a]

| Cases included | Equation number | Independent variables | | | | Constant | N (Spells)[b] |
		Government revenue/GNP	State authority index	Ethnic diversity	Log GNP/Cap		
Analyses of any change							
All countries	1	1.38(1.94)		.11(0.49)	−.74(.14)**	1.01(0.91)	113
Old countries	2	.39(3.33)		1.03(0.62)*	−1.01(.21)**	2.64(1.23)**	78
New countries	3	6.18(2.89)**		1.15(1.40)	−.98(.35)**	.33(1.63)	35
All countries	4	.69(2.28)	.014(.0087)*	−.07(0.63)	−.61(.18)**	−.35(1.43)	92
Old countries	5	3.52(3.48)	.027(.0107)**	1.22(0.65)**	−1.00(.24)**	.58(1.52)	78
Analyses of change toward centralized regime forms[c]							
All countries	6	2.45(2.41)		.61(0.67)	−.87(.19)**	1.23(1.16)	61
Old countries	7	.81(5.33)		1.96(0.95)**	−1.42(.39)**	4.59(1.93)**	45
New countries	8	6.27(3.24)**		1.74(1.74)	−.99(.46)**	.06(2.08)	16
All countries	9	.57(3.23)	.026(.014)**	−.49(0.88)	−.58(.25)**	−1.38(2.15)	53
Old countries	10	3.27(5.30)	.035(.016)**	1.90(1.01)**	−1.23(.41)**	1.14(2.48)	45

[a] Standard errors are in parentheses.

[b] Each regime form is treated as a separate spell. A given country can enter the analysis more than once if regime form changes occur. Cases, in terms of countries, are about two-thirds or three-fourths of the number of spells.

[c] Only cases starting with multi-party or two-party systems are included.

* $p < .10$ (one-tailed test of significance).

** $p < .05$ (one-tailed test of significance).

then where the dependent variable is movement from multi- and two-party systems to more centralized ones (Equations 6 through 10). The latter equations have many fewer spells because only those nations starting out with a multi- or two-party regime can be included.

The control variables show the expected effects. Log GNP/Capita consistently shows significant negative effects on regime turnover, as most theories and data have suggested. Again as the literature suggests, ethnic diversity positively affects regime change: This effect, however, disappears in the overall sample when the State Authority Index is included in the analysis.

The critical effects for our hypotheses are those of state power and authority. Equations 1, 2, and 3 show that government revenue as a percentage of GNP tends to have very weak effects on the rate of regime change in the whole sample and in the subsample of older countries: *but for new states it has a substantial positive effect on the regime turnover rate.* This clearly supports the argument that world-state-system expansion creates legitimacy problems for regimes in the newer nations. We do not have data over a long historical period, and cannot show whether this effect is especially due to the enhanced world model of the state in the present period or whether it has historically characterized any set of new states entering the world-system. In either case, the data support our larger argument that the state with exogenous origins in the wider system tends to create regime legitimacy and stability problems.

Equations 4 and 5 of Table 7.1 show that the level of constitutional state authority positively affects the rate of regime form change for the whole sample, and even for the older nations: Apparently, the world expansion of formal state authority and responsibility in the present period creates problems of regime stability even for established states (which were generally constructed and legitimated on a model of a weaker state).

The analyses of the rate of movement from multi- and two-party states to more centralized regimes are reported in Equations 6 through 10 of Table 7.1. The findings parallel the earlier results and show the same striking positive effect of state power on regime centralization in the new countries, as well as a positive effect of state authority on centralization in the whole sample. These analyses add further confirmation to our initial ideas, but cannot be taken as completely independent evidence, since the same data on regime turnover (which is frequently toward centralization) are included in both sets of analyses.

In analyses not reported here, we employed measures of other variables thought to affect regime turnover, but none showed consistent or significant effects. However, a measure of economic dependence (export partner concentration) showed positive effects approaching statistical significance in some models. In further research, it would be useful to consider other measures of national dependence, which is generally thought to weaken regime legitimacy.

All these analyses are exploratory; many more versions of them must be tried with more control variables and more points in time. But they provide tentative support for both subhypotheses of our first general argument. The organizationally expanded and ideologically extended state poses a problem for the stability of regimes, especially for those of new nations coming into existence after World War II.

These effects may disappear as effectively centralized regimes rise in the periphery of the world. By 1970, in many developing countries, regimes were in place that could delegitimate broader societal claims for state action (in the name of social order and economic progress). But during the transition period to more authoritarian regimes, we find evidence that the world-system's imposed and legitimated expanded state structure created problems of regime stability for the new states.

Problem 2

We turn now to our second main theme that, during the post World War II period, regime instability in the periphery, combined with the world forces legitimating stronger states, had the evolutionary effect of increasing state power in society. Our analyses here take a more conventional panel-analysis form and are estimated with ordinary least squares regression (Meyer and Hannan, 1979).

We perform analyses for all countries for which data are available, then for the subgroup of nations falling below a per capita Gross National Product of $278 in 1955 (the bottom 60%), and then for those countries above this point. The poor countries constitute our special interest in peripheral nations. The sample was divided on GNP per capita instead of recency of independence on substantive grounds. We argue that regime turnover increases state power in the periphery because these nations are poor and lack the organizational and material resources to fulfill the responsibilities defined in the world-state-system. The most important one being economic development. When the sample was divided on date of independence, little difference between new and old countries appeared in the results. Further, a variable dichotomizing the date of independence at 1945 shows no effects in the whole sample or in either subsample when added to the analyses reported in the following.

The bottom 60% of the countries on GNP per capita were used as the poor-country sample to provide enough cases for analysis. Data on other variables are frequently not available for the poorer countries, and many of them are consequently eliminated from the analyses. When even higher cutting points are used, the effects reported below still show the same differences, but are considerably attenuated (and not significant), perhaps because higher cutting points include too many countries in which regime turnover has the negative effects on state power that might conventionally be expected.

Only nations independent as of 1955 are included. We use Government Revenue as a percentage of Gross National Product, as previously described, for the measure of the dependent variable. It is again used as an indicator of the organizational power of the state. The variable is measured at an earlier point in time (1955) and then at a later point (1965) to permit longitudinal analysis. Government revenue is highly autocorrelated over time, but enough change occurs in it to permit investigation of the effects of other variables (see Rubinson, 1978).

The critical independent variable for our hypothesis is the number of regime form changes that took place around the earlier period of the analysis, since we want to see if such changes produce higher levels of state power at a later point, when earlier state power is held constant in the panel model. We simply count the number of regime form changes between 1950 and 1960 for each nation.

We employ as controls other variables known to affect state power as measured by the government revenue indicator (Rubinson, 1978): Gross National Product Per Capita, which has been found to positively affect state power (logged because it is highly skewed), and Export Partner Concentration, a measure of economic dependence, which has been found to negatively affect state power. The latter variable is taken from the *Yearbook of International Trade Statistics* (United Nations, 1951, 1963): It is the proportion of exports going to the country's largest trading partner.

The actual model used is shown in the following equation:

$$\text{(B)} \quad \text{Gov Rev/GNP}_{1965} = b_1 \text{ Gov Rev/GNP}_{1955} + b_2 \text{ Regime Changes}_{1950-1960}$$
$$+ b_3 \text{ Export Partner Concentration}_{1955}$$
$$+ b_4 \log \text{ GNP/Cap}_{1955} + a + e$$

Results

The findings are presented in Table 7.2. The control variables show the expected results. Government Revenue as a percentage of GNP is, of course, heavily affected by its earlier level in a country, as is common in such panel analyses; the finding is of little substantive interest. In the whole sample and among the richer countries, Log GNP per capita has the expected positive effects on state power: These effects disappear in the poor-country subsample, perhaps because the variance on national wealth is so much reduced

Table 7.2
Panel Regression Analysis of Factors Affecting State Power, 1955–1965 (Only Countries Independent by 1955)[a]

Cases included	Equation number	Independent Variables				Constant	N
		Regime change 1950–1960	Export partner concentration 1955	Log GNP/Cap. 1955	Government revenue/GNP 1955		
All countries	1	−.009(.008)		.029(.016)**	.78(.09)**	.009	56
All countries	2	−.003(.008)	−.084(.030)**	.028(.016)**	.80(.11)**	.033	53
Poor countries[b]	3	.001(.010)		−.034(.048)	.76(.14)**	.139	24
Poor countries[b]	4	.018(.008)**	−.194(.044)**	.018(.037)	.69(.13)**	.091	23
Rich countries[c]	5	−.037(.016)**		.059(.028)**	.82(.11)**	−.082	32
Rich countries[c]	6	−.039(.017)**	−.038(.038)	.051(.033)*	.86(.14)**	−.052	30

[a] Unstandardized slopes (standard errors). Dependent variable = Government Revenue/GNP 1965.
[b] Bottom 60 percent GNP per Capita, 1955 (under 278 1964 U.S. dollars).
[c] Top 40 percent GNP per Capita, 1955 (over 278 1964 U.S. dollars).
* $p < .10$ (one-tailed test of significance).
** $p < .05$ (one-tailed test of significance).

here. Export Partner Concentration has negative effects on state power, as previous research has led us to expect (Rubinson, 1978). The state organization tends to be weakened by economic dependence.

The crucial results for our hypothesis are those of regime form change. Equations 1 and 2 show that this variable has no effect on state power for the whole sample. Equations 3 and 4 show that for the poor countries, when economic dependence is controlled, *regime change has a positive effect on subsequent state power,* as our argument anticipated: This is the important finding in these analyses. The result appears only when economic dependence is controlled. This makes sense. The cross-sectional relation between regime change and dependence is rather high and positive, building a negative bias into the relation between number of regime changes and government revenue (Rubinson, 1978). When dependence is controlled, the masked substantial positive effects of regime turnover become manifest.

Equations 5 and 6 show the more commonly expected finding that regime change negatively affects government revenue in the richer countries. This makes sense in terms of the most obvious functional arguments; regime instability weakens the ability of a regime to build up a strong endogenous state. The surprise is our opposite finding for poor countries.

In further analyses, other relevant variables showed insignificant effects. Most notably, the type of regime (centralized or multi-party) had no effect on subsequent government revenue. We also analyzed models that used 5-year lags. Some of the findings are different: The effects of regime change are greatly attenuated whereas in some models the type of regime has small but usually not significant effects on state power. Clearly, more analyses are needed.

Overall, the findings give support to our second main hypothesis: Regime instability in the poor peripheral countries leads to stronger states in control of more resources relative to society; such turnover in the more developed countries decreases the level of state power.

Conclusions

Three concluding points must be made. The effects we note here result from a world political system legitimating and supporting strong states in the periphery. Without such supports, regime turnover would probably negatively affect the state's power (as it does in richer countries). And expanded states, built up by the same internal processes that construct strong and legitimate regimes to manage them, would show *less,* not more, regime turnover (and, indeed, the positive effects disappear among older countries). The tentative findings we report are creatures of a wider system that turns political events in the world periphery from reflecting internal life to reflecting the world political processes.

Second, the processes we study will not necessarily continue indefinitely; they capture the features of a transition period in which the number of new and peripheral states expanded very rapidly and through extraordinarily exogenous processes. During this period the establishment of strong, authoritative states has led to regime turbulence which in turn has resulted in even stronger, not weaker, states. However, the even stronger state may not subsequently further increase turbulence (although this must be decided empirically). Most new countries have now developed stable and centralized regimes that delegitimate broader societal and world claims, suppress internal turbulence, and limit the state. We expect state expansion in the periphery to occur more slowly in the future, as the lessons of its destabilizing consequences are built into peripheral polities. This process is reflected in the wave of centralist regimes that now dominates newer and more peripheral societies. It may also be reflected in the greater caution with which the state's authority and responsibility is ideologically expanded in the periphery. Boli-Bennett's data (1979) show that the long expansion in the authority typically claimed by states in their constitutions slowed by 1970. This may reflect the structural suppression of the revolution of rising expectations.

Finally, we again note the exploratory character of our findings. They run against most conventional reasoning about political processes and generally conform to our notion of the peripheral state as an exogenous construction. But they are tentative, both empirically, because more work needs to be done, and theoretically, because detailed mechanisms need to be articulated, and more alternative explanations need to be considered.

Acknowledgments

This paper was presented in the section on "Theoretical Issues in World-System Analysis," annual meetings of the American Sociological Association, Boston, August 1979. The authors are equal co-authors. We wish to thank Glenn Carroll for his help and substantive comments, and Nancy Tuma and Barbara Warsavage for their technical advice.

References

Banks, Arthur S.
   1971 *Cross Polity Time Series Data.* Cambridge: MIT Press.
Banks, Arthur S. (ed.)
   1976 *Political Handbook of the World.* New York: McGraw-Hill.

Boli-Bennett, John
  1978   "Human rights or state expansion? Cross-national definitions of constitutional rights, 1870–1970." Paper presented at the Conference on Global Human Rights, Denver and Boulder, Colorado. Spring.
  1979   "The ideology of expanding state authority in national constitutions, 1870–1970." Pp. 222–237 in J. Meyer and M. Hannan (eds.), *National Development and the World System*. Chicago: University of Chicago Press.
Ellul, Jacques
  1978   *The Betrayal of the West*. New York: The Seabury Press.
Fried, Morton H.
  1960   "On the evolution of social stratification and the state." In S. Diamond (ed.), *Culture in History*. New York: Columbia University Press.
Hannan, Michael T., and Glenn R. Carroll
  1979   "Dynamics of formal political structure: an event-history analysis." *Technical Report* No. 72, Department of Sociology, Stanford University.
Huntington, Samuel P.
  1968   *Political Order in Changing Societies*. New Haven: Yale University Press.
International Bank for Reconstruction and Development
  (various years)   World Tables. Washington: IBRD.
International Monetary Fund
  1972   *International Financial Statistics Supplement, 1972*. Washington: IMF.
Lipset, Seymour Martin
  1963   *The First New Nation*. Garden City, N. Y.: Doubleday.
Meyer, John W., John Boli-Bennett, and Christopher Chase-Dunn
  1975   "Convergence and divergence in development." *Annual Review of Sociology* 1:223–46.
Meyer, John W., and Michael T. Hannan
  1979   *National Development and the World System: Educational, Economic, and Political Change, 1950–1970*. Chicago: University of Chicago Press.
Meyer, John W., and Brian Rowan
  1977   "Institutionalized organizations: formal structure as myth and ceremony." *American Journal of Sociology* 83:340–63.
Ness, Gayl, and Jeannine Ness
  1972   "Metropolitan power and the demise of the overseas empires." Paper presented at the annual meetings of the American Sociological Association, New Orleans. September.
Polanyi, Karl
  1944   *The Great Transformation*. Boston: Beacon.
Riggs, Fred
  1964   *Administration in Developing Countries: The Theory of Prismatic Society*. Boston: Houghton Mifflin.
Rubinson, Richard
  1978   "Dependence, government revenue, and economic growth, 1955–1970." *Studies in Comparative International Development* 12:3–28.
Skocpol, Theda
  1979   *States and Social Revolutions*. Cambridge: Cambridge University Press.
Swanson, Guy
  1971   "An organizational analysis of collectivities." *American Sociological Review* 79:1–14.
Taylor, Charles L., and M. C. Hudson

1971   *World Handbook of Political and Social Indicators.* Vol. 2. Ann Arbor, Michigan: Interuniversity Consortium for Political and Social Research, University of Michigan.

Thomas, George M., Francisco O. Ramirez, John W. Meyer, and Jeanne Gobalet
1979   "Maintaining national boundaries in the world system: the rise of centralist regimes." Pp. 187–206 in J. Meyer and M. Hannan (eds.), *National Development and the World System.* Chicago: University of Chicago Press.

Tilly, Charles
1975   *The Formation of National States in Western Europe.* Princeton: Princeton University Press.

Tuma, Nancy B.
1979   *Invoking RATE.* 2nd ed. Menlo Park, California: SRI International.

United Nations
1951   *Yearbook of International Trade Statistics, 1950.* New York: United Nations.
1963   *Yearbook of International Trade Statistics, 1961.* New York: United Nations.

Wallerstein, Immanuel
1974   *The Modern World-System: Capitalist Agriculture and the Origins of the European World Economy in the Sixteenth Century.* New York: Academic Press.

Trade Dependence and Fertility in Hispanic America: 1900–1975

The importance of trade and foreign investment for peripheral states is not limited to the well known dependence effects on economic growth. Dependence alters the relationship between economic development and internal social processes like family formation and political change. For that reason the "multiplier effects" of economic development that are expected as the Third World becomes urbanized and literate often fail to appear. This fact is not widely recognized in the dependence literature. The focus of this chapter is on one such unrealized multiplier: the supposed fertility-reducing effects of economic development. However, the interaction uncovered here has implications for other anticipated multiplier effects that do not act quite as expected in Asia, Africa, and Latin America. I will return to the general issue in the concluding section.

Latin America has the highest rate of population growth in the world today. This growth is the result of a substantial reduction in mortality in the first half of the twentieth century that has not been followed by a comparable reduction in fertility.[1] Fertility in Latin America has been high throughout the twentieth century. The mean 1975 birth rate for the 18 former Spanish colonies analyzed here was 37 births per 1000 population, only 5 births per 1000 fewer than in 1915 (Collver, 1965). If one were to

---

[1] The rate of population growth is the difference between the birth rate and the death rate plus net migration. Unless rates of out-migration are extremely high, a large difference between birth and death rates results in rapid growth.

159

use prevailing demographic theory as a guide, this lack of change in fertility would be inexplicable. Massive increases in life expectancy coupled with significant economic development (see Meyer *et al.*, 1976) are supposed to lead to lower fertility. While demographic accounts of the lack of change illuminate its age-related aspects (e.g., Arriaga, 1970a, 1970b), an explication of the social structure underlying the demographic outcome is lacking.

The problem lies in prevailing demographic theory. It holds that as mortality declines and socioeconomic development increases, fertility decreases. This is the well known theory of the demographic transition. It is based on the experience of Europe in the nineteenth century. Basing theory on the experience of one region is not inherently troublesome. The problem of generalizing European experience to non-European settings arises because the wrong elements of the European experience are the focus of the explanation. The dominant position of Western Europe in the world economy and the subservient positions of other regions are typically ignored when the generalization is attempted.

The urbanization and other developmental trends associated with fertility decline in Europe were part of the industrialization of the core of the modern world economy. The same trends have not resulted in fertility reduction in Latin America because the context of those changes is so radically different. Latin America is a peripheral area that has provided the Northern core with minerals and foodstuffs throughout the period of core development. As a result of this economic relationship, social structures are fundamentally different from those found in Europe. Of particular importance for fertility analysis is the difference between core and periphery in the role of children within the family. The decline of family production and the child's role in it was a key factor in the association between industrialization and fertility reduction in Western Europe (Caldwell, 1976, 1978). Children in Latin American households have retained an economic role, despite socioeconomic change.

Also significant is the inequality of economic distribution typical of dependent states (Chase-Dunn, 1975; Bornschier *et al.*, 1978). Inequality blocks fertility reduction in two ways. By definition, high inequality means that some people are not touched by socioeconomic change; thus they do not limit their fertility because they are unaffected by socioeconomic change. Secondly, inequality distorts the linear form of the fertility–development relationship; a minimum level of development (or personal income at the individual level) must be attained before fertility starts to go down (Repetto, 1974, 1979). The net result is that it takes a larger increase in development to produce the same reduction in fertility.

My critique of demographic transition theory is that attempts to generalize from Europe to Latin America have failed because they concentrate on *internal* characteristics of the populations compared. Their failure to find *parallel* relationships has led demographic transition theorists to invoke ad hoc "cultural factors" to explain the differences (e.g., Beaver, 1975). These cultural factors are typically ill-specified and admit to ignorance about the causal forces at work. By including external factors such as dependent trade relations, which place conditions on development as part of the explanation, the account of fertility change in both Europe and Latin America can be improved. This chapter shows the fruitfulness of this dependence approach for the analysis of Latin American fertility. Tilly (1978) applies a similar perspective to Eastern Europe and discusses the possibility that dependence on foreign markets delayed fertility decline in Poland. The concluding section of this chapter returns to this topic and discusses the implications of the dependence perspective for Richards' (1977) analysis of German fertility.

Social Arrangements and Fertility

The social and economic roles of children in the family are crucial determinants of a society's fertility level (Caldwell, 1976, 1978).[2] Social arrangements within the family affect fertility in the following way: When the household is the focus of economic production, all household members— even very young ones—contribute to the household's production. Even where families have extended kinship ties, this relationship of children to production holds (Cain, 1977; Caldwell, 1978). When children contribute to the household economy, there is no motive for limiting births, even in high density areas like Bangladesh (Cain, 1977). With industrialization of the European sort, the focus of production shifts from the household to the factory. Households no longer generate income by selling what they produce; individual household members sell their labor and contribute their wages to the household.

Children can still contribute to the family under such circumstances. They do so by working for wages, as they did to a very significant degree in England. Or, more commonly, income from adult wages is supplemented by home production of food, clothing, or goods-for-sale (Wallerstein, 1978)— activities to which children contribute. These economic activities of children are only found when adult wages are low. When adult wages are high enough to provide subsistence, household production wanes. Children are

---

[2] The model presented here assumes that fertility is high at the onset of industrialization. In some instances, notably nineteenth century France and second generation frontier America, limited opportunities for agricultural expansion, coupled with inheritance customs, motivated couples to limit fertility prior to industrialization (van de Walle, 1978; Easterlin, 1976).

withdrawn from the labor market and they lose their economic role within the family. In Western Europe the rise in wages that accompanied industrialization was sufficient to initiate this decline in household production. It is a characteristic of dependency that wages not rise above subsistence (Lewis, 1977).

Regardless of their status as producers, children continue to be consumers, of course. Not only does children's consumption continue after the production declines, the cost of children's consumption increases as industrialization proceeds. The largest component of the increase is the cost of increased education. This cost increase is compounded by the prolonged dependence of children on parents that accompanies high educational attainment. Other increments to the cost of children come from increased overall costs for clothing, shelter, health care, etc. The overall cost of these items increases despite lower unit prices because more of each is consumed and the improved quality of consumer goods increases their overall cost in most instances (see Nerlove, 1974).

Because most nonmaterial rewards of having children can be as readily realized with few as with many children, the imbalance of this economic cost/benefit ledger provides couples with a motive for limiting their fertility (see Coale, 1973; Caldwell, 1978). Thus, when economic development alters social relations within the nuclear family, it can be expected to reduce fertility. However, when wages remain below subsistence so that children retain an economic role or when economic development is unequally distributed so that not all families are affected, the fertility-reducing effect of economic development is attenuated. The direct result of dependence is to keep fertility high by affecting the economic contribution of children; the indirect result operates through inequality by isolating a large segment from the development effects.

Dependence, Underdevelopment, and Fertility in Latin America

In this chapter I am concerned with the nature of the economic development-fertility relationship in Latin America, more specifically in the former Spanish colonies of Latin America. Considering the increased urbanization, literacy, and life expectancy in Latin America in the first half of the twentieth century, most demographic observers assumed that the 1950s would be marked by rapid fertility declines. For the most part, those expected changes have not been forthcoming. Despite repeated observations of strong negative correlations between socioeconomic development and fertility (e.g., Kirk, 1971; Beaver, 1975; Cutright *et al.*, 1976), the overtime relationship between the two is very weak: The rate of post-World War II economic growth averages four times the rate of fertility reduction.

Previous attempts to account for the lack of fertility change in Latin America in the 1950s and 1960s have referred to internal factors such as age composition (Arriaga, 1970a, 1970b) and religious ideology (Stycos, 1971). The age composition argument succeeds in its demonstration that the anticipated fertility decline could not have occurred in the 1950s, but it does not identify conditions under which fertility might decline.

The religious ideology argument requires more attention. It is true that most Latin Americans are Catholics and that the Catholic Church has traditionally opposed fertility regulation, but the empirical link between doctrine and fertility behavior is weak. Although countries with strong Catholic institutions have higher than average marital fertility, they have lower than average illegitimacy (Cutright *et al.*, 1976). Because illegitimacy is high in Latin America (averaging around 40% of all births [Johnson and Cutright, 1973]), the net effect of Church strength on overall fertility is not significantly greater than zero. At the individual level, fertility-related attitudes and behaviors are not correlated with church attendance and participation in the sacraments in seven of nine cities surveyed (CELADE, 1972:249–268).

In place of these incomplete explanations based on internal factors, I offer an explanation based on Latin America's ties to the core of the world economic system. Latin American is not an *un*developed region; it is *under*developed (Frank, 1969). The distinction is between primary economic production at the subsistence level and economic production organized for export to core developed countries. Dependent trade relations produce social structures that differ significantly from the social arrangements prevalent in the core. Social consequences of dependence important for the fertility analysis in this chapter are the low wages which necessitate supplementary, nonproletarian production on the part of workers' households (Wallerstein, 1978). This supplementary production is essential to the subsistence of the household. It gives children a positive economic role in the family. The low wages also result in extensive sectoral and household income inequality (Chase-Dunn, 1975; Bornschier *et al.*, 1978). The ways in which children's roles and income inequality affect fertility have already been discussed.

The importance of understanding dependence relationships for interpreting the economic history of Latin America is well documented (Furtado, 1970). This chapter presents an empirical case for also looking to dependence for an explanation of *internal processes that are linked to economic development*. In particular, this chapter shows that dependence on North American and Western European industrial powers impedes fertility decline in Latin America. The fertility-reducing effect of socioeconomic development (where and when such development occurs) is weaker when development is dependent on trade with a single core partner or in a single commodity than when it is not tied to a single partner or commodity. *The expected fertility-reducing effect of development emerges only where and when dependence is low.*

The possibility of a link between dependence and fertility has been suggested before. Goode (1960, 1961) cites the socially disorganizing effects of colonial penetration as an explanation of high fertility among never married women in the Caribbean. An article on which I collaborated (Cutright *et al.,* 1976) reports substantial indirect effects of Spanish colonial penetration on fertility in Spain's former colonies. Neither of these previous studies presents evidence on the link between postcolonial dependence and fertility. Tilly (1978) suggests that such a link may be important in his review of the fertility decline in Eastern Europe:

> Faint in the background flickers a fascinating possibility: that the high rates of population growth in today's Third World countries will turn out to be less consequences of their own peculiar internal organizations than effects of their economic relationships with the rich countries of the West [pp. 31–32].

Tilly (1978) cautions that his argument "is a chain of reasoning, not a chain of evidence" (p. 37). This chapter provides a link in the chain of evidence. Furthermore, it puts forth the argument that the internal organizations are not so peculiar but are themselves consequences of dependence. As such they carry the influence of dependence from the realm of international economic exchange to the realm of reproductive behavior.

Data and Measurement

The universe for this analysis is Hispanic America: Caribbean, Meso American, and South American countries that were colonized by Spain. The Hispanic restriction is imposed because this analysis is part of a larger project investigating Spanish colonialism, dependency, and economic and demographic change in these countries (see Hout, 1979). The only large country excluded by the Hispanic restriction is Brazil. The exclusion is of no practical consequence because Brazil would have to be excluded anyway due to missing data in all but the most recent period.

In all statistical analyses, weights proportional to population size at the time the independent variables were measured are used. The weights were constructed by dividing population size (Collver, 1965; supplemented by United Nations, 1975 and Banks, 1971) by the mean population size for the 62 populations in the analysis. Dividing through by mean population ensures that the proper degrees of freedom is used in computations. The weighting was done so that small countries would not dominate the analysis. Weighting has the additional salutary effect of giving more weight to more reliable, recent observations.

Fertility is indicated by the crude birth rate (births per 1000 population) in 1915–1919, 1945–1949, 1965, and 1975. The data source for the first two periods is Collver (1965; supplemented by United Nations, 1975); for the later points it is Mauldin (1978; supplemented by United Nations, 1975; Oeschli and Kirk, 1976). More data are available, but their inclusion has the ironic effect of reducing the temporal component of the total variance. The four measurements chosen maximize the length of the time series without reducing temporal variance to insignificance. An analysis of variance showed that 10% of the total variance in the crude birth rates used in this analysis is temporal. To use all available data would reduce that to 4%.

Table 8.1 presents the complete set of fertility data. There is little variance in initial fertility. Argentina and Uruguay have rates significantly below the others. The other populations all have rates between 41 and 46 births per 1000 population. Fertility in Argentina, Chile, Cuba, and Uruguay fell between 6 and 11 points between the first and second periods. Given the high rates of European immigration experienced by these states, this fertility decline and the low initial levels in Argentina and Uruguay are probably due to this compositional difference with the rest of Latin America. Cutright *et al.* (1976) report a significant effect of a dummy variable distinguishing these four from other Latin American states. The same dummy variable coding failed to improve fit over the preferred model presented below; however, given the pattern of residuals from the preferred model, it seems likely that a scaled migration variable that could distinguish among states more finely than the dummy variable does might show the immigration effect. Nearly all of the other states experienced fertility increases of 1 or 2 points during the first interval.

During the second interval fertility in Argentina, Chile, and Uruguay continued to fall. Birth rates rose significantly in Cuba and Honduras. No change was recorded in four of the six other Central American states for which 1945–1949 data are available. Venezuela also recorded no change. Fertility in the five other states fell by small amounts: an average of 1.6 births per 1000 population in 18 years.

The most recent interval recorded in Table 7.1 has been marked by widespread fertility declines, but fertility remains high relative to fertility in comparably developed countries in Asia and relative to Latin American mortality. Argentina and Uruguay continue to have the lowest birth rates in the region. They have been joined by Chile which recorded a 30% drop in the 10 years between 1965 and 1975. Five other countries experienced rapid

Table 8.1
*Crude Birth Rates and Rates of Fertility Change by Time Period: Hispanic America,
1915–1975*

Country	Births per 1000 population				Average annual rate of decline per cent[a]		
	1915–1919	1945–1949	1965	1975	1917 to 1947	1947 to 1965	1965 to 1975
Argentina	36	25	22	23	1.0	.7	−.5
Bolivia	–	47	44	44	–	.4	.0
Chile	43	37	33	23	.5	.6	3.0
Colombia	43	44	43	33	−.1	.1	2.3
Costa Rica	45	43	41	29	.1	.3	2.9
Cuba	41	30	34	29	.9	−.7	1.5
Dominican Republic	–	–	47	38	–	–	1.9
Ecuador	46	46	45	45	.0	.1	.0
El Salvador	43	45	46	40	−.2	.0	.4
Guatemala	43	45	45	43	−.2	.0	.4
Honduras	42	44	51	48	−.2	−.9	.6
Mexico	41	44	44	40	−.2	.0	.9
Nicaragua	–	–	49	46	–	–	.6
Panama	–	38	40	31	–	.0	2.2
Paraguay	–	–	42	39	–	–	.7
Peru	–	44	43	42	–	.1	.2
Uruguay	35	28	22	20	.7	1.2	.9
Venezuela	41	42	42	37	−.1	.0	1.2
Weighted[b] Mean	41.67	40.20	40.78	36.53			
Weighted[b] S.D.	3.28	6.98	8.14	8.62			

[a] A minus sign indicates an increase.

[b] Weighted by lagged population size divided by the mean population size for the 62 populations.

fertility reduction, dropping between 15 and 29% in the 1965–1975 interval. Most of the reduction occurred since 1972 (compare Table 7.1 with Nortman, 1974). Nonetheless, 8 countries, representing 52% of the region's Hispanic population still have birth rates of 40 or more per 1000. At these rates the 8 countries produce 4.3 million births a year compared with 2.8 million births in the 10 countries with low or declining fertility.[3]

Internal development is an index formed from (*a*) urbanization, (*b*) school enrollment, and (*c*) telephone use. It is measured in 1900, 1930, 1950, and 1960 (the reasons for lagging development behind fertility are discussed below and in Cutright *et al.*, 1976). Early urbanization is from

---

[3] There were 2.2 million births in the United States in 1975. The population of the U.S. at that time was about 220 million people—roughly 30 million more than the 1975 total population of all 18 Hispanic countries in this data set.

Banks (1971); it is the percentage of the total population residing in cities of over 50,000 residents. Later urbanization is from Davis (1970); it is the percentage of the total population residing in cities of over 100,000 residents. School enrollment and telephone use are from Banks (1971). School enrollment is the ratio of primary school students to population aged 6 to 12 years ($\times$ 1,000). Telephone use is the number of telephones per 100,000 population.

Ridit scaling (Bross, 1958; Lieberson, 1978) was used to combine these three variables into an index of internal development. First, the cumulative percentage distributions of each variable were computed. The urbanization distribution was adjusted to accommodate the change from 50,000 to 100,000 residents in the definition of urban (see Hout, 1979). Then the three percentages for each country were summed and divided by three. The scale has a possible range from 0 to 100; its actual range is from 6.67 to 96.67.

The internal development index values are plotted in Figures 8.1a−c. The plots separated the countries by 1930 population size ((a) over 3.5 million; (b) 1 million to 3.5 million; (c) less than 1 million). The increases shown in the figures are in line with the discussion of Meyer *et al.* (1976) regarding development trends in the Third World. The largest countries all exhibit increases that are nearly constant over time (as indicated by the nearly straight line for each). Furthermore, five of the six increase at almost the same average annual increment, averaging .95 points added each year. Argentina is the exception, increasing at an average of .34 points each year. Argentina's apparently slower growth is an artifact. The development scale has a maximum of 100. Argentina's initial value was 74; there simply is not enough room on the scale to fully record Argentina's growth.

Six of the seven medium-sized countries share a common pattern of accelerating development. The dashed line records predicted values from the equation:

$$D = 13.9 + .015(\text{Year})^2 \qquad [1]$$

which, when fitted to the pooled data for the six countries fit very well ($r^2 = .78$). The exception to the pattern is Uruguay which like Argentina, has a high initial scale value and is, consequently, subject to artifactual ceiling effects.

The smallest population category includes three of the fastest developing states (Costa Rica, Panama, and Paraguay) and the two slowest (Honduras and Nicaragua). The former all fit linear growth models very well ($r^2 > .95$) with average annual increments of more than 1.0 points each year. Honduras and Nicaragua, on the other hand, increase less than 50 points over the 60 year period. Nearly half of the increases for Honduras and Nicaragua are concentrated in the 1950−1960 interval.

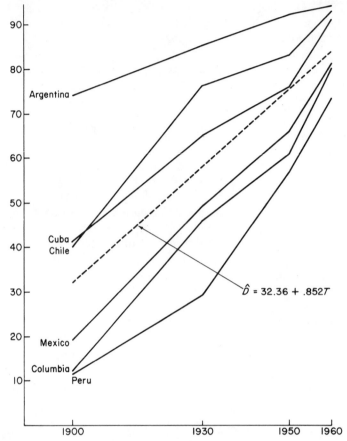

Figure 8.1a. *Internal development index values by time period for countries with over 3.5 million population in 1930.*

Figure 8.2 presents the joint distribution of fertility and internal development. It is clear from the figure that a significant negative relationship exists between the birth rate and internal development. But the relationship is not simple. Two other features of the graph merit comment. The relationship does not appear to be linear; the negative slope appears to be steeper at high levels of development. Second, the variance of fertility also increases as development increases. The increasing variance indicates one of two things: (*a*) heteroskedasticity, a statistical problem that requires an adjustment to the data before estimating the effect of development on fertility; or (*b*) an interaction between development and another independent variable, so that

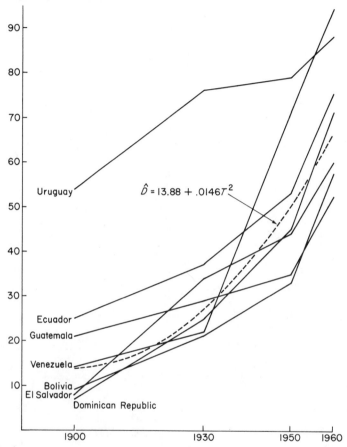

Figure 8.1b. *Internal development index values by time period for countries with between 1.0 million and 3.5 million population in 1930.*

instead of the graph showing one development–fertility relationship, it shows many.

The strategy I have followed is to let nonlinearity and interaction explain as much of the spread in Figure 8.2 as possible. Then, if necessary, I will make the adjustment for heteroskedasticity. This choice was made because the theoretical perspective as previously outlined (as well as past research) suggests interpretations for nonlinear and nonadditive effects while heteroskedasticity is simply a statistical malady. The nonlinearity, specifically a steeper rate of fertility decline at high values of development, corre-

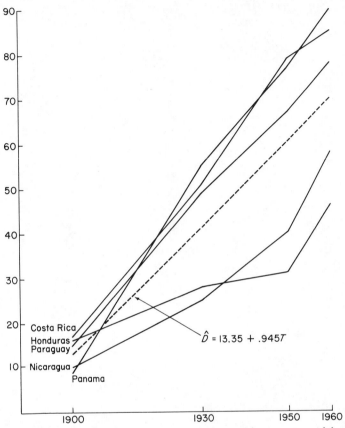

Figure 8.1c. *Internal development index values by time period for countries with less than 1.0 million population in 1930.*

sponds to the notion of a demographic transition threshold prevalent in the literature (e.g., Oeschli and Kirk, 1976); it is also a consequence of inequality effects (Repetto, 1977). If the suspected interaction is a positive one between dependence and development, it would indicate that the fertility-reducing effect of development is stronger at low dependence than at high. Therefore it would be a statistical representation of the central thesis of this chapter. Only if the residuals from a nonlinear, nonadditive model show the heteroskedastic pattern will the data be adjusted.

The world division of labor is defined by international trade. The principal empirical manifestation of dependence in trade is a specialization or concentration of trade. Two elements of trade concentration are measured: *partner concentration,* which is the ratio of imports from the largest trading

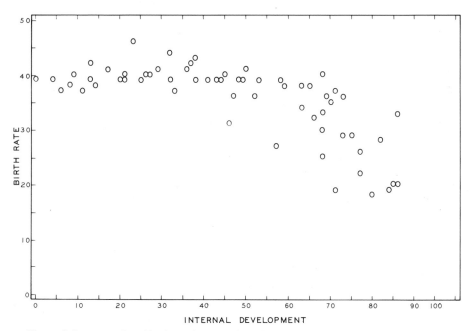

Figure 8.2. *Scatter plot of birth rate by internal development: Hispanic America, 1900–1975.*

partner to total imports and *commodity concentration,* which is the ratio of exports in the largest of five classes—agricultural produce, animal products, minerals, light manufactures, and all other—to total exports. They are measured in 1900, 1930, 1950, and 1960. Both measures are from the *Statesman's Yearbook* (1904, 1932, 1951, 1962). They are used as separate measures of dependence in this analysis.[4]

Table 8.2 presents the trade data. Partner concentration is less than commodity concentration in each year. The average percentage of trade with the leading partner is nearly the same in 1900 and 1930. It increased 30% between 1930 and 1950. The United States was the leading trading partner for all countries in 1950, so the increase most likely represents the effect of World War II on the trading capacities of the European economies. In 1960 partner concentration returned to its prewar level. Commodity concentration increased somewhat between 1900 and 1930 as mining waned

[4] Most previous empirical studies of dependence relations have focussed on foreign investment and debt dependence (Furtado, 1970; Chase-Dunn, 1975; Rubinson, 1976; Bornschier *et al.,* 1978). These analyses have revealed stronger dependence effects than the few which have focussed on trade concentration (Delacroix, 1977). In part it is because the overly specific coding scheme used by Delacroix dilutes the dependence effect by introducing extraneous variation among primary production categories (see Steiber, 1979).

Table 8.2
Trade Dependence Measures by Time Period: Hispanic America 1900–1960

Country	Partner concentration				Commodity concentration			
	1900	1930	1950	1960	1900	1930	1950	1960
Argentina	34	23	16	15	50	55	43	45
Bolivia	9	25	42	44	72	94	95	91
Chile	33	33	48	48	90	96	80	98
Colombia	40	45	68	61	51	64	80	75
Costa Rica	46	50	66	47	88	99	99	89
Cuba	43	57	79	52	73	99	89	90
Dominican Republic	56	56	75	52	99	99	99	99
Ecuador	29	40	67	48	81	84	86	90
El Salvador	71	80	67	48	99	99	99	96
Guatemala	50	59	68	46	96	99	86	99
Honduras	67	77	79	56	85	92	82	95
Mexico	54	45	84	72	66	70	67	75
Nicaragua	40	62	75	52	68	75	60	89
Panama	–	68	67	60	–	83	99	72
Paraguay	48	29	36	32	63	65	63	53
Peru	90	37	69	44	47	48	47	61
Uruguay	26	25	26	27	92	91	88	92
Venezuela	28	40	68	53	72	74	92	88
Mean[a]	43.5	47.0	61.1	47.4	74.5	83.2	80.6	82.8
Standard deviation[a]	14.8	18.2	19.2	13.2	20.6	17.1	17.6	16.8
N	12	15	18	17	12	15	18	17

[a] Weighted; see text (p. 164) for description. Only the 62 cases included in subsequent analyses were included in the computation of means and standard deviations.

and plantation agriculture spread in Meso America and Colombia. It changed little thereafter.

The independent variables were lagged 15 years to allow sufficient time for their effects to operate. Lags of 5 and 10 years were also examined. No significant differences among the lags were found. The 15 year lags were chosen because the measures for 1900, 1930, 1950, and 1960 are also used in other analyses of these data (reported in Hout, 1979).

Of the (18 × 4 =) 72 possible data points, 8 lack fertility data, one lacks trade data, and Period 4 Cuba is excluded because measurement of internal development for the fourth period is too close to the revolution to be comparable. The time series and cross-sections were pooled to yield 62 cases for analysis. This method maximizes variance in the independent variables and improves the efficiency of the regression analysis under the assumption that the coeffcients for particular countries or clusters of countries do not differ significantly from those for the others (Hannan and Young,

1977). This assumption was tested for regional clusters (Caribbean, Meso, and South) and three categories of 1930 population size. No significant interactions of that type were found.

Data Analysis

Specifying the Model

The routine way to proceed would be to correlate the birth rate with the indicators of internal development and trade dependence and use multiple regression to separate their effects. But as just stated, it is not clear that a simple linear, additive regression equation is the best representation of the dependency argument being advanced. I shall use a multiplicative term (trade × development) to represent the mitigating effect of dependence and square development to allow its effect to increase as development increases.

The effect of these changes can be seen by comparing the usual form with the modified form. The usual regression equation has the form:

$$B = a + b_1D + b_2T \tag{2}$$

where B is the birth rate, D is the development index, and T is the trade dependence indicator (partner or commodity concentration). The effect of development is measured by b_1, which is expected to be negative; the effect of dependence is measured by b_2, which is expected to be positive. The effects are independent of one another. By adding the squared development term (D^2) and the interaction between dependence and development (DT) to equation [1], the mathematical form of the model is brought closer to the theoretical formulation presented in the first section of this chapter:

$$B = a + b_1D + b_2T + b_3D^2 + b_4DT \tag{3}$$

The effects of development and dependence are not independent in equation [3]. As Stolzenberg (1980) shows, the effect of each can be obtained from the partial derivatives of [3] with respect to D and T, in turn:

$$\partial B/\partial D = b_1 + 2b_3D + b_4T \tag{4}$$
$$\partial B/\partial T = b_2 + b_4D \tag{5}$$

As long as b_3 is negative and b_4 is positive, the effect of development on fertility will become stronger as development increases and weaker as dependence increases, just as the theory says they should. Thus we have what amounts to an empirical test of the theoretical framework put forth at the outset of this chapter. If the coefficient for the squared development term is not significantly less than zero, then the simpler, more common arguments about development's effect on the birth rate suffice, and there is no need for the inequality argument advanced here. Regarding the consequences of dependence, if the coefficient for the interaction term is not positive, then dependence does not modify the development–fertility relationship. On the other hand, a positive interaction will support the central thesis of this chapter.

Several models were fitted using weighted least squares (the weights were described previously [p. 164]). A summary of the search is presented in Table 8.3. I began with a simple bivariate equation, added the trade dependence (T) terms, then the nonlinear and interaction terms (together and separately); then I deleted the main effects. The residual sum of squares and R^2 for each of the models is presented in the table. Models were fitted for partner and commodity concentration separately. They are viewed simply as interchangeable indicators of the one underlying concept: trade dependence. No attempt has been made to separate them theoretically. Empirically, they are not as highly correlated as one might expect ($r = .41$), but no

Table 8.3
Goodness of Fit and Tests of Significance for Various Models For Birth Rates:
Hispanic America 1900–1975

Model	Trade dependence indicator			
	Partner concentration	Commodity concentration	Partner concentration	Commodity concentration
	Residual Sum of Squares		R^2	
1. D^a	2212.85	2212.85	.461	.461
2. D, T^b	1055.27	1995.56	.743	.514
3. D, T, DT	933.32	1926.05	.773	.531
4. D, D^2, T	759.97	1181.93	.815	.712
5. D, D^2, T, DT	671.00	1129.62	.837	.725
6. D, D^2, DT	682.47	1153.62^c	.834	.719^c
7. D^2, DT	716.34^c	1417.79	.826^c	.655
	ΔRSS		ΔR^2	
[1]:[2]	1157.58	2.7.29	.282	.053
[2]:[3]	121.95	69.51	.040	.017
[2]:[4]	295.30	813.63	.072	.198
[3]:[5]	262.32	796.43	.064	.194
[4]:[5]	88.97	52.31	.022	.013
[5]:[6]	11.47	24.00	.003	.006
[6]:[7]	45.34	264.17	.012	.064

^{a} D = Development.
^{b} T = Trade dependence.
^{c} Preferred model.

attempt will be made to estimate the effect of each net of the other. Frankly, they are new measures, and not enough is known about them to interpret the results of such an exercise.

A preferred model is an equation that includes no extraneous terms and excludes no important ones. Usually inclusion and exclusion is determined by statistical significance tests. Because of the selective sample of countries coupled with the weighting scheme, the assumptions of such tests hold only approximately, if at all, in this case. Therefore, no formal tests were performed, but the residual sums of squares and R^2's can be used informally as guides to inclusion and exclusion of terms.

When the trade dependence indicator is partner concentration, a relatively simple two-variable model is preferred (Model 7 in the table). The included terms are the crucial ones for this analysis: the squared development index and the development–dependence interaction. Their inclusion bears out the speculations regarding nonlinearity and interaction advanced above. Adding either main effect does little to improve the model. When the dependence indicator is commodity concentration, a slightly more complicated model emerges; in addition to the squared and interaction terms, this preferred model includes a development main effect (Model 6 in the table).

Dependence and Development Effects

The equations for the preferred models are:

$$B = 43.40 + .00245DP - .00286D^2 \qquad [6]$$
$$(40.1) \qquad (9.1) \qquad (-16.3)$$

$$B = 34.03 + .00080DC - .00703D^2 + .515D \qquad [7]$$
$$(10.1) \qquad (1.9) \qquad (-6.3) \qquad (3.6)$$

where DP and DC are the interaction terms involving partner concentration and commodity concentration, respectively, and the numbers in parentheses are approximate t-ratios. The signs of the squared and interaction terms are in accord with the theoretical expectations. These equations are empirical support for the argument that *the fertility-reducing effect of socioeconomic development is strongest when dependence is low; it weakens as dependence increases.* Furthermore, the equations support the argument that development effects become stronger over the course of development. When partner concentration is the index used, the dependence effect is stronger than when commodity concentration is used. But it is noteworthy that *both equations support the theory.*[5]

---

[5] If the assumptions of the t-test were met, the DC interaction would be significant at the .06 level instead of the conventional .05 level.

Equations that contain a mix of linear and multiplicative terms are difficult to interpret. To aid in the interpretations of equations [6] and [7], some illustrative calculations have been graphed in Figures 8.3a and 8.3b. These figures show the relationship between fertility and development for three values of trade dependence. The middle line in each figure shows the predicted birth rate for each value of development when trade dependence is equal to its mean (50.9 and 72.2 for partner and commodity concentration, respectively). The upper and lower lines show the predicted birth rates when trade dependence is one standard deviation above and below its mean.[6]

The figures make the interaction between trade dependence and internal development explicit. When dependence is below the mean, the birth rate falls rapidly once it passes a development threshold. When dependence equals the mean, the threshold is at a higher development level, and the rate of decline is significantly less than when the dependence indicator is less than the mean. When dependence is above the mean, the threshold is even higher on the development scale, and the rate of eventual fertility decline is quite low. Comparing the two indicators of trade dependence shows that when commodity concentration is used, the threshold is at a higher development level than when partner concentration is used. The eventual rate of decline is greater in the case of commodity concentration.

The most important finding from an analysis of residuals (not shown) is that the preferred models explain nearly all of the change in fertility within countries. Roughly two-thirds of the residual variance is cross-sectional, indicating that most of the unexplained variance is due to persistent differences among countries. As suggested before, European migration might be one source of persistent difference. Mortality conditions and marital status distribution are two others.

Figure 8.2 depicted the relationship between fertility and development. In discussing this figure, I noted that variance in fertility was much greater at high values of development than at low. Such a condition suggests a violation of the homoskedasticity assumption of ordinary least squares regression. However, the existence of a strong positive interaction, such as the one between dependence and development in these data, is sufficient to produce increasing variance similar to that which was observed. To assess the extent to which the observed interactions reproduce the observed pattern, the predicted birth rates were superimposed on the observed joint distribution of fertility and dependence. The result is Figure 8.4. Each X represents a point expected under the model in equation [6], each O is an observed point. The

---

[6] Of course, development usually does not increase without a decrease in dependence. The figures are, in that sense, hypothetical. They are meant to represent the characteristics of the models. They do not purport to be projections of fertility for any specific country. Projections of that type would require assumptions about future values of both dependence and development.

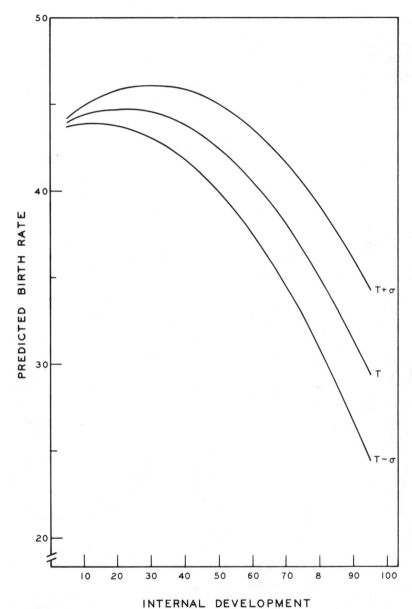

Figure 8.3a. *Association between predicted birth rate and internal development under conditions of high (T + σ), medium (T), and low (T − σ) dependence: Hypothetical results based on equation 6.*

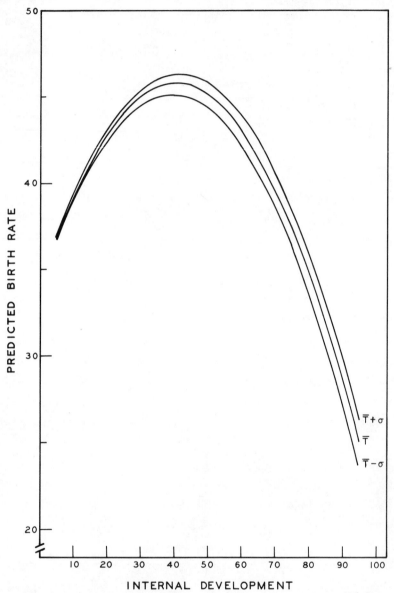

Figure 8.3b. *Association between predicted birth rate and internal development under conditions of high* (T + σ), *medium* (T), *and low* (T − σ) *dependence: Hypothetical results based on equation 7.*

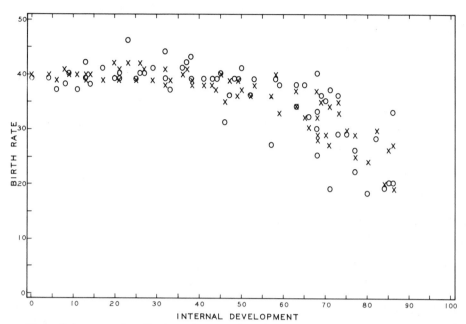

Figure 8.4. *Scatter plot of birth rate by internal development, observed (O) and predicted (X) birth rates: Hispanic America, 1900–1975.*

correspondence is striking. The apparent heteroskedasticity is not due to heterogeneous error variances; it is due to heterogeneous fertility-reducing effects of development.

A gross way to adjust for persistent differences is to include the birth rate in the previous period as an independent variable in the model. The lagged dependent variable method of adjustment produces unbiased estimates of effects if autocorrelation of residuals is insignificant. Autocorrelation is negligible when partner concentration is the trade dependence indicator, but it is substantial when commodity concentration is used. For that reason, only partner concentration is used in this section.

Adding the birth rate from the previous period to the model does not change the basic conclusion reached when analyzing the preferred models. The interaction between dependence and development is still significantly greater than zero, indicating that the fertility-reducing effect of development is weakened by dependence. The new equation is:[7]

$$B = 26.2 + .00109DP - .00201D^2 + .445B_{-1} \qquad [8]$$
$$(5.1) \quad (2.6) \quad (-6.1) \quad (3.8)$$

[7] Since no birth rate prior to 1915–1919 in included in the data set, inclusion of past birth rate reduces sample size to 45 cases.

where B_{-1} is the symbol for previous birth rate. The magnitude of the inter-action effect in this model is only about half of what it is in the preferred model. This is because trade dependence is very stable over time (Hout, 1979). This stability means that some of the dependence effect in the pre-ferred model reflects an earlier effect of initial dependence on initial birth rate.

Previous dependence affects previous birth rate and current depen-dence; previous birth rate and current dependence affect current birth rate. The previous dependence affects the current birth rate indirectly through previous birth rate and current dependence. When previous birth rate is left out of the current birth rate equation, as it is in equations [6] and [7], some of the indirect effect through previous birth rate is represented as a direct effect of current dependence, so the current dependence effect is larger when pre-vious birth rate is left out (see Duncan, 1966). The coefficient for D^2 is also smaller in absolute magnitude for similar reasons. The large coefficient for previous birth rate reflects the large country component of the residuals from the preferred model. Inclusion of previous birth rate increases R^2 to .88.

Changes in the Birth Rate

Much attention has been given to identifying factors that influence the *rate* of fertility decline. Most of the articles addressing this issue relate to the formulation of population policy (e.g., Mauldin *et al.*, 1978). Therefore, since it is important to know what the perspective developed in this chapter offers those concerned with population policy, I have undertaken an anal-ysis of changes in fertility.

There are two ways to proceed. The first is to algebraically transform equation [8] by subtracting B_{-1} from both sides, dividing through by B_{-1} and multiplying by 100. This series of manipulations yields:

$$\widehat{\Delta\%B} = (2624/B_{-1}) + (.109DP/B_{-1}) - (.201D^2/B_{-1}) - 55.5 \qquad [9]$$

This is an unsatisfactory model for policy interpretation because of the com-plicated nonlinearities. All effects depend on the level of previous fertility.

The second approach is to reestimate effects in a simpler model. That was done by using the same independent variables as in equation [8]. They were regressed on percentage change in the birth rate. This approach implies a very complex model for B,[8] but a more straightforward model for $\widehat{\Delta\%B}$.

---

[8] The model for B implied by equation [10] is:

$$\hat{B} = 1.64B_{-1} - .0136B^2_{-1} + .0000307DPB_{-1} - .0000517D^2B_{-1}.$$

The resulting equation, as estimated by ordinary least squares, is

$$\widehat{\Delta\%B} = 64.0 + .00307DP - .00517D^2 - 1.36B_{-1} \qquad [10]$$
$$\phantom{\widehat{\Delta\%B} =} (4.5) \qquad (2.7) \qquad (-5.6) \qquad (-4.2)$$

This model has the same basic features as equation [8], and thus offers further support for the theory advanced here. Most important, the interaction term is significantly greater than zero, so that the fertility-reducing effect of development becomes weaker as dependence increases. Like the other models, this model also shows that fertility falls faster in the upper range of the development scale than in the lower range.

What can policy makers learn from this model? First, they cannot expect development to affect fertility much unless the increase in development is accompanied by a decrease in dependence. Second, they can expect greater changes after substantial development than in the early stages. Third, they can expect larger percentage decreases in countries with higher initial fertility than in others. This suggests that the change is more adequately modeled by an absolute change model than by a percentage change one. In sum, equations [6]–[8] are good guides to policy makers.

Summary and Discussion

Demographic Issues

The demographic issue addressed in this chapter is the apparent irregularity of fertility decline in Latin America. While fertility declined in some countries during or shortly after the period of increasing urbanization, literacy, and Northern-style consumption, it remained high in most, including those that experienced development comparable to the countries with falling fertility. The key to understanding this demographic pattern lies in the world context in which the observed socioeconomic development took place. Socioeconomic development in Latin America as a whole is dependent on trade with the core of the capitalist world system. But some states are more dependent than others.

Solving this equation for $B_{-1} = \bar{B}_{-1} = 39.3$ yields:

$$\hat{B} = 43.0 + .00121DP - .00203D^2$$

which is very close to what would be obtained by solving equation [8] for the same value of B_{-1}:

$$\hat{B} = 43.7 + .00109\bar{D}P - .00201D^2.$$

However, the models diverge substantially for values other than $\bar{B}_{-1}$.

The most important finding of this chapter is that the fertility-reducing effect of socioeconomic development is significantly less in those countries where development (such as it is) is tied to a high concentration of trade in a single commodity type or with a single trading partner. Dependence, at least trade dependence, blocks the fertility-reducing effect of development. This finding underscores Keyfitz' (1978) observation that understanding the local social context is essential to understanding the development—fertility relationship. There is no immutable law of developmental incentives that universally results in fertility decline.

This chapter is not without implications for other regions, however. The only treatment of another region that is comparable to the analysis presented here is Richards' (1977) appraisal of fertility decline in Germany. She found that the effect of development on fertility increased over the period 1880–1905. This followed a period of rapidly declining dependence in Germany during which unification and protective tariffs thrust Germany into competition with England as a core power (Rubinson, 1978). An issue worth pursuing is the extent to which the falling dependency is tied to the increased fertility-reducing effect of development observed by Richards. As an explanation of her findings, Richards suggests that as experience with industrialization accumulates, individuals become more sensitive to economic change and adopt rational planning in a wider sphere of personal activities—including family planning. Thus she sees her results as representing a fertility reduction process that is spread out over time.

An increase in industrialization decreases current fertility directly and subsequent fertility indirectly. This interpretation is consistent with the results presented here regarding nonlinear development effects in Latin America. In addition, this chapter shows another important process at work: the mitigating effect of dependence. This effect may well have been working in late nineteenth-century Germany as well. Germany's industrialization was significantly boosted by aggressive severance of dependence ties, particularly regarding the grain trade of the Prussian Junkers with Britain (Rubinson, 1978). It is likely that the lessened dependence contributed to the strengthening of the fertility-reducing effect of industrialization. In that way, the increased economic independence of Bismark's Germany may well have influenced the fertility reduction that followed. Tilly's (1978) discussion of Eastern European fertility suggests that the role of dependence in fertility reduction may have been similar in Poland and elsewhere in Eastern Europe. If so, the dependence—development interaction may be a very general pattern.

This has important implications for those Third World states that are waiting for economic development to reduce fertility levels. The dependence

–development interaction means that the anticipated fertility-reducing effects of development will not be forthcoming if that development is tied to foreign dependence.

Methodological Issues

Latin America is generally viewed as a dependent region, and rightly so. All of the countries are fundamentally dependent on trade with a few countries in a few commodities. Their economies are highly penetrated by foreign investors. But this chapter shows that there is variation in the dependence within Latin America. Furthermore, the differences have significant consequences for the individual states and for the region as a whole. Related research (Hout, 1979) shows that these differences have, over the course of the twentieth century, produced a differentiation within Latin America.

Differences among Latin American states in the level of economic development are greater today than they were in 1900. Much of that variance in development is attributable to variance in trade dependence. Few have taken seriously Furtado's (1970:253) admonishment that the time had come to abandon notions of Latin American homogeneity. This chapter shows the gains to be made from the exploration of Latin American heterogeneity. Furthermore, these gains can be made using a methodology designed to simultaneously confront comparative and temporal differences in a multivariate framework.

Dependence Issues

The findings presented in this chapter are important for more than just the demographic process examined. It is usually assumed that economic development transforms many social and economic institutions. The literature on economic development takes these "multiplier effects" for granted. On the assumption of substantial multiplier effects, development is recommended as the solution to an array of problems from over-urbanization to political disorganization to debt. This is in addition to the cry for development as a solution to population growth stemming from high fertility. Sociologists (e.g., Lenski, 1966) and economists (e.g., Nash, 1978) almost uniformly assume them in constructing theories of development. The demographic findings presented here show that multiplier effects are not universal. In showing that dependence blocks the fertility-reducing effects of development, this chapter suggests the possibility that dependence may block the effects of development on other, nondemographic variables. Once one of the key multiplier effects is called into question, the others are not above suspicion.

The consequences of dependence are only beginning to be understood. The consequences for economic development are well documented. Dependence on the industrial core (whether in the form of indebtedness, investment, or trade) depresses economic development. The implication of this study of Latin American fertility is that dependence effects are more far-reaching than previously thought. Rapid population growth, spurred by the dependence-related high fertility, has its own multiplier effects. Housing and food supply problems are the most obvious, but maldistribution of income, poor education for those enrolled and difficulties enrolling those at home, and loss of investment and debt service revenue all result from long periods of rapid population growth (Coale and Hoover, 1956; Coale, 1976).

If the dampening of multiplier effects is a general consequence of dependence, then the scope of dependence effects is wider than it was previously thought to be. Several writers have linked the political instability in Latin America to dependence. Chirot (1977; Chirot and Ragin, 1976) links political violence to characteristics of class structure typical of peripheral states within the capitalist world system. Other variables may show a similar relationship to dependence.

Socioeconomic development and educational expansion are proceeding rapidly in the Third World (Meyer *et al.*, 1976, 1977). The trends may not have the broad consequences generally anticipated if what is reported here is not a unique relationship.

Acknowledgments

This research ·vas supported by the University of Arizona. Thanks to Albert Bergesen, Phillips Cutright, Stanley Lieberson, Charles Tilly, and Wendy Wolf for comments on an earlier draft. Thanks also to Phillip Morgan and William Lockwood for their assistance in gathering the data.

References

Arriaga, Eduardo E.
   1970a   *Mortality Decline and Its Demographic Effects in Latin America*. Berkeley: Institute of International Studies.
   1970b   "The nature and effects of Latin America's non-western trend in fertility." *Demography* 7:483–502.
Banks, Arthur S.
   1971   *Cross Polity Time Series Data*. Cambridge, Mass.: MIT Press.

Beaver, Steven E.
 1975   *Demographic Transition Theory Reinterpreted.* Lexington, Mass.: D. C. Heath.
Bornschier, Volker, C. Chase-Dunn, and R. Rubinson
 1978   "Cross-national evidence of the effects of foreign investment and aid on economic growth and inequality." *American Journal of Sociology* 84:581–583.
Bross, I. D. J.
 1958   "How to use ridit analysis." *Biometrics* 14:18–38.
Cain, Mead T.
 1977   "The economic activities of children in a village in Bangladesh." *Population and Development Review* 3:201–229.
Caldwell, John C.
 1976   "Toward a restatement of demographic transition theory." *Population and Development Review* 2:321–366.
 1978   "A theory of fertility: From high plateau to destabilization." *Population and Development Review* 4:553–578.
Centro Latino Americano de Demografía (CELADE)
 1972   *Fertility and Family Planning in Metropolitan Latin America.* Chicago: Community and Family Study Center.
Chase-Dunn, Christopher
 1975   "The effects of international economic dependence on development and inequality." *American Sociological Review* 40:720–738.
Chirot, Daniel
 1977   *Social Change in the 20th Century.* New York: Harcourt, Brace and Jovanovich.
Chirot, Daniel, and C. Ragin
 1975   "The market, tradition, and peasant rebellion." *American Sociological Review* 40:428–444.
Coale, Ansley J.
 1973   "The demographic transition reconsidered." Pp. 53–72 in *International Population Conference,* 1973, Vol. I. Leige, Belgium: International Union for the Scientific Study of Population.
 1976   "Population growth and economic development: The case of Mexico." *Foreign Affairs* 56:415–429.
Coale, Ansley J., and E. M. Hoover
 1958   *Population Growth and Development in Low Income Countries.* Princeton: Princeton University Press.
Collver, O. Andrew
 1965   *Birth Rates in Latin America: New Estimates of Historical Trends and Fluctuations.* Berkeley: Institute of International Studies.
Cutright, Phillips, M. Hout, and D. R. Johnson
 1976   "Structural determinants of fertility in Latin America: 1800–1970." *American Sociological Review* 41:511–527.
Davis, Kingsley
 1970   *World Urbanization* 1950–1970 (two volumes). Berkeley: Institute of International Studies.
Delacroix, Jacques
 1977   "The export of raw materials and economic growth." *American Sociological Review* 42:795–808.
Duncan, Otis Dudley
 1966   "Path analysis: sociological examples." *American Journal of Sociology* 72:1–16.

Easterlin, Richard A.
    1976   "Population change and farm settlement in the Northern United States." *Journal of Economic History* 36:45–75.

Frank, André Gunder
    1969   *Latin America: Underdevelopment or Revolution.* New York: Monthly Review Press.

Furtado, Celso
    1970   *Economic Development of Latin America:* New York: Cambridge University Press.

Goode, William J.
    1960   "Illegitimacy in the Caribbean social structure." *American Sociological Review* 25:21–30.
    1961   "Illegitimacy, anomie, and cultural penetration." *American Sociological Review* 26:910–925.

Hannan, Michael T., and A. A. Young
    1977   "Estimation in panel models: Results on pooling." Pp. 52–83 in David R. Heise (ed.), *Sociological Methodology,* 1977. San Francisco: Josey-Bass.

Hout, Michael
    1979   "Persistent dependence: The case of Latin America from colonial times to the present." Paper presented at the meetings of the American Sociological Association, Boston, Mass., September, 1979.

Johnson, David R., and P. Cutright
    1973   "Problems in the analysis of Latin American illegitimacy." Pp. 377–408 in Allen D. Grimshaw and J. Michael Armer (eds.), *Comparative Social Research: Methodological Problems and Strategies.* New York: Wiley.

Keyfitz, Nathan
    1978   "Causes and consequences of population change." Paper presented at the annual meetings of the American Sociological Association. San Francisco, CA., September 4–8, 1978.

Kirk, Dudley
    1971   "A new demographic transition?" Pp. 123–147 in National Academy of Sciences (ed.), *Rapid Population Growth: Consequences and Policy Implications.* Baltimore: Johns Hopkins University Press.

Lenski, Gerhard
    1966   *Power and Privilege.* New York: McGraw-Hill.

Lieberson, Stanley
    1978   "A reconsideration of the income differences found between migrants and northern-born blacks." *American Journal of Sociology* 83:940–966.

Lewis, W. Arthur
    1977   *The Evolution of the International Economic Order.* Princeton: Princeton University Press.

Mauldin, W. Parker
    1978   "Patterns of fertility decline in developing countries 1950–75." *Studies in Family Planning* 9:75–84.

Mauldin, W. Parker, B. Berelson, and Z. Sykes
    1978   "Conditions of fertility decline in developing countries, 1965–75." *Studies in Family Planning* 9:89–147.

Meyer, John W., J. Boll-Bennett, and C. Chase-Dunn
    1976   "Convergence and divergence in development." *Annual Review of Sociology* 1:223–246.

Meyer, John W., F. O. Ramirez, R. Rubinson, and J. Boli-Bennett
 1977 "The world educational revolution, 1950–1970." *Sociology of Education* 50:242–
   258.
Nash, Manning (ed.)
 1978 *Economic Development and Cultural Change.* Chicago: University of Chicago
   Press.
Nortman, Dorothy
 1974 *Population and Family Planning Programs: A Factbook.* New York: Population
   Council.
Nerlove, Marc
 1974 "Toward a new theory of population and economic growth." Pp. 527–545 in
   Theodore W. Schultz (ed.), *Economics of the Family.* Chicago: University of Chicago Press.
Oeschli, Frank W., and D. Kirk
 1976 "Modernization and the demographic transition in Latin America and the Caribbean." *Economic Development and Cultural Change* 23:391–419.
Repetto, Robert
 1974 "The interaction of fertility and the size distribution of income." Unpublished man-
   uscript. Harvard Center for Population Studies, Paper No. 8.
 1977 "Income distribution and fertility change: A comment." *Population and Development Review* 3:486–489.
 1979 *Economic Inequality and Fertility.* Baltimore: Johns Hopkins University Press.
Richards, Toni
 1977 "Fertility decline in Germany." *Population Studies* 31:537–553.
Rubinson, Richard
 1976 "The world economy and the distribution of income within states." *American Sociological Review* 41:638–659.
 1978 "Political transformation in Germany and the United States." Pp. 39–74 in Barbara
   H. Kaplan (ed.), *Social Change in the Capitalist World Economy.* Beverly Hills:
   Sage Publications.
Statesman's Yearbook
 1904 London: Macmillan.
 1932 London: Macmillan.
 1951 London: Macmillan.
 1962 London: Macmillan.
Steiber, Steven R.
 1979 International Trade and Domestic Development. Unpublished Ph.D. dissertation.
   Department of Sociology, University of Arizona.
Stolzenberg, Ross M.
 1980 "Interpreting direct and indirect effects in nonlinear and nonadditive models."
   Forthcoming in Karl F. Schuessler (ed.), *Sociological Methodology,* 1980. San Francisco: Jossey-Bass.
Stycos, J. Mayone
 1971 *Ideology, Faith, and Family Planning in Latin America.* New York: McGraw-Hill.
Tilly, Charles
 1978 "The historical study of vital processes." Pp. 3–56 in Charles Tilly (ed.), *Historical
   Studies of Changing Fertility.* Princeton: Princeton University Press.
United Nations
 1975 *Demographic Yearbook.* New York: United Nations.

Van de Walle, Etienne
    1978   "Alone in Europe: The French fertility decline until 1850." Pp. 257–288 in Charles Tilly (ed.), *Historical Studies of Changing Fertility.* Princeton: Princeton University Press.
Wallerstein, Immanuel
    1978   "World-system analysis: Theoretical and interpretive issues." Pp. 219–235 in Barbara H. Kaplan (ed.), *Social Change in the Capitalist World Economy.* Beverly Hills: Sage Publications.

The Development of Core Capitalism in the Antebellum United States: Tariff Politics and Class Struggle in an Upwardly Mobile Semiperiphery

In the context of an expanding and deepening capitalist world-economy, "national development" can be understood as upward mobility in the hierarchical division of labor between the core and the periphery. Most areas that are incorporated into the expanding world-economy become organized as peripheries and are unable to escape this position. The process of peripheralization, or as André Gunder Frank calls it, the "development of underdevelopment," reproduces the structures that perpetuate peripheral capitalism and block the emergence of core capitalism. Occasionally, however, a nation is able to overcome the forces of peripheralization and develop core activities by which it reorganizes its relationship to the larger world-economy.

In the late sixteenth and early seventeenth centuries, core capitalist manufacturers and farmers in semiperipheral England were able to recapture the home market from core producers in the United Provinces. This was the beginning of England's long rise to world hegemony culminating in the nineteenth century. Similarly, shipbuilders and merchants of New England and the middle colonies in the eighteenth century were able to begin the process of capital accumulation in types of production which allowed them to compete with producers of core products in England. The later rise of the United States to core status and world hegemony stems from these developments.

This chapter summarizes recent work, which reinterprets the original

STUDIES OF THE
MODERN WORLD-SYSTEM

successes of the New England merchants and shipbuilders from the world system perspective, but its main task is to investigate the struggles in the antebellum period (1815–1860), which allowed U.S. core producers to expand and attain political hegemony in the Federal state. It is the story of core production and how the controllers of core production struggle for sufficient state power to realize their coreness over the long haul. The particular focus of this investigation is the politics of the import tariff. Tariff politics are one reflection the class forces that were contending for state power in the antebellum period. Domestic core producers seeking to compete with British products in the home market needed tariff protection. Peripheral producers (exporting raw materials to England and importing manufactured goods) opposed tariffs because they raised the price of the imports and because they feared British retaliation. Thus, the conflict which eventually led to the Civil War was not "sectional" except insofar as geography contributed to the emergence of classes which had contradictory interests vis á vis the world-economy.[1] This class struggle between core capitalists and peripheral capitalists within the United States is the focus of this paper. The problematic here is not, then, the emergence of core activities, but rather their survival. The establishment of shipbuilding firms and textile factories in New England did not inexorably lead to the rise and triumph of core capitalism, but rather the forces of peripheral capitalism and competing interests in England constantly challenged the very survival of these core producers.

---

[1] This theoretical perspective calls our attention to the importance of larger forces, such as the world market and international political and economic power, but it does not, as Robert Brenner (1978) claims, ignore the importance of class struggles. On the contrary, class relations are seen to exist at the level of the whole system, and class struggles are understood to take place across, as well as within, state boundaries (Wallerstein, 1976a). State boundaries overlay the structure of world classes and are an important influence on the subjective and organizational interests of classes. Capitalist production relations include both wage labor in the core and various forms of coerced labor in the periphery, as well as the relationship between these different types of labor control. From this perspective class formation, state formation, and nationbuilding are processes that occur *within,* not exogenous to, the operation of the capitalist mode of production. Brenner's (1978:88–90) contention that it was class forces *in Virginia,* rather than in the world-system, which determined the direction of development ignores the question of how the class structure of Virginia came into being.

The working out of the logic of capitalist development is, of course, influenced by exogenous variables, such as climate, soil fertility, geographical features, and the institutional structures of precapitalist societies which are incorporated into the world division of labor. These exogenous factors influence the outcomes of struggles between classes, states, firms, and so on. But the main determinants of success or failure come from the process of uneven development itself, and the success of some means the failures of others. The opportunities for increases in income are limited by the socially created and sustained scarcities, which the interests of superordinate world classes place on the production and distribution of surplus product.

Definitions of Core and
Peripheral Types of Production

Immanuel Wallerstein's world-system perspective involves a reinterpretation of the nature of capitalism. For Wallerstein, the capitalist system is constituted by an economic division of labor between core areas and peripheral areas. The political side of capitalism is the institution of unequal and competing nation-states which political scientists call the "international system." The capitalist world-economy has expanded and deepened since its emergence in Europe in the long sixteenth century, but its basic nature has not changed (Chase-Dunn and Rubinson, 1977).

Core areas of the system are areas where core types of production are most concentrated. Peripheral areas are areas where peripheral production is most concentrated. At the most analytic level, core activities are those types of production that employ relatively capital-intensive techniques and utilize skilled, highly paid labor. Peripheral activities are those types of production that use relatively labor-intensive techniques and employ coerced, low-wage labor. At a less abstract level, we can usually identify core production as the production of highly processed goods. But this is not always the case. As Arghiri Emmanuel (1972) has pointed out, textile manufacturing, a key core activity in the nineteenth century, has become a peripheral activity in the twentieth century relative to the capital intensive production currently occurring in core. Similarly, peripheral activities cannot always be identified in terms of the production of raw materials. Wheat production in the twentieth-century United States is more capital intensive than much manufacturing activity occurring in the contemporary periphery.

Peripheral production often creates a class of merchants in the periphery who exchange peripheral products for core imports. These merchants align themselves with the political interests of peripheral producers and the core areas for which they are producing. Thus, they often oppose the development of domestic core activities that would threaten their import–export business. These mediators of the core–periphery exchange occasionally have reason to support the development of core activities in peripheral areas, however. These exceptions are worthy of attention, especially in the case under investigation.

Wallerstein (1978) argues that there are no semiperipheral activities as such, but rather there are semiperipheral states which incorporate within their boundaries a relatively equal mix of core and peripheral types of production. Upwardly mobile semiperipheral states are ones in which core producers are in the ascendance, while downwardly mobile semiperipheral states are dominated by peripheral producers or former core producers who were pushed out of the world market. The state in the semiperiphery is more crucial than in core or peripheral areas, and class struggle for the control of the state is intense because of the very contradictory interests of the core producers and peripheral producers.

The conceptualization of classes utilized in this study focuses on production relations which are both national and worldwide. Arghiri Emmanuel's (1972) theory of unequal exchange provides a basis for understanding world classes that is grounded in the production and distribution of surplus value. This theory implies that wage differentials beyond differences in productivity create unequal exchange between core states and peripheral areas of the world economy, and that this affects the interests of classes. Nicos Poulantzas (1975) has argued that class position is determined not only by the relationship between the direct producer and his or her immediate overseer, but also by the political, legal, organizational, and ideological structures in which each producer is located. The state, then, is a major constituent of production relations, and, in the world-economy, one's relationship to states (foreign and domestic) is an important determinant of class position. I would argue that the wage differentials, which cause unequal exchange, are a consequence of class struggle and political processes that are not exogenous to capitalist development, but are rather an integral part of it.

The Origins of Core Capitalism in North America

From the world-system point of view, one of the main effects of the capital accumulation process is to reproduce the core–periphery division of labor through unequal development. The mechanisms by which the "development of underdevelopment" occurs have been studied in operation in Eastern Europe, Latin America, Asia, and Africa. Yet some areas have managed to escape the process of peripheralization.[2] Although a general explanation for these exceptions has not yet been formulated, there are case studies that form the basis for a theoretical understanding.[3]

A great deal has been written about the development of capitalism in

[2] The conditions that allowed Japan to avoid peripheralization and develop core activities are described by Frances Moulder (1977). England's upward mobility is analyzed by Wallerstein (1974) and Frank (1978). Wallerstein (1980) also explains the emergence of semiperipheral Sweden and Prussia, as well as New England in the late seventeenth and early eighteenth centuries.

[3] This is an ironic reversal of approach when compared to the modernization literature, which sought to understand and promote the development of "backward" nations in the basis of generalizations derived from the history of "advanced" ones.

North America, and much of this has had an implicitly comparative perspective. It has been asserted that the protestant ethic of the Puritans inclined them toward thrift and investment, and that the democratic ideas of the Glorious Revolution in England encouraged those bold embattled farmers to resist exploitation. These ideas, it is held, led to the creation of a new society in which individualism and competitive capitalism expanded unfettered by the feudal remnants of the Old World. While it would be unwise to neglect the effects of ideology, the world-system perspective directs us to the institutional and structural conditions under which such ideologies contribute to social development. Not all Puritans, and not all English subjects, were able to establish core industries in the late seventeenth and early eighteenth centuries.

Karl Marx understood that the colonists of North America did not arrive empty handed. They brought with them a recipe for the creation of a purified form of capitalism.

> In these colonies, and especially in those which produced only merchandise such as tobacco, cotton, sugar, etc. and not usual food stuffs, where, right from the start, the colonists did not seek subsistence but set up a business. . . . They did not act like the Germans, who settled Germany in order to make their home there, but like people who, driven by motives of *bourgeois production,* wanted to produce commodities, and their point of view was, from the outset, determined not by the product but by the sale of the product [Marx, 1863/1968:239; italics in the original].

Samir Amin (1976) argues that "simple commodity production"[4] was established in North America and allowed to develop unfettered by the existence of feudal remnants which survived in European society. But he distinguishes between peripheral capitalism, which developed under the influence of the core, and the proto-core capitalism, which developed independently of the core. Wallerstein (1980) points out that the colonists of New England did not produce exports for the core during the first 40 years of their existence. Instead, simple commodity production developed without regard to the core—periphery division of labor.

André Gunder Frank (1979) argues that it was the combination of a relatively egalitarian distribution of land (with most farmers engaged in both subsistence and commodity production) and the "benign neglect" of British mercantile policy during the turmoil of the Glorious Revolution and its aftermath that allowed core capitalism to develop in New England. He contends that an agrarian class structure composed mostly of yeomen is a

---

[4] Simple commodity production exists when there is no differentiation between capital and labor. Producers own the means of production and produce commodities for sale on a market. The free farmers working their own land and producing cash crops constituted a large part of the colonial economy in the Northern and middle colonies.

necessary, but not sufficient, condition for the emergence of core capitalism. Other peripheral areas, such as Costa Rica, the Spanish West Indies, Argentina, and Jamaica (before its development as a sugar island) as well as Canada, had a yeomanry without developing core industry.[5] Such a class structure provides the basis for the development of a diversified domestic market for core commodities. This potential home market, however, does not automatically lead to the development of core industries. In areas where there is a strong colonial administration, industries that are potential competitors with producers in the mother country are discouraged. In addition, merchants mediating the core—periphery exchange often oppose the development of domestic core industries.

Why did this not happen in New England? Wallerstein (1980) argues that the key core industry which developed in seventeenth century New England was the shipbuilding industry and its associated fishing industry and carrying trade. How and why was the shipbuilding industry able to develop in New England, and why did it not develop elsewhere in the periphery? Wallerstein agrees with Frank that part of the answer is benign neglect. The British were preoccupied with political struggles at home; this prevented them from realizing their mercantile grand plan to develop colonies that would enrich the mother country. The wave of colonization, which started under the Tudors, developed with little direct interference—or support.

In the southern colonies and the British West Indies, soil and climate facilitated the creation of classical peripheral capitalism using coerced labor (slaves) to produce agricultural commodities for export to the core. But in the less hospitable North, the production of staple exports was much less profitable. In New England, poor soil and climate were capable of sustaining only subsistence production and production for the local market on small owner-worked farms. Thus, the agrarian class structure of New England was characterized by a relatively equal distribution of land tenure and income. In the middle colonies soil and climate were more favorable and larger farms produced cash crops such as wheat, some of which was ex-

---

[5] These are the areas that were least profitable in terms of the exploitation of raw materials and labor, and thus subsistance farming created a relatively egalitarian class structure. In areas where mines or plantations created an incentive for labor exploitation, either indigenous or imported coerced labor forces were utilized, resulting in a much more hierarchical class structure. Mintz (1969) supports this analysis with his comparison of Puerto Rico and Jamaica in the early nineteenth century. The two islands, which are very similar geographically, were going through a transformation of class structure in exactly opposite directions. Jamaica, which had been a sugar colony for 150 years was, because of soil exhaustion, returning to a rather egalitarian subsistence economy, while Puerto Rico, which had been a neglected Spanish colony with a subsistence economy, was in the process of becoming a plantation economy based on coerced wage labor.

ported. With the exception of the Hudson River valley,[6] these farms were worked by their owners and the distribution of land tenure was fairly equal. The attempt by the Dutch West India Company to introduce slaves into agriculture in New Amsterdam was thwarted by the greater demand for slaves from southern planters. The slaves imported in the North were quickly sold to higher bidders and reexported. Governor Stuyvesant's tax on the export of slaves was to no avail. The economics of slavery favors a long growing season since the slaves must be fed all year round. The great land owners of the Hudson Valley preferred tenants who were responsible for their own subsistence through the winter.

The upper South is another intermediate case. In the Chesapeake tidewater, natural conditions favored the growing of tobacco. This was most efficiently done on middle-sized plantations using small slave labor forces. These plantations were smaller than the great agrarian enterprises producing indigo, rice, and sugar further south, but larger than the farms of the middle colonies or New England. The ruling class of the upper South was a larger percentage of the population than in the deep South. There was also a large number of small owner-worked farms growing tobacco in the upper South. The adoption of more republican and less aristocratic political institutions in the upper South stems from this (Greene, 1976). Thus, the God-given conditions of agronomy seem to have had more effect on the class structure than the revealed knowledge of the Puritans or the Catholic doctrine of Maryland. Soil and climate favorable to the employment of slave labor would quickly have transformed Boston into Charleston.

Stein and Stein (1970) suggest that part of the success of the British colonies was due to their extermination of indigenous populations and the creation of culturally homogenous settlements in which the working classes were paid relatively high wages. This argument confuses what Frank's treatment makes clear. First, a yeoman-based, culturally homogenous class structure is insufficient by itself and is not solely the product of *British* colonialism. The less profitable (and more neglected) areas of the Spanish empire also evolved such a class structure. Second, the British lost no time in importing African slaves when they found conditions favorable to plantation agriculture. Finally, British, Dutch, and French colonists in northern North America made every effort to extract wealth from the indigenous peoples (seen most vividly in the fur trade) but the less hierarchial indigenous social

---

[6] Dutch settlements (of Protestants) in the Hudson River valley evolved an agrarian class structure of large landlords and leasehold tenants who worked on the estates (Kim, 1978). This land tenure pattern remained after the British took control of the area (Lynd, 1964). This indicates that, in regions where soil productivity and climate is intermediate, political and institutional factors more easily affect the type of class structure that develops.

organization of the native North Americans rendered them particularly un-suitable as slaves or serfs. As it was, New England had to fall back on the one natural resource it had: timber (Clark, 1916). The export of lumber was not as profitable, however, as the building of ships with the lumber. The shipbuilding industry was stimulated by the fishing industry and the oppor-tunities for entering the carrying trade among the colonies and between the core and the periphery.

Shepherd and Walton (1972) have shown that the so-called "triangle trades" were not usually carried on by individual shippers. Most shippers shuttled between the northern colonies and England, while some traded with southern colonies and the West Indies, and others sailed to Southern Europe and Africa. As Shepherd and Walton (1972) have stated

> trades involving two or more overseas areas, such as from the West Indies to Great Brit-ain and back to the colonies, were not typical. It is possible, of course, to describe the pattern of international settlements as triangular or multilateral (for example, the West Indies earned surpluses in their trade with Britain, the continental colonies earned sur-pluses in their West Indies trade, and Britain earned surpluses in its American trade) [p. 156].

By 1770, the negative balance of trade of the American colonies with Britain was largely compensated by so-called "invisible exports" such as merchan-dising and shipping services, and these incomes returned largely to the mer-chant shippers of New England and New York. Thus, the merchant ship-pers accumulated investment capital from their profitable mediation between the European core and the American, West Indian, and African peripheries.

But buying cheap and selling dear (merchant capitalism) does not in it-self create the basis of core production, and the merchants who mediate the exchange between core and peripheral areas most often come to have a stake in the exchange, leading them to resist changes in the division of labor. For example, the merchants of New England and New York often opposed tariff protection of domestic core manufactures and sided with peripheral capitalists in the early nineteenth century. What led the eighteenth century merchants of New England, New York, and Philadelphia to invest their profits in production that would compete with core industries (e.g. ship-building) rather than invest in peripheral production? And why were they allowed to do so?

The answer to the first question is that they had a comparative advan-tage in shipbuilding and profits were high. Even though labor costs were higher than in England, the low cost of raw materials encouraged New En-glanders to build ships for their own use and for export. Shepherd and Walton (1972:244) report that an estimated 57% of the shipping tonnage built in the colonies during 1769–1771 was sold abroad.

But why was this North American industry—and the complementary carrying trade and fishing industry—allowed to compete with similar producers from the mother country? Competitive advantage in production (the ability, in this case to produce ships more cheaply than others) is no guarantee that such production will be allowed to develop, especially in a mercantile world of monopoly protection. Shipbuilders, fishermen, and merchant mariners in England were undoubtedly opposed to the competition from the colonies.

Benign neglect was undoubtedly part of the answer. The political turmoil in England and the rivalry between England and France allowed the emerging Yankees some space. But it was also the eighteenth century upturn in the world-economy, and especially the rapid increase in trade in the Atlantic economy, which facilitated the emergence of core production in New England. In an expanding economy the interests of consumers in buying cheaply come to outweigh the interests of producers in maintaining monopoly, at least relative to periods of contraction. The development of the shipbuilding industry and the ability of the New England merchants to insert themselves into the core–periphery Atlantic economy in a semiperipheral (intermediate) position allowed them to accumulate capital rapidly and to expand their operations. The increased space for core production was a function of expansion of the world economy as a whole.

This explains why core production survived outside the previously core areas during this period. But why did this development occur in New England as opposed to elsewhere? Wallerstein suggests that it was to New England's benefit, relative to other areas in the periphery, that it was a *British* colony. Britain was uniquely Britain, but it was also *the* emerging hegemonic core power of the world-economy and was experiencing a rapidly accelerating industrial revolution. It was less important that the colonies inherited British cultural and institutional characteristics (such as parliamentary democracy) than that Britain had a unique location in the world economy. During the colonial period, the British colonies had greater access to the most advanced technological developments through information flows and immigration of skilled labor than did the colonies of other core powers. After the War of Independence, the North Americans were suspicious of, and resistant to, British attempts to influence and control them. This is in contrast to the Latin American new nations, which made their anti-imperial revolts with the aid of the British and in order to do business with them.

The settler colonialism of the British—sending whole communities rather than only overseers to direct the extraction of surplus from natives—

is due in part to the racism of the English who, unlike the French, insisted on bringing their women with them rather than marrying daughters of the local chiefs.[7] Settler colonialism was also due to the intensified commercialization of agriculture in Britain, which drove migrants to the cities and to the colonies.

To summarize, five factors contributed to the emergence of core activities in New England: (a) the natural conditions of New England which discouraged peripheral agriculture and encouraged the shipbuilding and maritime industries; (b) a relatively egalitarian class structure; (c) the expansion of the Atlantic economy which created space for the emergence of the core producers and lessened the resistance of those already engaged in these industries; (d) the benign neglect of the British during the seventeenth and early eighteenth centuries; and (e) the advantage of being a British colony rather than a colony of another core power.

The Expansion of Core Capitalism in the Antebellum Period

We have reviewed arguments about the original emergence of core activities in New England and the middle colonies. Here we turn to the question of how these activities were expanded and politically protected in the period between 1815 and 1860. The discussion will focus on the issue of tariff politics. The state is understood to be the main mechanism by which classes and alliances of classes distort market forces in their own interest.[8] From the world-system point of view, this is not exogenous to the workings of capitalism. The state system and the utilization of state structures by competing and conflicting classes in the world-economy are understood to be the political side of capitalism. The arena of market competition is always larger than the political domain of any single state, and so the differentiation between economic and political institutions occurs at the level of the whole system rather than at the national level.

The politics of import duties reflects the struggle between classes that

[7] The conscious policy of separation from indigenous peoples evolved from the earlier experience in Ireland where English overlords had become completely merged with the Gaelic population and thus beyond control.

[8] This description of the role of the state as reflecting the combined interests of dominant classes does not exclude the possibility that the state apparatus itself occasionally exercises influence in its own behalf. My position is not a vulgar "instrumentalist" one (Gold, Lo, and Wright, 1975). For the case under investigation, however, a sophisticated structuralist theory of the state is hardly required. The "relative autonomy" of the U.S. Federal state in the antebellum period is out of the question. The state apparatus itself was small (Crenson, 1975); thus the vectors of class interest operated on state policy relatively unmediated by a government bureaucracy.

have different interests in relation to the larger world economy. This does not imply that these interests are perfectly reflected, or that individuals always know their own economic interests. As Marx pointed out, politics often reveals only a shadowy relationship to the underlying class forces operating in society. This investigation of tariff politics tends to confirm that insight. Yet the outlines of the struggle between core capitalists, peripheral capitalists, and the other classes which ally with or oppose them, can be discerned in the tariff history of the United States between 1815 and 1860. As to the correspondence between the attitudes of individuals and their class interests, we do not assume a naive "economic man" model. In a study of recent United States tariff politics and attitudes, Bauer, Pool, and Dexter (1968) have shown that individuals often do not know what their interests are, and that, in response to social pressures, they often act in ways which are inconsistent with their own interests. Benjamin Franklin, as a Philadelphia manufacturer, supported free trade and the doctrine that agriculture is inherently superior to industry.

On the other hand, aggregate political processes do tend to reflect the economic rationalities of conflicting interests. This will be seen in the following account of nineteenth century tariffs, but it is also illustrated in the study by Bauer, Dexter, and Pool. They document the transition from the long-standing policy of protectionism to free trade in the late 1950s. Then the U.S. economy had attained economic hegemony in the larger world and producers shared a common interest in expanding to foreign markets, rather than in protecting the home market. As such, it was similar to the British adoption of free trade in the 1840s and the Dutch advocacy of free trade in the seventeenth century.

From the point of view of U.S. core capitalists, what had been accomplished by 1815? The main political accomplishment was the construction of a sovereign state, independent of imperial control and capable of protecting the interests of its producing classes—both core and peripheral—in the larger world economy. The contrasting case of Canada and the other northern colonies shows the importance of political independence. The continuation of the colonial system in Canada stimulated the export of timber with "differential duties" until the British adopted free trade in 1846 (Lower, 1973). Wood (1977) compares nineteenth-century India and the United States to show the different effects of British influence. Direct colonial control of India led to the perpetuation of that country's peripheral position in the world-economy. The railroad system that the British built created an infrastructure that entrenched colonial control but did not promote independent economic development. British investment in U.S. railroads was much more at the behest of U.S. core capitalists, and had a beneficial effect on the integration of the national economy.

   The American Revolution and the process of early state formation need to be reinterpreted from a world-system perspective but I will not attempt to do so here. Clearly core and peripheral producers and colonial merchants supported the formation of an independent state.[9] Core producers did not dominate the new state, but neither were they excluded from it. The anticolonial victory did not, in itself, guarantee the upward mobility of the United States in the world-economy. After all, the Latin American republics successfully established formal political independence in the early nineteenth century, but economic "neo-colonialism" continued to produce the development of underdevelopment and they remained in a peripheral position in the world division of labor (Stein and Stein, 1970). This leads us to consider the upward mobility of the United States as problematic, and to inquire how the class forces supporting the development of domestic core production were capable of winning out over the interests that supported the maintenance of peripheral production for export to the established core in Europe.

   The creation of the Federal state and the Constitution in 1789 was a necessary step in the direction of further upward mobility (national development), but did not guarantee it. The Constitution institutionalized the interests of property owners (both core and peripheral capitalists, as well as merchants) in the state. It consolidated the power of the planters, the merchants, and the nascent manufacturers over the small farmers, artisans, and slaves and created a semiperipheral state capable of enforcing its own mercantile policy to protect the international interests of these dominant classes. At first this was evidenced by tariffs and navigation laws favorable to the carrying trade of the merchants and shippers. A navy was necessary to enforce these laws and to protect American ships. The war with Tripoli in 1801 was an effort to halt piracy of U.S. vessels in the Mediterranean, as well as to

   [9] From a world-system perspective it is understandable why emergent core producers in a peripheral area and small commodity producers relatively independent of the core–periphery division of labor might support a War of Independence. But why would Southern planters and Northern merchants tied to the core–periphery exchange support it? Of course, many large property owners did not. Tory sentiment in the South and in the commercial cities of the middle colonies (especially New York) was high. But many merchants and planters were in debt to British creditors (Thompson, 1978). The planters shared with Northern farmers a resentment of the increase in what was perceived as illegitimate taxation. Merchants resented the reorganization and attempted enforcement of the Navigation Acts. And the planters also resented British attempts to limit expansion westward with the Proclamation Line of 1763. Plantation agriculture quickly exhausted the soil and necessitated expansion to fresh areas. Aptheker (1960) suggests that rivalry between British and planter land companies in the Ohio Valley contributed to Whiggish sentiment in Virginia. But Frank (1978) argues that none of the above grievances would have been sufficient in the absence of the cyclical economic slump which followed the expansion of the first half of the eighteenth century. This, and the defeat of the French by the British in the Seven Years War (and consequent French support for the Americans) made the anti-imperial revolt possible.

demonstrate to the European powers that the U.S. could intimidate Barbarians as well as any core power (Field, 1969).

The interests of potential core producers were not strongly supported by the Federal state prior to the tariff of 1816, but there had been an intellectual defense of the protection of core activities. Alexander Hamilton, as Secretary of the Treasury in 1791, addressed to Congress an eloquent pre-Listian defense of import substitution entitled "A Report on the Subject of Manufactures". Hamilton's argument was partly a defense against the claim of the Phisiocrats that agriculture is inherently more productive than industry. But Hamilton also argued for protection against core imports on the grounds that the core powers discriminated against U.S. agricultural exports.

> In such a position of things, the United States cannot exchange with Europe on equal terms; and the want of reciprocity would render them [the U.S.] the victim of a system which would induce them to confine their views to agriculture, and refrain from manufactures. A constant and increasing necessity, on their part, for the commodities of Europe, and only a partial and occasional demand for their own, in return, could not but expose them to state of impoverishment compared with the opulence to which their political and natural advantages authorize them to aspire [Cole, 1928:265].[10]

The significance of Hamilton's position is made clear by a comparison with the Latin American republics. In the United States after the War of Independence, as in Latin America, politics became polarized around the issue of centralization versus local autonomy. But there was one essential difference. For example, in Argentina the centralizers were based on urban merchant interests in Buenos Aires who mediated the core–periphery exchange. The ideology of these centralizers was free international trade (and their own monopoly over this trade) (Burgin, 1946).[11] In the United States, on the other hand, some of the centralizers argued for protection of domestic industry against competition from core imports. This difference reflects the different prior histories of the areas, which allowed fledgling core activities to develop in the U.S. but not in Latin America.

The contention between Hamilton and Jefferson was, in part, over different visions of the future of the United States. Although Jefferson later

---

[10] The theory of unequal exchange (Emmanuel, 1972) does not appear full-blown here, but the argument bears a striking similarity to the "instability and inelasticity of demand" formulations of United Nations economists concerned with contemporary Latin American dependency.

[11] The "free trade" postures of the Latin American regimes did not preclude all tariffs, but rather avoided a policy which systematically protected domestic core producers from British competition (Burgin, 1946). The occasional regimes that did advocate independent national development and protection were ineffectual and short-lived due to the strong opposition of peripheral producers supported by the British (Frank, 1967; Hale, 1968).

opted for a policy of expansion and competition for power in the larger world economy, his original vision was of an arcadian society composed of gentleman farmers, isolated from the vicissitudes of world market competition but freely importing and exporting to meet the needs of a stable, no-growth agricultural republic. It has been pointed out that Jefferson's own arcadia, contrary to all his Jacobin sympathies, was based on slave labor (Vidal, 1973). The struggle between the Federalists (Hamiltonian centralists) and Republicans (Jeffersonian decentralists) resulted in the political victory of the Virginians and their subsequent adoption of most of the Hamiltonian program, including territorial expansion, a permanent navy, a sound fiscal basis for the Federal State, the creation of the first United States Bank.

The Napoleonic Wars were a great stimulus to the carrying trade because the U.S. was granted neutral status by the European powers. Merchants enjoyed a virtual monopoly over the carrying trade between the West Indies, Latin America, and Europe. The interruption of this profitable business by Jefferson's Embargo and Non-Intercourse Acts and Madison's declaration of war against Britain caused New England to consider secession from the Union at the Hartford Convention in 1814. But these Acts and protection from import competition afforded by the war with Britain stimulated the growth of import-substituting manufactures, especially in Pennsylvania, Massachusetts, and Rhode Island. Peacetime was a disaster to these new industries as the post-war market was flooded with cheap English "gee-gaws" auctioned in New York City at prices below their cost of production. Dumping of core products in New York was a conscious policy of British manufacturing interests. As Lord Brougham explained to Parliament in 1816, it was "well worth while to incur a loss upon the first exportation, in order, by the glut, to stifle in the cradle those rising manufactures in the United States, which war had forced into existence, contrary to the natural course of things." (Forsythe, 1977: 69). The newly established cotton textile manufacturers were shut down until the tariffs of 1816 and later years provided protection from English imports.

The United States tariff policy between 1815 and 1860 can be roughly outlined as follows. The war duties (intended for revenue) were replaced in 1816 with a tariff which, although not high, was intended to be protective. The average rate in 1816 was 25% ad valorem. This was increased in 1824 to 33%, and again in 1828 to 50% (Freehling, 1967). In 1833, Southern planter and Northern merchant opposition forced the adoption of the Compromise Tariff which lowered rates slowly until 1842. In 1842 protection was renewed until 1846 when the Walker Tariff, a victory for the free traders, was adopted. In 1857 tariffs were lowered even further. The Republicans passed the ultra-protectionist Morrill Tariff and protectionism reigned from then until after World War II.

This tariff history reflects the process of class formation in the antebellum period. Core manufacturers expanded after the War of 1812 and, in alliance with farmers, succeeded in passing protectionist legislation. The peripheral capitalism of King Cotton expanded even more rapidly and the core and peripheral interests contended for power in the Federal state by making alliances with other classes: merchants, workers, and yeoman farmers. Peripheral capitalism in the South was by no means moribund. Indeed it was a dynamic and differentiated economy based on commodity production with slave labor. By the 1840s the upper South had become a slave-breeding and semi-industrial region (Bateman and Weiss, 1976). But the main form of appropriation in this slave-based peripheral economy remained the production of cotton for the European core of the world-economy. The plantocracy of the South was able to dominate the Federal state during most of the antebellum period by allying with Western farmers and Northern workers in the Democratic Party. This alliance, which ushered in the period of low tariffs in the 1840s and 1850s, eventually foundered on the issue of the legal status of slavery in the new territories of the West.

The access of core producers to state power before 1815 can be assessed by examining tariff politics. As argued, tariff politics and tariff policies are a reflection of the strength of classes with conflicting interests in the world economy. Pennsylvania created protective tariffs during the period of the Articles of Confederation (Eiselen, 1932) but the tariffs enacted by the Union from 1789 to 1816 were, with few exceptions, designed only as a source of revenue. Other state policies, such as the Navigation Acts and creation of the permanent navy to defend shipping, clearly benefited shipping interests and merchants, but these policies were supported by the planters. The interests of Northern merchants and Southern planters were harmonious, but they came into conflict with the core capitalist manufacturers who were spawned by the dearth of imports during the Embargo and the War of 1812.

The post-war slump and flood of British imports showed that the United States remained an economic neo-colony of Britain. In 1815 the success of the manufacturers was by no means certain. The Tariff of 1816 was a crucial turning point because the Federal state began to use its power for the first time to foster core capitalism.

The Rise of Protectionism

Protectionism became the policy of the Federal government between 1816 and 1832 for several reasons. Core producers were strong enough to flood Congress with memorials demanding relief from the influx of cheap foreign goods, and there was little opposition to such pleas. The War of

1812 made obvious the dependence of the United States on European imports and there was wide support for the development of manufacturing that would lessen this dependence. John C. Calhoun, later the champion of the Southern anti-tariff cause, supported protectionism for national development until the mid-twenties. The Tariff of 1816 passed the House 88 to 54. It was not a party line bill and sectional divisions were only faintly visible. The 8 Southern states were split 25 for and 39 against. There was strong support from Kentucky and a majority in favor in South Carolina and Tennessee. New England was split. The only solid protectionist area was the middle states, New York, Pennsylvania, New Jersey, and Delaware. Ohio voted solidly for the bill (Forsythe, 1977).

What determined which commodities would be protected and how high the rates would be for different commodities? If the theory of protection for "infant industries" had been followed we would expect those industries that were weakest but most essential for national security and economic development to be the ones given the most protection. Eiselen's (1932) thorough study of the politics of protection in Pennsylvania concludes, however, that it was not generally the weakest industries that received protection, but rather those that were strong enough to exercise influence on Congress. Pincus's (1977) econometric study of the Tariff of 1824 shows that industries which were concentrated in a particular geographical area, rather than spread over a wide area, were more likely to organize political pressure and receive protection. Competition within a particular industry could also influence the height of the tariff wall. Zevin (1971) reports that in 1816 Francis Lowell, a cotton textile manufacturer who had recently observed production techniques in England and returned to invent his own power loom, lobbied against the high rate proposed by the less efficient textile producers in Providence. The tariff that was adopted was high enough to allow Lowell and the other producers who adopted mechanized production to make a profit, but low enough to drive out the less efficient producers.

The Panic of 1819 followed the post-war boom. The price of agricultural commodities fell rapidly and unemployment in the cities of the North reached alarming proportions. The last great Corn Law was passed by Parliament in 1815 to protect English agriculture from foreign imports. This, and the recovery of agriculture in Europe, caused American exports of grain to fall. The declining price of their produce induced the farmers of Pennsylvania and other Northern states to rally to the cause of industrial protection. Similarly the unemployed mechanics and workingmen were told by the Philadelphia protectionist, Matthew Carey, that a high tariff would promote industrial employment and raise wages (Taylor, 1953). Eiselen (1932) in reflecting on the ebb and flow of Pennsylvania protectionist enthusiasm during the antebellum period, notes that economic slumps always resulted in a clamoring for tariffs as prices fell, while good times reduced tariff enthusiasm.

Henry Clay of Kentucky proposed his "American System" to promote the alliance between agriculture and industry based on the protected development of the diversified national market. In Clay's scheme the Federal government would stimulate manufacturing by applying a protective (but not prohibitive) tariff. The revenues resulting from the tariff would enable the government to sell Western land cheaply and to finance internal improvements in transportation between the agricultural West (and, presumably, the South) and the industrial East. Clay's program created the political alliance among core capitalists, farmers, and labor, which supported increasing protectionism until Southern opposition reversed this trend in 1833. The program of internal improvements began in 1818 with the completion of the National Road, a Federally built highway which connected Baltimore with the Ohio Valley (Broude, 1964). The General Survey bill of 1824 proposed an elaborate national transportation system of roads and canals, most of which were later built under the auspices of the separate states, but with Federal encouragement (Goodrich, 1960). The Erie Canal was completed in 1825.

The maritime and commercial interests of New England were against protection at first. To his later embarrassment, Daniel Webster made spirited free trade speeches at the behest of the shipping concerns of New Hampshire. Commercial interests were opposed to import tariffs because their profits were gained mainly from the core–periphery trade. Financial connections with London led many New York and New England merchants to oppose protection of American core industries throughout the antebellum period.

The shipbuilders of New England, formerly the most developed core capitalists in America, also opposed the tariff bills which Congress passed during the first era of protection. They did this in part because some of the commodities protected were raw material inputs into their industry, particularly hemp and iron. Core products were not the only protected commodities. Indeed core producers obtained protection by making alliances with other producers. Logrolling resulted in tariff bills which supported both core products, such as textiles and glass manufactures, and also raw materials, such as coal, iron, hemp, and lead. Shipbuilders were understandably unwilling to support legislation which increased their costs. In addition, the "Tariff of Abominations" (1828) was intentionally constructed by the Jacksonians to be unpalatable to New England in order to embarrass the Adams administration. It included tariffs on sugar and molasses, which were offensive to the New England distilleries.

New England eventually came over to protectionism, however. "In 1825, the great firm of W. and S. Lawrence of Boston turned its interest and capital from importing to domestic manufacturing, and the rest of State Street fell in behind it. So did Daniel Webster, who was now to become Congress' most eloquent supporter of protection [Forsythe, 1977]."

What were the effects of the tariffs? Free traders, as we shall see, claimed broadly evil consequences. Advocates of protection argued that it stimulated industrial growth and enhanced both profits and wages. Henry C. Carey, the first American contributor to the science of political economy, blamed every economic slump in the antebellum years on free trade and attributed every period of prosperity to protection (Stanwood, 1903). Taussig's (1964) classic study of tariff history and industrial growth, first published in 1892, concluded that, especially after 1824, tariffs did not greatly contribute to the growth of particular industries. According to Taussig the protection afforded by the War of 1812 and the Tariffs of 1816 and 1820 were helpful to some infant industries, but probably not essential for their survival and growth.

The onslaught of British imports after the War of 1812 was only partly affected by the tariffs, which—although protectionist in intent—were not very effective (Pincus, 1977:102). An exception was the protection of cotton textiles. Most protected items were given an ad valorem rate based on a percentage of their import price. In 1816 cotton textiles were also given a "minimum" rate, which meant that, no matter how low the market price dropped, they would be treated as if their price was a certain minimum. This minimum rate proved to be extremely important when the price of British textiles dropped rapidly in the years following 1816.

Eiselen (1932) argues that for most industries the effect of protection on prices was only temporary. A price rise due to a tariff increase encouraged new firms to enter production and the increased competition tended to drive prices back down again. David (1975) argues that the temporarily higher profits may have allowed manufacturers of cotton textiles to "learn by doing," that is, to experiment with production techniques and to increase efficiency.[12] His econometric analysis of six firms during the period from 1834 to 1860 does not provide much support for this argument, however, and he concludes that Taussig's contention about the tariff effect is basically correct. Zevin's (1971) econometric study of the causes of

---

[12] Whereas it has often been assumed that high wages were the main incentive for investment in machinery in the textile industry, David (1975:146) cites an unpublished work by Zevin which contends that one large firm held a monopsony (buyer's monopoly) in the local labor market, and that this circumstance, probably shared by other leading firms, enabled manufacturers to pay workers less than their marginal productivity even though labor was scarce. So it was labor scarcity rather than high wages that motivated these firms to employ additional machinery.

growth in the textile industry finds that the largest portion of the phenomenal growth of factory cloth production in New England in the period from 1815 to 1833 is due to change in the composition of total production between home and factory, that is, the growth of demand for manufactured cloth as a replacement for homespun.[13] He concludes that the tariff made a negligible contribution to the growth of American demand for New England mill products.

On the other hand, Fogel and Engerman (1971), studying the growth of iron production between 1842 and 1858, estimate that reductions in the tariff rate caused a 10.8% fall in the price of domestic iron and a 29% reduction in output. Taussig never claimed, however, that the tariff had no effects, but rather that it was not essential to the establishment and growth of particular industries. Protection undoubtedly affected the timing and rate of growth of industry, and, from the perspective of the competitive world-economy, timing can be very important. The advances made by the core industries in the 1820s and 1830s enabled them to survive and prosper in the period during the 1840s and 1850s when peripheral producers reestablished their control of the Federal state. Zevin (1971) reports that between 1820 and 1830 American consumption of cotton cloth increased from 50 to 175 million yards, while the share of that consumption supplied by New England increased from about 30% to about 80%. By 1825 even Hezekiah Niles, the ardent Baltimore protectionist, admitted that American coarse cotton textiles no longer needed protection. By 1832 these coarse cottons were competing with British products in the markets of the Far East. Thus further protection of cotton textiles was redundant.

Even though Taussig's careful study of individual industries led him to the conclusion that protection was not essential to the birth and survival of any single industry by itself, he nevertheless acknowledged the importance of the protectionist movement in stimulating the overall transition from the agricultural and mercantile economy that existed before 1815 to the more diversified manufacturing economy that developed thereafter. This observation helps us understand the ambivalence of the shipbuilders and commercial interests of New England who were the key core industries of the earlier era.

Shippers and mercantile capitalists were hurt badly by the ending of the

---

[13] Zevin (1971) assumes that most of the increased demand for manufactures came from the rapidly expanding West, whereas North (1966) emphasizes the importance of the growing Southern market. But Lindstrom's (1978) study of the composition of demand and interregional trade demonstrates that most of the demand for manufactures came from the East itself. The rapidly growing old maritime cities (Boston, New York, Philadelphia, and Baltimore), the new industrial centers (Pittsburgh, Wilmington, Providence), and the increased use of manufactures by the rural populations of the East were the main consumers of American core products in this period.

Napoleonic Wars. Their semimonopoly over the Atlantic Trade and the incredibly profitable "business" of privateering came to an end. The post-war slump was not followed by a new expansion of the maritime industry until the thirties. Nevertheless, there was considerable United States support for the Latin American independence wars against Spain, especially from the traditionally Catholic city of Baltimore (Bornholdt, 1949).[14] In 1823 President Monroe refused Canning's proposal for a joint British–United States declaration in support of Latin American independence and issued the precociously paternalistic Monroe Doctrine forbidding European interference in Pan-American affairs.

In the 1820s world shipping revived and increased competition caused freight rates to fall. The maritime industry recovered slowly from the post-war slump. Nevertheless, regularly scheduled packet lines leaving at designated intervals connecting New York City with the ports of Europe were established, but profit rates were lower than in manufacturing (North, 1966). This explains the growing integration of the maritime interests with domestic manufacturing, and the increasing support for protectionism. But, at the same time, the forces of opposition were gathering.

The Rise of Opposition to Protection

The peripheralized colonial Southern economy based on tobacco, rice, and indigo seemed to have reached its zenith before the turn of the century. It was predicted by contemporaries such as Jefferson that slavery would wither away; others thought that the South would turn toward maritime and industrial activities. But the invention of the cotton gin and the demand for cotton to feed the mills of the English midlands gave plantation slavery a new lease on life. The cotton gin made cultivation of the short fiber, upland cotton commercially profitable with the application of slave labor.

The growth of the new core–periphery division of labor between the South and England also had effects on the maritime and commercial interests of the North, particularly New York City. New York merchant shippers bought most of the cotton from the planters, at first transporting the cotton to New York for inspection before shipment to Liverpool. Later the New York merchants established factors in the port cities of the South that enabled them to ship directly (Buck, 1925). But they maintained financial control of most of the trade between the South and England. Credit facilities by which American merchants could purchase English goods with drafts on

---

[14] The clue which led me to Bornholdt's (1949) article was a small, seemingly incongruous, bust of Simón Bolívar encountered on a walk up Baltimore's North Charles Street.

London banks were established by specialized merchant-banker firms such as Baring Brothers and George Peabody and Company. Peabody, a Baltimore dry goods merchant, established a firm in London for this purpose and hired another dry goods importer, Junius Spencer Morgan of Boston; through this connection, the Morgan family entered the calling of high finance (Hidy, 1951).

Opposition to protectionism arose in the South after the Panic of 1819. Cotton prices fell from 31¢ a pound in 1818 to 14¢ in 1920; 10¢ in 1826; and 8¢ in 1831. This was due to the world-wide expansion of cotton production. The cotton planters of South Carolina were hit particularly hard by this fall in prices because it corresponded with increasing soil exhaustion on their upcountry plantations. Cotton planters further west and low country rice planters were less severely affected (Freehling, 1968). The antiprotectionist movement in South Carolina began to develop after 1819 — particularly among the cotton planters.

Pincus (1977) points out that, in a democratic polity, a minority with a great deal to win or lose can frequently have its way when the cost to the majority of individuals is small and dispersed. Thus producers often exert more influence over the state than consumers because they stand to gain much more than consumers (individually) stand to lose. This is part of the explanation of the fact that most nations most of the time have protectionist tariffs. It is also consistent with the development of strong opposition to protection among Southern "consumers" in the antebellum United States. These consumers were not simply individuals buying for their own use. Tariffs on coarse woolen and cotton textiles came to be opposed by the Southern planters who were purchasing these commodities to clothe their slaves. It was not that these buyers, and the New York merchants who were their agents, were too small and dispersed to mobilize, rather they were simply unmobilized in 1816.

Both Northern merchants and Southern planters came to fear that their British customers would retaliate against U.S. protection by obtaining their raw materials from other than U.S. producers. Also Southern exporters were made aware that, as international economists have demonstrated, a tariff on imports is not only a tax on consumers of imports but is also effectively a tax on exporters. Dr. Thomas Cooper, a disciple of Adam Smith and President of the College of South Carolina, suggested that the time had come for the South to "calculate the value of the Union." This suggestion that the marriage between the states was somewhat less than a transcendent relationship received a great deal of criticism from the patriots of the North, but Cooper's logic was based on this inflammatory, but not entirely inaccurate, appraisal:

> There is not a petty manufacturer in the Union, from the owner of a spinning factory, to the maker of a hobnail, . . . from the mountains of Vermont to the swamps of Patapsco, who is not pressing forward to the plunder; and who may not be expected to worry Congress with petitions, memorials and querulous statements for permission to put his hands into the planter's pocket. The avowed object now is, by means of a drilled and managed majority in Congress, permanently to force upon us a system, whose effect will be to sacrifice the South to the North, by converting us into colonies and tributaries . . . to tax *us* for their own emolument . . . to claim the right of disposing of our honest earnings . . . to forbid us to buy from our most valuable customers . . . to irritate into retaliation our foreign purchasers, and thus confine our raw material to the home market . . . in short, to impoverish the planter and to stretch the purse of the manufacturer [Bancroft, 1928:32].

Southern memorials to Congress complained bitterly of the unequal effects of the tariff and the failure of the program of internal improvements to benefit the South. Senator George MacDuffie argued that, of every 100 bales of cotton produced in the South, 40 of them were stolen by the North. This was an exageration but Van Deusen's (1928) study shows that the costs to the South were by no means insignificant.

The Tariff of 1828 raised rates and extended protection to a large number of commodities not protected before, including a number that angered New England. Antiprotectionist sentiment was growing and free traders hoped that the election of Andrew Jackson would bring relief. But Jackson did not act to lower the duties. Southern planters organized an unsuccessful boycott of Northern products and leading politicians appeared in public in homespun to dramatize their cause. The most rabid of the South Carolinians were talking of secession when Calhoun devised what he thought to be a compromise that would preserve the Union. Antitariff politicians had argued that tariff protection was unconstitutional. Calhoun (anonymously at first) proposed the doctrine that states have the right to nullify Federal laws that they deem unconstitutional (Bancroft, 1928). Nullification received enthusiastic support in South Carolina, but not in the other Southern states. In 1832 the South Carolina legislature called a convention and adopted nullification unilaterally, but President Jackson stood firm against this challenge to the sovereignty of the Federal state and, after some sabre-rattling, the South Carolinians backed down.

The controversy over the tariff is often portrayed as being based on sectionalism, and indeed the Congressional voting record on the tariff acts from 1820 on shows that it was increasingly the Southern states that opposed protection. I would argue, however, that it was largely a class conflict between core capitalists interested in creating a diversified and integrated national economy and peripheral capitalists specializing in the exchange of raw materials for European core products. These two groups contended throughout the antebellum period for the support of other politically important classes: merchants, farmers, and increasingly, workers. Evidence for this contention can be seen within sections as well as between them.

Boucher (1968) shows that the backcountry, non-slave-owning yeomen of South Carolina did not support the political actions taken by the anti-tariff forces in the state. And Freehling (1968) demonstrates that the merchants of Charleston were much more likely to support the Unionist cause than the planters. Farmers in the North and West alternately supported protection or opposed it as their fortunes in the world market changed. The closing of the European markets for their produce caused them to support protection and the development of the home market. But later growth of grain exports to Europe brought them to the cause of free trade. The middle states, with the biggest concentration of manufacturers producing for the home market, were staunch supporters of protection. Kentucky, a slave state, was strongly protectionist not only because its hemp was in competition with foreign peripheral producers for the shipbuilding market of the maritime states, but because it was a manufacturer of cotton bagging. And as we have seen, the merchants of New England shifted their support to protection when they became interested in investments in domestic manufacturing.

It is interesting to ask what differences there were in the 1820s between the farmers of Pennsylvania and the upcountry cotton planters of South Carolina that caused them to respond in exactly opposite ways to the falling prices of their export commodities. In theory, the planters could have supported Clay's scheme on the basis that an internal demand for cotton would be created by domestic textile production. Similarly the farmers of Pennsylvania could have opposed protection in the hope that the European market would again buy their commodities—not necessarily a worse bet than the growth of the home market demand for food. There are many differences between the planters and the yeomen. The farmers were employing only themselves and their families, while the planters were employing slave labor. Freehling (1967) reports that planters recognized in the 1820s that the abolition movement would eventually pose a threat to their "peculiar institution." The Denmark Vesey conspiracy in Charleston, a planned slave revolt foiled in 1822, was attributed to the antislavery sentiments expressed in Congress during the debate over the Missouri Compromise in 1820 (Genovese, 1976).

Another difference between yeomen and planters, which may account for their divergence on the tariff question, was the nature of British trade regulation. The Corn Law was directed against grain, but not against cotton. Thus the British state, in reflecting its own class coalitions, was exercising political power against the Pennsylvania farmers but not against the cotton planters of the South. This most probably affected opinions about the proper policy of the United States government.

Compromise and the Jacksonian Economy

In 1828 part of Calhoun's strategy against the tariff was to split the alliance between Northern manufacturers and Western farmers. He envisioned a coalition in which Southern and Western agriculture would oppose tariffs and support liberal land policies. Northern manufacturers tended to oppose cheap land policies that drew away their employees, which created a labor shortage and upward pressure on wages. Western Senator Thomas Hart Benton, in response to a Connecticut Senator's proposal to limit the sale of public lands, suggested the similarity between restrictions on land sales and the protective tariff—both were indirect subsidies to manufacturers (Forsythe, 1977). Senator Robert Hayne of South Carolina proposed a combined program of low tariffs and low land prices, but Daniel Webster temporarily forestalled this alliance by transforming the discussion into a debate about states rights. His stirring invocation of patriotism carried the day, but the rise of Jacksonian democracy was not to be halted by a single debate.

The regime crisis (Forsythe, 1977) over nullification caused by the unhappy Southerners resulted in the Compromise Tariff of 1833, the first of Henry Clay's political recipes for balancing the contradictions between core and peripheral capitalism. The bill was supported by the South and the West and opposed by New England and the middle states. It was mostly a face-saving device for the South, however. The principle of protection was abandoned and henceforth tariff advocates had to couch their proposals in terms of "incidental protection." But the bill specified that tariff rates were to be lowered slowly until 1842, when they were to be drastically reduced to an average of 20% ad valorem. The stated object of the slow reduction was to give manufacturers a period of adjustment before opening the ports. But many protectionists expected that the Southern opposition would cool and the proposed reduction in 1842 would never come to pass.

Cotton exports were the largest export commodity from 1815 to 1861, increasing from 32% of all exports in 1815 to 56% in 1835, and then varying from 40% to 57% from 1835 to 1860 (North, 1966). Wheat flour exports to England, which would become one of the most important export commodities after the Civil War, began to grow rapidly in 1829 (Potter, 1960: Table IV). This new interest in the foreign market undoubtedly lessened the enthusiasm of U.S. wheat growers for protectionism. The convergence of interests between the planters of the New South and the farmers of the Ohio Valley was also facilitated by the development of New Orleans as their common entrepot, and by the growing importance of the South as a market for Western produce.

In addition, both farmers and planters were increasingly dissatisfied with the tight money policies of Eastern bankers; the 1830s saw the growth of labor organizations opposed to municipal monopolies and restrictive land sales policies that were associated with Eastern financial and manufacturing interests. The Democratic Party chose Andrew Jackson, an Indian fighter from Tennessee, to symbolize the new coalition of farmers, laborers, and planters.[15] Jackson was not sympathetic to free trade, nor did he yield to nullification, but his election was the beginning of the coalition between the South and the West, which was to increasingly delimit the power of the domestic core capitalists in the Federal state in the 1840s and 1850s.

The Bank War, in which Jackson and the soft money forces refused to recharter the Second United States Bank, was the first attack on the institutionalized power of the indigenous core capitalists. The dissolution of the U.S. Bank and the growth of state banks has been alleged to have caused the rampant inflation of the 1830s. Temin (1969), however, argues that most of the credit expansion and inflation was actually caused by an increase in the supply of silver specie from an influx of investment capital from Britain and a change in the balance of payments in the China trade. The reduced need to pay for Chinese exports in silver (because of increased opium smuggling into China) allowed Mexican silver, previously used in the China trade, to be imported into the United States. This increased bank reserves and allowed the expansion of credit. Temin may be correct that the dismantling of

---

[15] Part of the Jacksonian coalition involved an agreement to expand at the expense of the American Indians. Jackson's fame as an Indian fighter and his toleration of the abrogation of treaties and removal of Indians from the lands of the South was an early example of the dark side of American democracy. An alliance between popular forces and large investors touted as democracy was cemented by a common front against an underclass, in this case indigenous peoples. It is characteristic of upwardly mobile semiperipheral states that the class coalition upon which they are based is relatively progressive in that it includes a larger percentage of the "lower orders" than the class coalitions upon which other contemporary states are based. And, as well, the ideologies used to mobilize development in these countries are usually relatively egalitarian. Citizenship is cemented by treating some groups as noncitizens. In the U.S., it has been blacks, Indians, and recent immigrants. In Britain, it was first the propertyless Englishmen and later the Irish, Scots, and Welsh (Hechter, 1975). In the Soviet Union, it has been certain national minorities and political deviants. Thus the upwardly mobile countries mobilize national development by incorporating rather larger numbers of the population within the political community and the scope of development, and this is an advantage relative to other countries because it solves some of the Keynesian problems of effective demand by creating a large home market. The exclusion of an internal underclass does not function primarily as a mechanism of economic exploitation, but rather to maintain the solidarity of the larger "egalitarian" alliance.

the U.S. bank was *not* the cause of the credit expansion and the influx of specie, but the decentralization of banking did eliminate the only institution that might have been able to modify the effects of international economic forces. As such, it was symptomatic of the decline of the political power of core capitalists and their policies of economic nationalism.

The 1830s saw an incredible economic boom based mainly on the expansion of cotton production in the New South, but also on the growth of the West and the continued growth of manufacturing in the East. The price of cotton rose from 8¢ a pound in 1831 to an average of 14¢ a pound between 1834 and 1837. This, along with Jackson's easy land policy and easy credit, caused land sales to rise dramatically in 1835 and 1836. In Mississippi and Louisiana plantation banks were established to finance the expansion of slave-grown cotton. English capital was invested in the securities of these banks. In the West, extensive state-sponsored canal projects were undertaken by floating bonds in London; in the East, the first railroad expansion was financed by British rail sales in exchange for stock in the newly created railroad firms. Speculation in land and cotton trading was heavy.

In an attempt to slow the land boom and "excessive trading," Jackson declared the Specie Circular, which required that all further public land sales be paid for with specie—gold or silver. Many historians have seen this as the act which brought about the Panic of 1837, but Temin (1969) argues that it was the contraction of credit initiated by the Bank of England that punctured the bubble. The monetary crisis of 1837 had no real affect on production, but the Crisis of 1839 initiated a depression which, according to North (1966), was as severe as great depression of the 1930s.

The increasing interdependence of the economies of the United States and Britain in this period has been documented by Potter (1960, 1976). The new core–periphery division of labor was based primarily on slave-grown cotton exports, but the agricultural produce of the free farmers played an increasing role from 1830 onward. British investment capital flowed into the U.S. in the 1830s but was stung by the crash of 1839 in which thousands of firms failed and nine states defaulted on securities held by English investors. Domestic manufacturing continued to expand but was faced with stiff competition from a growing influx of British imports.

In the 1830s, the cities of the East saw the growth of labor unions, city centrals, and labor parties opposed to municipal monopolies and in support of the 10-hour day and the extension of free public education (P. Foner, 1975). The depression that followed the crisis of 1839 saw the demise of most of these early labor organizations and the rise of Utopian movements and religious sects. Waves of Irish and German immigrants from Europe and the massive movement of population toward the West discouraged stable working class political organization and encouraged both ethnic poli-

Table 9.1

Ratio of British General Imports to the United States[a] to the U.S. Realized National Income in Manufacturing[b]

Year	Ratio	Year	Ratio
1821	.365	1869	.146
1829	.249	1879	.104
1839	.387	1889	.078
1849	.191	1899	.039
1859	.241		

[a] United States Bureau of the Census, 1975 part 2:907.
[b] Martin, 1939, tables 1 and 17.

tics and Utopian escapism, which have been recurring features of American political life.

The maritime and shipbuilding industry of the East experienced a new expansion as a result of the growth of the Atlantic economy and the trade with China and Latin America. Philadelphia, New York, and Boston merchants joined the British in opium smuggling and the tea and porcelain trade with the Chinese treaty ports (Basu, 1979; Goldstein, 1978). American clipper ships set new speed records in an era when time was becoming an increasingly important element in economic calculation.

Even though manufacturing continued to grow, the core capitalists of the United States faced an increasingly difficult battle against British imports. The struggle for the home market was by no means yet won. Table 9.1 shows that the ratio of imports from the United Kingdom to the United States Realized National Income in manufacturing increased dramatically between 1829 and 1839.[16] This was not a result of the Compromise Tariff

[16] In order to study the development of core capitalism in the United States we need to know the extent to which the home market was dominated by British imports. None of the studies that examine the relationship between the United States and Britain in the nineteenth century organize their comparisons in a way which would reveal this. North (1966) and Potter (1960, 1976) stress the importance of the Atlantic economy in explaining U.S. economic development, but they never directly examine the trend in the proportion of the commodities consumed in the U.S. that are imported from Britain. Rather, they show the trend in the value of imports by itself. Potter examines British exports to the U.S. as a percentage of all British exports, but neither combines the British imports with data on U.S. production or income. Table 9.1 does this. It shows the ratio of U.S. Realized National Income in manufacturing to the value of British imports. We do not have data on imports from Britain before 1821, but if it is correct to extrapolate the trend in Table 9.1 backward in time, then the proportion of the home market served by imports from Britain was high until 1839. Then this proportion declined until 1849, experienced a small rise to 1859, and then declined continuously. The years are not exact as data on Realized National Income for intervening years are not available, but we can safely conclude that the peak of British domination of the home market was around 1839 or earlier, and this domination declined from then on, except for a slight recovery during the 1850s. Data on Realized National Income in manufacturing are computed from Martin (1939) and British imports from U.S. Bureau of the Census (1975).

of 1833 since rates were only mildly reduced. Imports were encouraged by favorable terms of trade, as U.S. prices were high and British goods correspondingly cheap. The growth of imports created a negative trade balance but this was offset by the inflow of British investment capital.

The reduced influence of indigenous core capital over the Federal state was not due to its absolute decline. Indeed, manufacturing continued to expand throughout the antebellum period. The loss of power in the state came from the shifting of alliances and the increasing importance of Southern cotton production as the major export commodity. Core capitalists achieved a protectionist Federal policy in the early part of the period—from 1816 to 1833—because of the unmobilized Southern opposition and because the free farmers supported the notion of developing the national market. Also some agricultural and mining raw materials were brought into the protectionist camp through logrolling. The weakening of the protectionist forces in 1833 was due to the desertion of the farmers, who saw a new opening in the world market, and also to the increased mobilization of the Southern planters, rather than to an actual decrease in the power and prosperity of the manufacturers. The Crisis of 1839 brought new demands for protection and the tariff was renewed at a high rate until 1846. But in that decisive year the nation and the world turned toward free trade.

Free Trade

The Compromise Tariff of 1833 prescribed that tariffs should be cut drastically in 1842. The low rates were in effect for only two months before Congress, responding to new clamoring for protection, doubled the rates for textiles, iron goods, and many other products. Since the South opposed the bill, Northern and Western Democratic votes were necessary to enact it as law. As had happened before, the years of depression influenced farmers and workers to support protection, and the bill passed with considerable support from the West. But this was the last protectionist bill to be passed until the enactment of the ultra-protectionist Morrill Tariff in 1861.

By 1846 the economy was recovering and with it the Southern–Western alliance against protection. The peripheral producers of the South achieved their last ascendancy in the Federal state in an alliance with the West cemented in the Democratic Party. In the election of 1844 protection was an issue; Polk had tried to be on both sides of the question. But his appointment of Robert J. Walker from Mississippi as Secretary of the Treasury made his true sentiments plain. The Walker Tariff, which was passed by Congress in 1846, lowered rates drastically and was considered a great victory for free trade. Its support was more along party lines than along sectional ones. It passed the House 114 to 95 with 18 Democrats voting against it: 11 from Pennsylvania; 4 from New York; 2 from New Jersey; and 1 from Maryland. Only 2 Whigs supported the bill. Thus the Western Democrats, and many Northern ones, supported the bill (Stanwood, 1903).

Secretary Walker argued that the bill would be good for farm prices because it would expand the foreign market. He claimed that adoption of the bill would bring reciprocity from England in the repeal of the Corn Law. In fact the Corn Law was repealed prior to the final passage of the Walker Tariff, and Anti-Corn Law League propagandizing in the United States was thought by some to have had an illegitimately large influence on the decision. Protectionists disparaged the bill as a product of foreign intervention in American politics (Eiselin, 1932).

Walker also attacked the argument that protection raises the wages of the working class, and argued, on the contrary, that it increases the power of capital over labor. "When the number of factories is not great, the power of the system to regulate the wages of labor is inconsiderable; but as the profit of capital invested in manufactures is augmented by the protective tariff there is a corresponding increase of power, until the control of such capital over the wages of labor becomes irresistible [quoted in Stanwood, 1903:47]." This argument was apparently successful in obtaining the support of Northern Democrats from labor constituencies.

In 1845 the potato famine in Ireland caused prices of American agricultural commodities to rise due to increased foreign demand. The recovery of the West from the crash of 1839 had been slow but the new demand caused a renewal of expansion and brought the West back into the free trade coalition with the South.

This raises the question of the world class position of the free farmers of the United States. Were they core producers or peripheral producers? As

WORKING MEN!
You Pay a Tax of Tenpence

*Upon every Stone of Flour you and your wives
and little ones consume.*

If there was not the Infamous CORN LAW you and your Families might buy THREE LOAVES for the same money that you now pay for Two.

Upon every Shilling you spend for Bread, Meat, Bacon, Eggs, Vegetables, &c., you pay 4d. Tax for Monopoly.

DOWN, DOWN
WITH THE
Infamous Bread Tax!

Figure 9.1. *Handbill. (From* Free Trade *by Norman McCord, Newton Abbot, Great Britain: David & Charles, 1970, p. 75.)*

producers of raw materials for export they had political interests in common with the planters. But agricultural production is not necessarily peripheral production. Capital-intensive, high-wage wheat grown in the twentieth century U.S. is clearly a core product. Nor is the determination of class location in the world-system simply a matter of the formal nature of production relations. Yeomen in seventeenth century England were core producers relative to the larger world economy, but this was not due entirely to their legal status as middlesize, self-employed capitalist farmers. Yeomen in twentieth century Africa producing cash crops for export are peripheral producers selling the labor of themselves and their families to a world market that is coercive in the sense that the prices at which they sell their products and buy core products are determined by a political structure which exploits them (Lipton, 1977).

So we cannot answer the question about the free farmers of the antebellum period by looking at their formal legal control over property, nor by determining whether they sell primarily to the national or the world market. We must ask about the returns of their labor from the exchanges in which they were engaged. Unfortunately, I have not been able to locate data on the "wages" of the free farmers. It seems likely that their average incomes, including subsistence production in an abundant natural environment, were high compared to the wages of other core workers. At least they were high enough to cause migration from England, Germany, and the Atlantic states.

It is also known that the terms of trade of the free farmers varied over time with the rise or fall of the prices of their products relative to the prices of the goods they bought on the market. If the yeomen were peripheral producers we might expect them to have the same reaction to changes in the terms of trade as the planters had. In fact, as we have seen, reactions were just the opposite. Hard times caused farmers to support protection, while planters were driven to greater efforts in favor of free trade. Thus, even though careful analysis of the relative incomes of the antebellum farmers has not been done, it seems reasonable to conclude that they were core producers.

Was the period of free trade from 1846 to 1861 a period of crisis for core capitalist manufacturers? Clearly, their power over the Federal state was reduced. There is evidence that some were hurt by the tariff reduction. Fogel and Engerman (1971) attribute the slow growth of iron production to the effects of the low tariff. Table 9.1 shows that the conquest of the home market by domestic core producers was temporarily forestalled. The ratio of British imports to Realized National Income in manufacturing increased from 1849 to 1859. This import boom was financed by a new wave of British capital investment—especially in railroads—and also by the export to London of much of the gold produced by the California gold rush. Exports of wheat and cotton to Europe grew, but not nearly enough to cover the new expansion of imports.

Nevertheless, the conclusion that manufacturers were badly hurt by their temporary loss of power in the Federal state would be unjustified. The growth rate of manufacturing industry between 1844 and 1854 was 69%, higher than any other decade in the antebellum period. And manufacturers recovered much more quickly from the slump of the early 1840s than did the agriculturalists of the South or the West (North, 1966).

Many industries in the U.S. no longer needed protection from imports. Cotton textiles were cheaper in New York than in Manchester. The home market had been conquered by 1839, and the temporary setback of the decade from 1849 to 1859 does not contradict the conclusion that core production was so well established by this period as to be able to succeed in the world market without direct protection from the state.

The 1840s and the 1850s saw changes in the world economy that reduced the salience of the protection issue to core capitalists in the United States. Schumpeter (1939) points out that this period saw a long-term upswing in the pace of economic growth throughout the world. There was a reduction in tariff barriers all across Europe as the benefits of trade came to outweigh the injuries done to domestic producers (Fielden, 1969). As the British economy shifted from the production of mass consumption goods toward the production of capital goods (Hobsbawm, 1968), the capitalists of other core states developed their own mass consumption industries by importing British machinery and railroad equipment.

The Crystal Palace Exhibition of 1851 was a great promotional effort to expand the export of British technology, a reversal of the earlier attempt to monopolize production techniques (Landes, 1969). The international division of labor between core producers became less autarchical and protectionist as a result (Krasner, 1976). Cobden and Bright traveled widely, lecturing on the beneficial effects of a world free market. Their arguments were acted upon because the actual gains from free trade to consumers came to outweigh the costs to producers. And the producers, including core capitalists in the United States, had less to lose because the pace of growth was expanding and they wanted to import capital goods from England.

But free trade among core powers does not necessarily mean the relaxation of political coercion over peripheral areas. The 1840s was a decade of U.S. expansionism. Texas was annexed in 1845; a treaty with Britain brought Oregon into the Union in 1846; and, the war with Mexico gained California in 1848. The South was the main supporter of the war with Mexico but the manufacturers' opposition to territorial expansion and cheap land was reduced by the great influx of Irish immigrants willing to work in the urban industries of the East for low wages. One consequence of the territorial expansion was a renewal of the conflict over the status of new states. Though temporarily resolved by the Compromise of 1850, this was the issue which finally divided the forces of core capitalism from those of peripheral capitalism.

The Tariff of 1857 lowered rates even further. The politics of this tariff bill illustrate well the decline in the salience of the tariff issue for many manufacturers. The main debate was between producers of woolen textiles and wool growers. The woolen manufacturers argued that the tariff on raw wool was driving them out of business and advocated a reduction. Except for Pennsylvania iron masters and the wool growers, there was very little protectionist sentiment in 1857.

Hofstadter (1964) used the Tariff of 1857 to attack the Beard and Beard (1964) thesis that the tariff was an important economic issue dividing the North and the South. He points out that this tariff act was called the "manufacturers bill" because the woolen manufacturers succeeded in lowering the duties on raw wool, and that the bill was also supported by the commercial interests of New York. The tariff issue had been an important source of conflict between Northern manufacturers and Southern planters earlier in the century, but Hofstadter was correct that this issue was no longer as volatile by 1857. His case that economic interests were not involved in the coming conflict is hardly supported by the example of the commercial interests of New York, however. These were the same mercantile interests who had previously supported the politics of the Southerners because of their involvement in the core—periphery trade. And these same New York merchants were to threaten secession in 1861 because of their ties to the South (P. Foner, 1946). The Beards were correct that the conflict had an economic and a class basis, but it was not a war primarily between the capitalists of the North and the "precapitalist" South.

Protection Again: The Irrepressible Conflict

The Panic of 1857 came a few months after the passage of the tariff bill. It was similar to the depression of 1839 in that it followed a period of rapid inflation, economic expansion, foreign investment, importation, and Westward movement. But the expansionary phase was based on the growth of manufactures and Western free agriculture rather than slave-grown cotton as the growth of the 1830s had been. And, as before, the fall of grain prices (partly resulting from the end of the Crimean War which allowed Russian wheat back on the world market) and the fall of wages and employment renewed the spirit of protectionism.

The new growth of the labor movement (especially among immigrant

German workers), the opposition to the extension of slavery to the Western states, and the renewed enthusiasm for cheap land led to the birth of the Republican Party. The greatest issue of the new party was "free soil" and the passage of the Homestead Act (E. Foner, 1970). The Republicans attracted Democratic voters with the slogan "vote yourself a farm" and they supported prolabor legislation. Lincoln avowed the principle that labor is the source of all wealth and won the support of immigrant workers by his opposition to an alliance between the Republicans and the Know-Nothings (P. Foner, 1975). The Republicans were antagonistic to the "money power" of the East, but they eventually adopted protectionism in order to appeal to the manufacturers.

The success of the Republicans and the split between the Northern and Southern Democrats broke the alliance between the farmers of the West and the planters of the South, which had allowed the Southerners to control the Federal state through the Democratic party. The crumbling of this alliance provoked the Civil War[17] even though the Republicans never advocated the abolition of slavery but only prevention of its extension to the West. Southern peripheral capitalism was expansionist because of its extensive nature and the quick exhaustion of the soil, but this was not the main reason why the South desired the extension of slavery to the West. The main issue for the South was control over the Federal state. Planters opposed the creation of free states because the alliance with free farmers was tenuous and they felt they would have less and less power in the Federal state. The result would be a direct attack on their "peculiar institution" and their subjugation to the North as an internal colony. Therefore, when the South–West coalition crumbled and Lincoln won the election in 1860, South Carolina did not even wait for him to take office. As Rubinson (1978) has pointed out, the Presidency was everything because there was hardly a Federal bureaucracy in which the South could have institutionalized control. South Carolina seceded immediately, and most of the other slave states followed when it became clear that the North would make war in order to preserve the Union.

The argument that the conflict between the North and the South was due to the economic inefficiency of slavery has been sufficiently demolished. Let me only add that plantation slavery remained highly profitable and the Southerners were well aware that emancipation in the British West Indies in 1834 had increased the cost of sugar production considerably. Slavery was not simply the basis of an aristocratic civilization, it was a profitable business. The plantocracy of King Cotton was probably the most successful pe-

---

[17] Northern sympathizers called it the Civil War. Southerners called it the War for Southern Independence. A neutral name is the War between the States.

ripheral capitalism in the whole history of the world-system because it was less encumbered by precapitalist institutions than the Hispanics, Germanics, Slavs, or even the British, and French colonies had been. This was truly successful capitalist agriculture and its very success led to dreams of slave empire and the challenge to the Northern and Western interests (Genovese, 1965). After all, the slaveholders started the Civil War. The core capitalists, workers, and farmers of the North only grudgingly made war to keep the Union intact.

The contention that capitalism and slavery were incompatible for political or cultural reasons simply does not fit with the historical facts. Barrington Moore's (1966) observation that the legal and political legitimation of slavery contradicted the more opaque form of exploitation that existed in the North is true, but insufficient to explain the violent conflict which developed. Similarly Eugene Genovese's (1969) characterization of the divergence between the political culture of the aristocratic and precapitalist South from that of the fully developed capitalist mode of production based on wage labor in the North does not explain the Civil War. Regardless of cultural differences both the North and the South were capitalist, only the North had become an area of core capitalism employing relatively high wage labor, while the South had remained an area of peripheral capitalism utilizing coerced low "wage" slave labor (Wallerstein, 1979b).

The evidence that supports the foregoing contention is to be seen in the political history which led to the Civil War. Northern manufacturers were not against slavery. In fact, in the face of increasing labor struggles they may have been envious of it. Their biggest conflict with the South had been over the tariff issue, and that was no longer crucial to them by 1860. The main cause of the Civil War was the opposition of the free workers and farmers to the extension of slavery to the West. These core workers and farmers were not abolitionists. The main issue for them was the threat of competition with slave labor for the lands of the West. Their unhappiness with the Compromise of 1850 was seen most vividly in the battle for Kansas and in the fight against Southern opposition to the Homestead Act.

The Lincoln Administration did not contemplate emancipation until well after the war had begun, and then mainly to head off English and French support for the South (Case and Spencer, 1970). Queen Victoria adopted a formally neutralist stance. The cotton famine caused by the blockade of Southern ports resulted in massive unemployment in the English midlands. English support for Southern naval raiders allowed them to sink a large portion of the Northern merchant marine.[18] The Emancipation

[18] This injury and the emerging British superiority in ocean steamships caused the American maritime industry to go into a decline from which it did not recover until the end of the century.

Proclamation generated enough support for the Northern cause in England and France to prevent further aid to the South.

It was not slavery that was the main issue but the question of who would dominate the Federal state. Free farmers and workers found themselves at odds with the interests of the peripheral capitalists of the South on the issue of the frontier, and so cast their lot with core capital. In so doing, they destroyed the plantocracy and created a strong core state. The Civil War and Reconstruction firmly established the hegemony of core capitalism and core labor over the Federal state. The upward mobility of the United States was hereafter assured by the alliance between classes which was only disturbed by quibbling over shares of an expanding pie, rather than by the regime crisis that had characterized the antebellum period.

Conclusion

What can be concluded from this examination of antebellum tariff politics? The world-system perspective led us to expect that class forces contending for state power would be important to the success or failure of core capitalism in the United States. This study confirms that there was a great deal of conflict between core and peripheral producers over the tariff and that the nascent core capitalists needed alliances with other classes in order to overcome the opposition of peripheral capitalists and the influence of extant core states. But the prevalent conclusion among economic historians that the tariff was not crucial to the survival of individual core industries does not support the idea that protection was essential to the upward mobility of the United States in the world-economy. This conclusion is supported by the research of Zevin (1971), Taussig (1964), and David (1970) and is only partly contradicted by Fogel and Engerman's (1971) study of the iron industry. What has not been done is an analysis of the overall sectoral effects of protection. It is possible, as Taussig implies, that protection was not crucial for any single industry but was nevertheless important to the manufacturing sector as a whole. Further research needs to be done before a definite conclusion can be reached.

Nevertheless, the tariff issue is significant as a reflection of contradictory class interests as perceived by the actors. The world-system perspective helps us interpret the changing political alliances of classes and interest groups. As mediators of the core—periphery trade the merchants often sided with the peripheral capitalists, but when the imperial core state (Britain) became unusually hostile, or when manufacturing became more profitable than the maritime trade, they supported the politics of the domestic core capitalists.

The class alliances of the free farmers were a function of their changing position in the larger world-economy. This is not to say, as did Weber, that class location is reduceable to market position. The repeal of the Corn Law changed the world market position of American farmers, but this was not a consequence of the "sphere of circulation." It was a change in the politically structured conditions of agricultural production.

The world-system perspective also reinterprets the class position and alliances of American wage workers, thereby shedding some new light on "American exceptionalism." As Aglietta (1978) has argued, the original reliance of the propertied classes on farmers and mechanics for support against the British in the War of Independence created a political constitution that allowed the extension of citizenship and political rights to men of little or no property. In addition, the conflict between core and peripheral capitalists caused both to try to mobilize the farmers and mechanics behind them. As we have seen, both free traders and protectionists argued that adoption of their tariff policy would raise wages.

In addition, the dynamism of American economic growth was both a cause and consequence of the interaction between capital and labor. The open frontier allowed expansion and—even with massive immigration—kept wages higher than they were in Europe. This encouraged capitalists to utilize labor-saving machinery, and also provided an expanding home market for manufactures and agricultural commodities. Thus the political constitution, the class structure, and the rate of economic growth created the relative harmony between capital and labor which Henry C. Carey elevated to a universal economic truth (Marx, 1858/1973). It also created the tendency for the reproduction of an underclass excluded from the mainstream of economic development.

The end of continental expansion created the contradiction that led to the Civil War. It was not the cultural incompatibility of slave society and wage–labor capitalism, but the diminishing amount of new territory in which to expand that led to the confrontation between core capitalism and peripheral capitalism. And this was less a struggle between core capitalists and peripheral capitalists (as the earlier controversy over the tariff had been) than a fight between peripheral capital and core labor and farmers. The victory redounded to the favor of the manufacturers, but it was not primarily their interests which led to the conflict.

It may be argued that the world-system perspective would lead us to expect that the Civil War was caused by the conflict between core capitalists and peripheral capitalists over the foreign policy of the Federal state, and indeed this was my expectation when I began this study. The foregoing conclusion focusing on conflict between core labor and peripheral capital over the "internal" policies of the state is not inconsistent with a sophisticated version of the world-system perspective, however. The examination of class conflict as it occurs in the context of the world-economy seeks to eliminate the internal–external distinction, which has confused much previous analysis. The confrontation was caused by "internal" scarcities only because the policy of annexation had come upon natural and political limits. And the alliance between core capital and core labor, which is one of the most interesting hypotheses of the world-system perspective, can be seen in formation in the Civil War. This class coalition made possible the creation of a strong core state that could rise to hegemony in the world-economy.

This study also reveals that tariff politics are not always an ideal indicator of struggle between core and peripheral producers. This is because the salience of international boundaries and state regulation of trade varies with changing conditions in the larger world-economy. State boundaries and other institutions that are used to intervene politically in the market are more crucial during periods of economic contraction than in periods of expansion. Class conflicts are generally less severe in expansionary periods and so tariffs do not accurately reflect contradictory class interests in these periods.

A more complete understanding of the rise of core capitalism in the United States requires the investigation of the world class basis of other types of state intervention in the economy. Federal land policy, Indian removal, immigration policy, regulation and deregulation of currency and credit, the extension of suffrage, internal improvements, and the expansion of public education are all important issues that reveal the nature of class contradictions and harmonies. Further research should combine an analysis of these with our knowledge of tariff politics in order to provide a fuller explanation of the rise of core capitalism in the antebellum period.

Acknowledgments

I would like to thank William P. Quinn for his help on this chapter.

References

Aglietta, Michel
   1978   "Phases of U.S. capitalist expansion." New Left Review 110:17–28.
Amin, Samir
   1976   Unequal Development. New York: Monthly Review Press.
Aptheker, Herbert
   1960   The American Revolution. New York: International Publishers.
Bancroft, Frederic
   1928   Calhoun and the South Carolina Nullification Movement. Baltimore: Johns Hopkins University Press.

Basu, Dilip
    1979   "The peripheralization of China: Notes on the opium connection." In Walter L.
            Goldfrank (ed.), *The World-System of Capitalism, Past and Present*. Beverly Hills,
            Calif.: Sage.
Bauer, Raymond A., Ithiel de Sola Pool, and Lewis A. Dexter
    1968   *American Business and Public Policy: The Politics of Foreign Trade*. New York:
            Atherton Press.
Bateman, Fred, and Thomas Weiss
    1976   "Manufactures in the antebellum South," in Paul Uselding (ed.), *Research in Eco-
            nomic History*, Vol. 1. Greenwich, Conn.: Jai Press.
Beard, Charles, and Mary Beard
    1964   "The tariff as a cause of sectional strife and the Civil War." In Gerald D. Nash (ed.),
            Issues in American Economic History. Boston: D. C. Heath. [Originally published
            in 1927.]
Bornholdt, Laura
    1949   "Baltimore and Early Pan-Americanism." *Smith College Studies in History*, 34.
            Northampton, Mass.
Boucher, Chauncey S.
    1968   *The Nullification Controversy in South Carolina*. New York: Russell and Russell.
            [Originally published in 1916.]
Brenner, Robert
    1977   "The origins of capitalist development: A critique of neo-Smithian Marxism." *New
            Left Review* 104:25–92.
Broude, Henry W.
    1964   "The role of the state in American economic development, 1820–1890." In Harry
            N. Sheiber (ed.), *United States Economic History*. New York: Knopf.
Buck, Norman S.
    1969   *The Development of the Organization of Anglo–American Trade*. Hamden, Conn.:
            Archon Books. [Originally published in 1925.]
Burgin, Miron
    1946   *Economic Aspects of Argentine Federalism*. Cambridge: Harvard University
            Press.
Case, Lynn M., and Warren F. Spencer
    1970   *The United States and France: Civil War Diplomacy*. Philadelphia: University of
            Pennsylvania Press.
Chase-Dunn, Christopher, and Richard Rubinson
    1977   "Toward a structural perspective on the world-system." *Politics and Society* 7:453
            –476.
Clark, Victor S.
    1916   History of Manufactures in the United States 1607–1860. Washington, D.C.: Car-
            negie Institute of Washington.
Cole, Arthur H. Ed.
    1928   *Industrial and Commercial Correspondence of Alexander Hamilton Anticipating
            His Report on Manufactures*. Chicago: A. W. Shaw.
Crenson, Matthew A.
    1975   *The Federal Machine: Beginnings of Bureaucracy in Jacksonian America*. Balti-
            more: Johns Hopkins University Press.
David, Paul A.
    1975   "Learning by doing and tariff protection: A reconsideration of the case of the ante-
            bellum United States cotton textile industry." In *Technical Choice, Innovation and*

    Economic Growth. London: Cambridge University Press.

Eiselen, Malcolm R.
  1932   *The Rise of Pennsylvania Protectionism.* Philadelphia: University of Pennsylvania Press.

Emmanuel, Arghiri
  1972   *Unequal Exchange: A Study of the Imperialism of Free Trade.* New York: Monthly Review Press.

Field, James A.
  1969   *America and the Mediteranean World 1776–1882.* Princeton: Princeton University Press.

Fielden, Kenneth
  1969   "The rise and fall of free trade." In C. J. Bartlett (ed.), *Britain Preeminent.* London: Macmillan.

Fogel, Robert W., and Stanley L. Engerman
  1971   "A model for the explanation of industrial expansion during the 19th century: With an application to the American iron industry." In R. W. Fogel and S. L. Engerman (eds.), *The Reinterpretation of American Economic History.* New York: Harper and Row.

Foner, Eric
  1970   *Free Soil, Free Labor, Free Men: The Ideology of the Republican Party Before the Civil War.* New York: Oxford University Press.

Foner, Philip
  1946   *Business and Slavery: The New York Merchants and Irrepressible Conflict.* Chapel Hill: University of North Carolina Press.
  1975   *History of Labor Movement in the United States,* Vol. 1. New York: International Publishers. [Originally published in 1947.]

Forsythe, Dall W.
  1977   *Taxation and Political Change in the Young Nation. 1781–1833.* New York: Columbia University Press.

Frank, André Gunder
  1967   *Capitalism and Underdevelopment in Latin America.* New York: Monthly Review Press.
  1978   *World Accumulation, 1492–1789.* New York: Monthly Review Press.
  1979   "On the roots of development and underdevelopment in the New World: Smith and Marx vs. the Weberians." In *Dependent Accumulation and Underdevelopment,* Chapter 3, New York: Monthly Review Press.

Freehling, William W.
  1968   *Prelude to the Civil War: The Nullification Controversy in South Carolina, 1816–1836.* New York: Harper and Row.
  1967   *The Nullification Era: A Documentary Record.* New York: Harper and Row.

Genovese, Eugene D.
  1965   *The Political Economy of Slavery.* New York: Random House.
  1969   *The World the Slaveholders Made.* New York: Random House.
  1976   *Roll, Jordan, Roll.* New York: Vintage.

Gold, David A., Clarence Y. H. Lo, and Erik O. Wright
  1975   "Recent developments in Marxist theories of the capitalist state." *Monthly Review* 27(5):29–43.

Goldstein, Jonathan
  1978   *Philadelphia and the China Trade 1682–1846.* University Park, Pennsylvania: Pennsylvania State University Press.

Goodrich, Carter
 1960 *Government Promotion of American Canals and Railroads 1800–1890*. New York: Columbia University Press.
Greene, Jack P.
 1976 "Society, ideology and politics: An analysis of the political culture of mid-18th century Virginia." In Jack P. Greene, R. L. Bushman, and Michael Kammen, *Society, Freedom and Conscience*. New York: Norton.
Hale, Charles A.
 1968 *Mexican Liberalism in the Age of Mora, 1821–1853*. New Haven: Yale University Press.
Hechter, Michael
 1975 *Internal Colonialism: The Celtic Fringe in British National Development 1536–1966*. Berkeley: University of California Press.
Hidy, Muriel
 1951 "The capital markets" in Harold F. Williamson (ed.), *The Growth of the American Economy*. Englewood Cliffs, N.J.: Prentice-Hall.
Hobsbawm, E. J.
 1968 *Industry and Empire*. Baltimore: Penguin.
Hofstadter, Richard
 1964 "The tariff issue on the eve of the civil war" in Gerald D. Nash (ed.), *Issues in American Economic History*. Boston: D. C. Heath.
Kim, Sung Bok
 1978 *Landlord and Tenant in Colonial New York: Manorial Society, 1664–1775*. Chapel Hill: University of North Carolina Press.
Krasner, Stephen D.
 1976 "State power and the structure of international trade" *World Politics* 28,3:317–347.
Landes, David
 1969 *The Unbound Prometheus*. Cambridge: Cambridge University Press.
Lindstrom, Diane
 1978 *Economic Development in The Philadelphia Region 1810–1850*. New York: Columbia University Press.
Lipton, Michael
 1977 *Why Poor People Stay Poor*. Cambridge: Harvard University Press. .
Lower, Arthur R. M.
 1973 *Great Britain's Woodyard: British America and the Timber Trade 1763–1867*. Montreal and London: McGill-Queen's University Press.
Lynd, Staughton
 1964 "Who should rule at home?: Dutchess County, N.Y. in the American revolution." In Harry N. Scheiber (ed.), *United States Economic History*. New York: Knopf.
Martin, Robert F.
 1939 *National Income in the United States 1799–1938*. New York: National Industrial Conference Board.
Marx, Karl
 1968 *Theories of Surplus Value*, Part 2. Moscow: Progress Publishers. [Originally published in 1863.]
 1973 "Bastiat and Carey." In *Grundrisse*. New York: Vintage. [Originally published in 1858.]
 1974 "Articles on the North American Civil War." In *Surveys From Exile*. New York: Vintage. [Originally published in 1861.]

Mintz, Sydney
  1969   "Labor and sugar in Puerto Rico and in Jamaica, 1800–1850." In Laura D. Foner, and Eugene D. Genovese (eds.), *Slavery in the New World.* Englewood Cliffs, N.J. Prentice-Hall.
Moore, Barrington
  1966   *Social Origins of Democracy and Dictatorship.* Boston: Beacon Press.
Moulder, Frances
  1977   *Japan, China and the Modern World Economy.* Cambridge: Cambridge University Press.
North, Douglass C.
  1966   *The Economic Growth of the United States 1790–1860.* New York: Norton.
Pincus, Jonathan J.
  1977   *Pressure Groups and Politics in Antebellum Tariffs.* New York: Columbia University Press.
Potter, James
  1960   "Atlantic economy, 1815–60: The U.S.A. and the industrial revolution in Britain." In L. S. Pressnel (ed.), *Studies in the Industrial Revolution. London:* Athlone Press.
  1976   "The Atlantic economy in the mid-19th century." *Atti del I Congresso Internazionale di Storia American,* May 29. Genoa.
Poulantzas, Nicos
  1975   *Classes in Contemporary Capitalism.* London: New Left Books.
Rubinson, Richard B.
  1978   "Political transformation in Germany and the United States." In Barbara H. Kaplan (ed.), *Social Change in the Capitalist World Economy.* Beverly Hills, Calif.: Sage.
Schumpeter, Joseph
  1939   *Business Cycles,* Vol. 1. New York: McGraw-Hill.
Shepherd, James F., and G. M. Walton
  1972   *Shipping, Maritime Trade and Economic Development of Colonial North America.* Cambridge: Cambridge University Press.
Stanwood, Edward
  1903   *American Tariff Controversies of the Nineteenth Century,* Vol. 2. Boston: Houghton-Mifflin.
Stein, Stanley J., and Barbara H. Stein
  1970   *The Colonial Heritage of Latin America.* New York: Oxford University Press.
Taussig, F. W.
  1964   *The Tariff History of the United States.* New York: Capricorn.
Taylor, George R.
  1953   *The Great Tariff Debate 1820–1830.* Boston: D.C. Heath.
Temin, Peter
  1969   *The Jacksonian Economy.* New York: Norton.
Thompson, Tommy R.
  1978   "Personal indebtedness and the American Revolution in Maryland." *Maryland Historical Magazine* 73:13–29.
United States Bureau of the Census
  1975   *U.S. Historical Statistics from Colonial Times to the Present, Part 2.* Washington, D.C.: U.S. Government Printing Office.
Van Deusen, John G.
  1928   *The Economic Basis of Disunion in South Carolina.* Columbia University Studies in History, Economics and Public Law, no. 305.

Vidal, Gore
    1973   *Burr*. New York: Random House.
Wallerstein, Immanuel
    1978   "World-system analysis: Theoretical and interpretive issues." In Barbara H. Kaplan
           (ed.), *Social Change in the Capitalist World Economy*. Beverly Hills: Sage.
    1979a "Class conflict in the world-economy." Pp. 283–294 in *The Capitalist World-Economy*. Cambridge: Cambridge University Press.
    1979b "American slavery and the capitalist world-economy." Pp. 202–221 in *The Capitalist World-Economy*. Cambridge: Cambridge University Press.
    1980   "Semi-peripheries at the crossroads." In the *Modern World-System: Mercantilism and the Consolidation of the European World-Economy, 1600–1750*. Vol. 2. New York: Academic Press.
Wood, Harold D.
    1977   "Imperialism and economic development: England, the U.S. and India in the 19th century." In P. Uselding (ed.), *Research in Economic History*. Vol. 2. Greenwich, Conn.: JAI Press.
Zevin, Robert B.
    1971   "The growth of cotton textile production after 1815." In Robert W. Fogel, and Stanley L. Engerman (eds.), *The Reinterpretation of American Economic History*. New York: Harper and Row.

Albert Bergesen
Ronald Schoenberg

Chapter **10**

Long Waves of Colonial Expansion and Contraction, 1415–1969

At the heart of the world-system idea lies the assumption that there are structures and collective dynamics at a level of analysis higher than that of discrete national societies. There is a world-*system* with a life of its own, which in turn has important consequences for the national societies embedded within it. Most of our efforts, though, have gone into identifying the effects of this world-system upon the development or underdevelopment of national societies, rather than specifying the distinctive collective dynamics of the system itself. In this chapter, one set of world-system dynamics, the long waves of colonial expansion and contraction will be examined.

Central to any understanding of the modern world-system is colonialism. It has existed from the inception of the system in the sixteenth century until the 1960s, and it has encompassed at one time or another much of the world's territory. By 1800 some 35% of the world was, or had been, under European control; by 1878 the figure was up to 67% and by 1914 it reached 84% (Fieldhouse, 1973:3). But most important, colonialism is a structural feature of the system itself, a linkage between core and periphery, and as such, a property of the system as a whole.

We have examined the significance of colonialism from the point of view of the core, spurring its development and reproducing its position in the overall world economy. We have also viewed colonialism from the point of view of the periphery, creating dependent development and similarly reproducing its dependent position in the world economy. We have, though,

231

STUDIES OF THE
MODERN WORLD-SYSTEM

rarely looked at colonialism from the point of view of both core and periphery at once. As a structural linkage between core and periphery, colonialism can be seen as a property of the world-system as a whole; as such it can be studied in its own right, independent of its effects upon either of the economic zones—core and periphery—that it links. This is not to argue that colonialism does not affect either core or periphery, but only that it can be studied on its own, and that this study allows an understanding of some of the distinctive collective dynamics of the world-system.

Measuring Colonial Activity

Measuring colonialism in some constant metric from its inception in the sixteenth century through the 1960s is difficult. What do we measure? The land mass under colonial control, or possibly the number of people under colonial rule? These things are hard to accurately determine. The extent of control obviously varies from colony to colony, and within colony from region to region. Similarly population estimates would be difficult to acquire, and besides it is not entirely clear that colonies should be weighted any more by population than by, say, wealth or military importance. There is, in short, no clear cut way to measure colonialism.

In this chapter, the presence of a colonial governor will be used as a measure of colonialism because it provides a constant unit of measure over some 500 years, and because of the availability of an exhaustive study of the dates of colonial rule by Henige (1970). He provides the dates of colonial administrations of 412 colonies from the establishment of a colony at Ceuta in 1415 through 1969 when his study was completed.[1] As the 1960s was a decade during which most of the colonization of the previous century disappeared,[2] Henige's study virtually encompasses the whole history of colo-

---

[1] Twenty-two of the colonial governors Henige lists were functions of colonial reorganization, the *intendencia* system initiated by Spain in the 1780s to eliminate corruption and raise revenues. The reorganization took place within the existing viceroyalties of Neuva España, Peru, and Río de la Plata. Since these administrative reorganizations were not indicative of new colonial expansion they were not counted. This left us 390 colonies divided accordingly: Britain (172), France (65), Spain (59), Portugal (38), Netherlands (23), United States (8), Germany (7), Italy (5), Japan (5), Denmark (3), Belgium (2), Sweden (2), Russia (1).

[2] Even though most of the decolonization of Africa and Asia that began after 1945 was completed by 1969, there still remain some 58 colonial governors in 1969. These include colonies that will later become independent, like Angola and the Seychelles Islands; French colonies that voted to remain with the French community as overseas territories, like the Comoro Islands, French Polynesia (Tahiti, etc.), St. Pierre and Miquelon, or the Wallis and Futuna Islands; British Crown colonies, like Bermuda, Bahama and Hong Kong, along with other British colonies and protectorates; American possessions such as Guam, American Samoa, the Micronesian Trust Territory, and the Virgin Islands; and some possessions that were settled relatively recently, such as the French Southern and Antarctic lands settled in 1950 for scientific purposes.

nialism. Henige listed the years during which colonial governors held office; this will provide our indicator of the duration of each colony's existence.[3] This list of colonial administrators does not take into account questions of informal colonialism, neo-imperialism, and so forth; we will be dealing only with territories that are formally administered by a core state. From his list of dates during which governors held office, we recorded (a) the total number of colonies established each year between 1415 and 1969 (the year in which the colony's first governor began his term); (b) the total number of colonies terminated each year (the last year in which a governor served in office); and (c) the cumulative net number of colonies in existence for each year (years during which governors held office). As we are interested in relations between core and periphery as a whole, we did not examine the rates of colonial activity for specific core states. We are examining only the aggregate amount of colonial activity. This raw data is presented in the Appendix.

Rates of Establishing and Terminating Colonies

The first colony was established by the Portuguese at Ceuta in 1415, and from then until the end of the century only five more colonies were established (in 1480, 1482, 1485, and two more in 1496). After 1500 the rate of colonization increased dramatically. This can be seen in Figure 10.1, which presents an 11 year moving average of the number of colonies established from 1415 through 1969. The largest spurt of colonization came toward the end of the nineteenth century, but there were also outbursts of activity during the seventeenth century, the second half of the eighteenth and the middle of the nineteenth century.

The establishment of colonies seems a more stationary process than the termination of colonies. As Figure 10.2 shows, terminations come in two very distinct and well-pronounced spurts: the first quarter of the nineteenth century, centering on the collapse of the Spanish empire in Latin America, and the post-1945 decolonization of Africa, India, and Asia. The first wave of decolonization peaked in 1821 with the termination of 30 colonies, and the second wave had 2 peaks, with 17 terminations in 1947 and 23 in 1960.

---

[3] In recording the dates of colonial rule, we used the earliest and latest administrative officer he listed, whether this was a commandant, chief commissioner, high commissioner, chief political resident, chief magistrate, lieutenant governor, or governor. The purpose here was to determine when control was first established, regardless of the precise title employed.

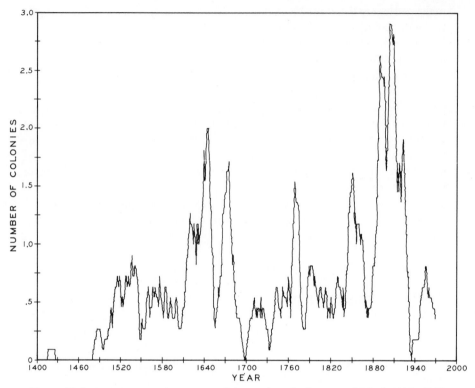

Figure 10.1. *An 11-year moving average of the number of colonies established, 1415–1969.*

Long Waves of Colonial Expansion and Contraction

The cumulative net number of colonies is presented in Figure 10.3, which clearly shows the first and second wave of colonialism. The smoothness of these waves is not a function of smoothing by moving averages; these are the raw numbers. We can view these waves of colonial activity as cycles, as they represent the repetition of explicit political domination of peripheral areas by the core.

INCREASING AMPLITUDE AND FREQUENCY OF GLOBAL CYCLES

By looking at the movement of colonialism over the long duration, we can identify certain minimal collective properties of the system itself. Although there are only two cycles, their amplitude and frequency is increasing. The first cycle began in 1415 and reached its peak in 1770 at 147 colo-

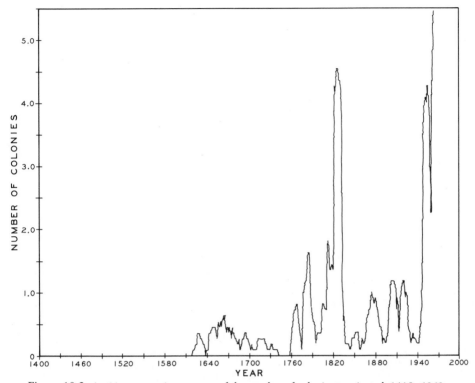

Figure 10.2. *An 11-year moving average of the number of colonies terminated, 1415–1969.*

nies. The decline begins shortly thereafter with the American and Latin American revolutions, and reaches a low point of 81 colonies in 1825. The second cycle begins in 1826 and reaches its peak in 1921 with 168 colonies. It then declines to 58 colonies in 1969. Nineteen sixty nine is not a real trough in the sense of being an absolute low point before the next upswing. This is only the place where our particular data set ends. By 1969, though, most of the decolonialization of Africa and Asia was completed, and few major colonies remained.

The frequency of these cycles is also increasing. The first cycle lasted 410 years (1415–1825), while the second only lasted 143 years (1826–1969). During the upswing of the first cycle, from its beginning in 1415 to the peak in 1770, 188 colonies were established at a rate of .530 colonies per year. During the upswing of the second cycle, from the trough of 1826 to the peak of 1921, 138 colonies were established at a rate of 1.452 per year, a little less than three times as fast as during the upswing of the first cycle. Also, during the upswing of the first cycle, 41 colonies were termi-

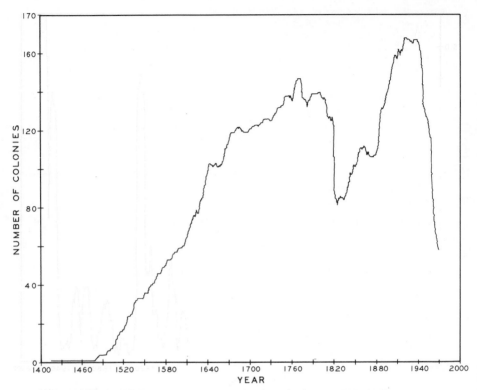

Figure 10.3. *The cumulative net number of colonies, 1415–1969.*

nated at a rate of .115 per year, while during the upswing of the second cycle, 53 colonies were terminated at a rate of .558 per year. The net difference between the number of colonies established and terminated was twice as great during the upswing of the second cycle, when .894 colonies per year were being established compared with only .415 per year during the upswing of the first cycle.

The downswing was also quicker during the second cycle. During the downswing of the first cycle, from 1775 to the trough of 1825, 95 colonies were terminated at a rate of 1.900 each year. This rate increased during the downswing of the second cycle, from the peak year 1926 through 1969, when 127 colonies were terminated at a rate of 2.953 per year. There were also colonies being added during these downswings. During the first downswing 28 colonies were added at a rate of .560 per year, and 17 were added during the second downswing at a rate of .395 per year. The net change though was an overall loss of colonies. During the first downswing there

Table 10.1

The Number of Colonies Established and Terminated per Year and the Net Change during the Upswing and Downswing of the First and Second Waves of Colonialism

Yearly average	First Wave, 1415–1825		Second Wave, 1826–1969	
	Upswing 1415–1770[a]	Downswing 1775–1825	Upswing 1826–1921[b]	Downswing 1926–1969
Colonies established	.530	.560	1.452	.395
	(N = 188)	(N = 28)	(N = 138)	(N = 17)
Colonies terminated	.115	1.900	.558	2.953
	(N = 41)	(N = 95)	(N = 53)	(N = 127)
Net change	+.415	−1.340	+.894	−2.558

Source: Appendix.
[a] The peak lasted from 1770 through 1774.
[b] The peak lasted from 1921 through 1925.

was a net loss of 1.340 colonies per year, and an even greater loss of 2.558 colonies per year during the second downswing. (See Table 10.1.)

While it is not exactly clear at this point what fundamental processes increasing amplitude and frequency reflect, we can say that they are properties of the world-system itself. It is not just the core, or periphery, let alone any particular national society that has this cyclic rhythm, but the system as a whole. Also, these movements could not have been identified without viewing the totality of the system—the aggregation of all colonial links— over virtually the entire length of its existence (1415–1969). There is a collective reality to the world-system that is only apparent when the whole system is examined. The methodological lesson here is that by viewing either smaller pieces of the system or shorter lengths of time, one misses these distinctly systemic dynamics.

The Theoretical Model

As we are only dealing with two waves of colonialism, the idea of cycles may be premature. Let us suppose, though, that we have uncovered a repetitive process at the world level. If this is so, exactly what is it that is repeating itself and why? We begin with two constraints. First we want a model that is as applicable to the world-system of the early sixteenth century as it is to the second half of the twentieth century—for colonialism spans over five centuries of world history. Second, we want a model that views colonialism from the point of view of the world-system as a whole, reflecting our earlier concern of dealing with the system sui generis.

The key to understanding changes in core–periphery relations lies with certain repetitive changes within the core itself. We can conceive of a pure model of the core's structure in terms of a continuum. At one end, the core would be composed of a number of perfectly equal states; at the other end the core would be composed of a single dominant state. Here core and state would be one. Where there is a hegemonic state, such as mid-nineteenth-century Britain and the United States of 1945–1973, the core as a whole takes on more of a corporate existence. It appears as a single interest and entity, which becomes represented in the policies and structures of the dominant state.

Since there is no core-wide state apparatus to formulate and act upon the class interests of the core as a whole, the expanded influence, or hegemony, of a dominant state provides the mechanisms through which the collective interests of the core can be realized. The decomposition of the core into a plurality of rivalrous powers occurs with the decline of the dominant state and the rise of serious competitors. In this situation, the ability of one state to singularly represent and enforce the class interests of the core as a whole declines. The various other core states are now less penetrated by the interests of the dominant state, and accordingly come to represent more of their own discrete interests, rather than those of the hegemonic power. This situation, in which each state pursues its own interests rather than the common interest, appears inherently more unstable.

Over the long history of the world-system the core has moved back and forth along this unicentric–multicentric continuum, and most importantly this repetitive movement coincides with the repetitive expansion and contraction of colonialism. During those periods when power is dispersed over a number of core states (a multicentric core) colonialism expands, and during periods when one hegemonic state dominates (a unicentric core) colonialism contracts. If you view the world-system as a whole, over the long duration of its existence, the correlation of these two movements becomes visible. From the sixteenth through the early nineteenth century, the core can be characterized as multicentric and unstable as seen in the incessant warfare among the Absolutist States (Anderson, 1974). During this period we see the first wave of colonial expansion led by Spain and Portugal and centered in the Americas. Then, during the mid-nineteenth century the structure of the core changes. Britain emerges as the dominant hegemonic power creating a unicentric-stable core. The endless conflicts of the earlier centuries cease, and there is a period of peace among the major core powers, a Pax Britannica. With this stability in the core, colonialism contracts with the decolonization of the Americas.

Toward the end of the century Britain's hegemony declines, Germany and the United States emerge as powerful core states, and the core again becomes more multicentric and unstable. As the structure of the core changes so does the nature of core–periphery relations. During the last quarter of the nineteenth century, we have the second wave of colonialism centered this time in Africa, India, and Asia. These colonial empires remain largely intact until after 1945, when the structure of the core once again shifts form a plurality of competitive states to one dominant hegemonic state, the United States. With this shift in the core there is another wave of decolonization and colonialism once again contracts. This then is the general movement of the world-system: core instability and expanded colonialism; core stability and contracting colonialism.

Is there a causal connection between transformations in the core and the changing substance of core–periphery relations? The answer we think is yes. To speak of a world-system is to speak of something more than just a system of interrelated, but self-contained and separable, components. There is a collective reality and distinctly organic quality to the world-system, such that when internal difficulties arise—like instability and conflict within the core—the system pulls itself together and reaffirms its fundamental social relationships. Colonialism, then, is an extra-economic mechanism for resetting the basic core–periphery division of labor in times of disorder and stress. When there is stability within the core the more explicit political regulation of core–periphery relations collapses, as seen in the waves of decolonization. The integration of the system now resides with the more distinctly economic linkages of the world-economy and less with the more political linkages of colonialism. When trouble appears, colonialism reappears, as a means of more explicitly—and forcefully—realigning and resetting the hierarchial structure of the world-system.

So far we have spoken very generally about instability and systemic response. There are two additional sources of support for this level of abstraction. First, the idea that it is the whole system which is regenerating itself suggests that the response to core difficulties should not be limited to only one kind of core–periphery linkage. The political regulation of core–periphery relations should appear in other kinds of linkages, like trade relations. The realignment of core and periphery is manifested in all the ways the system binds itself together, which obviously must also include economic transactions. When there is instability in the core there is also a more explicit political regulation of trade relations between core and periphery.

Periods of mercantilism, rising tariffs, import restrictions, and protectionism in general, correspond to the very same periods of core instability and expanding colonialism. The mercantile regulation of colonial trade persisted through the first phase of core instability and colonial expansion (roughly 1500–1815); then, with the rise of British hegemony and the subsequent core stability, there appeared both the decolonization of the

Americas and the rise of Free Trade policies from the 1820s through the 1870s. With the decline of British hegemony and the second wave of colonialism, there was also a dramatic rise in tariffs and protectionism which ended the free trade policies of mid-century. These economic restrictions lasted until shortly after 1945 when we again have a new hegemonic power, America, peace in the core, decolonization, and a decline in tariffs and a rise in free trade epitomized by the General Agreement on Tariffs and Trade (GATT) negotiated in 1947. Colonialism and trade regulation rise and fall together (Figure 10.4) and most importantly correlate with core instability.

The second source of support for the generality of this model can be seen in the fact that core and periphery are once again becoming more explicitly politically linked, even though colonialism has largely disappeared. The model is general; it is not tied to particular historical forms. If the general conditions are met—a multipolar–unstable core—then we expect in-

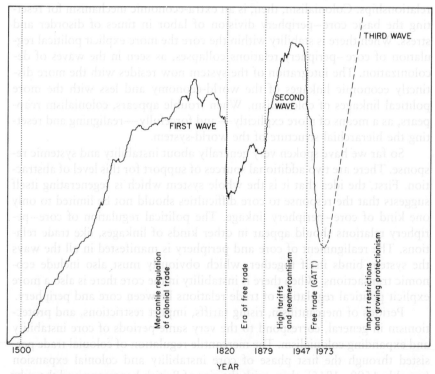

Figure 10.4. *Mercantile and free trade periods compared with the expansion and contraction of colonialism.*

Table 10.2
A *Summary of the Effects of Changes in the Structure and Stability of the Core upon Changes in Core–Periphery Relations*

Years	Core structure	Core–periphery relations
1500–1815	Multicentric–unstable A plurality of competing states resulting in commercial rivalries, dynastic struggles and balance of power conflicts within the European state system.	More explicit political regulation *Colonialism.* The first colonial expansion led by Spain and Portugal centered in the Americas. *Trade.* Mercantile regulation of Colonial trade.
1815–1870	Unicentric–stable One hegemonic power, Britain, and an absence of major conflict among the core powers. A Pax Britannica.[a]	Less explicit political regulation *Colonialism.* Decolonization of Latin America *Trade.* The decline of mercantilism and the rise of free trade.
1870–1945	Multicentric–unstable A plurality of competing states, created by the decline of British hegemony and the rise of Germany, the United States and Japan, and resulting in rivalry, conflict, and eventually two world wars.	More explicit political regulation *Colonialism.* The second colonial expansion this time led by Britain and France and centered in Africa, India and Asia (the Age of Imperialism). *Trade.* The decline of free trade and the rise of tariffs, protectionism and neo-mercantilism in general.
1945–1973	Unicentric–stable One hegemonic core state, the United States, and an absence of major conflicts among core powers. A Pax Americana.	Less explcit political regulation *Colonialism.* Decolonization of Africa, India, and Asia. *Trade.* Lowered tariffs (GATT) and increasing free trade.
1973–	Multicentric–unstable A growing plurality of competitive states created by the decline of American hegemony and the growth of the EEC, Japan, and the Soviet Union.	More explicit political regulation *Newer forms of Core Domination.* Arms dependence creating client states which undermines the nonaligned status of peripheral states. *Trade.* Import restrictions and increasing protectionism.

[a] There was one major conflict between core powers, the Crimean War of 1854–1856.

creased political regulation of core–periphery relations; with the decline of American hegemony in the 1970s, this is exactly what we are observing.

> The multipolarity emerging from the Sino–Soviet split, as well as the increased power of Europe and Japan, may contribute to a mutual balance of power strategy similar to that known in the period preceding World War I . . . the balance of power, however, is inherently unstable and has not guaranteed peace in the past; and there is no reason to believe it will necessarily do so in the future [Frank, 1977:136].

We are, in effect, beginning a third wave or cycle. The general conditions of core multicentricity are being met—Europe and Japan are challenging the United States economically, and the Soviet Union is challenging militarily. And, as before, core–periphery relations are once again becoming politically regulated. Import restrictions and protectionism began to rise in the 1970s and the nonaligned status of the Third World is declining as peripheral states fall under the sway of one or another major core power. The process of political domination can be handled in a number of ways. Arms dependence and client states provide the means for extending core control that was previously managed by colonialism.

In sum then, we have suggested a model of some of the long term repetitive dynamics of the world-system as a whole. The pure form of the model relates changes in the distribution of power within the core to changes in the substance of core–periphery relations. When power is distributed over a number of core states, this condition is referred to as multicentricity: The core is unstable; the system as a whole responds by reordering and resetting its fundamental structural relationships. The hierarchial core–periphery division of labor is reestablished through extra-economic mechanisms, like colonialism and mercantile trade policies. When the instability passes, the extra-economic means of integration retreat, and free trade emerges. This does not mean that domination and dependency cease. Neocolonialism and the imperialism of free trade function to reproduce the basic core–periphery division of labor and unequal development on a world scale. What is different is that extra-economic mechanisms, like colonialism, are less prevalent. This model is of necessity abstract and general, for it encompasses large scale long term historical movements. The pure model is itself determinate. Actual historical time and space, though, only more or less approximate this model (see Table 10.2). We will now turn to a closer look at these historical approximations.

1500–1815: Core Instability and Politically Regulated Core–Periphery Relations

Core Instability: Dynastic Struggles and Balance of Power Conflicts

This first period centers on the emergence of both core and periphery and as such the basic framework of the modern world-system (Wallerstein, 1974). The historical origin of the core was feudal Europe, which when considered as a whole, was in the process of undergoing a dual transformation of disintegration at the top—the collapse of a homogenous Latin Christendom and the rise of various religious persuasions after the Reformation and Counter Reformation—and a consolidation of political authority from below—the growth of centralized monarchies in the form of the Absolutist State which replaced the parcelized sovereignty of feudalism (Anderson, 1974). This dual transformation began the modern European state system by constituting ultimate political authority at a middle level—above the localism of feudal ties, yet below the universality of the Church and Latin culture. The differentiation of state structures out of the parcelized sovereignty of feudalism began with the budding centralized states of the "new monarchs" in late fifteenth-century Spain, France, and England. For most of the history of the modern world-system the core is composed of the European state system, to which in later centuries other strong states will join, such as the United States and Japan.[4]

The plurality of states representing the emerging European state system constituted a molecular structure that was inherently unstable, as no one state was in a position to exercise *enough* hegemony to give the system any long term stability. Even when some states were stronger than others the emerging principle of the "balance of power" provided opposing coalitions and ever shifting alliances of weaker states, which kept any one power from exercising long term dominance.

The inherent instability of a core composed of a plurality of competitive states is reflected in their almost endless conflicts and warfare. Modern conflict within the European state system began with the Hapsburg (Spain) and Valois (France) struggles over the control of Renaissance Italy during the Italian Wars (1495–1504). From then until the end of the Napoleonic Wars in 1815, the major core powers are involved in almost constant conflict. There were the wars of Spanish expansion under Charles V and Phillip II (1521–1604) and the wars of religion between Reformation and Counter Reformation states beginning in 1520 and culminating in the Thirty Years War (1618–1648). There were the Anglo–Dutch commercial rivalries culminating in their wars of the 1650s and 1660s, and there were the balance of power wars against the expansionist policies of Louis XIV, from 1672 to the Treaty of Utrecht in 1713. During the middle of the eighteenth century the Seven Years War (1756–1763) was followed by the American Revolution, which became a general European war (1775–1783) when France,

---

[4] This is a broad conception of the core, and some lesser core states would be considered more semiperipheral or peripheral (like Poland) in other schemes. By definition those states holding colonies—Britain, France, Portugal, Netherlands, Germany, United States, Italy, Japan, Denmark, Belgium, Sweden, and Russia—are part of the core, since they are, to a greater (Britain, Spain, Portugal, France) or lesser (Sweden, Italy, Denmark, etc.) degree part of the mechanisms of core domination over peripheral areas. Where a lesser core power ends and a major semiperipheral power begins is both a vexing empirical problem and a reflection of the coarse nature of our early attempts at specifying hierarchial structures on a world scale.

Spain, and the Netherlands along with the American colonies opposed Britain. Finally, there were the French Revolutionary Wars (1792–1802) that preceded the Napoleonic Wars of 1805–1815. The emergence of Britain after 1815 as the hegemonic core power brings stability to the core and an end to some 300 years of intermittent dynastic struggles, balance of power conflicts, and commercial rivalries.

This relationship between core instability, as reflected in major wars, and the expansion of colonialism can be seen in Figure 10.5, where we have plotted Wright's (1942) list of major European Wars since the inception of the modern state system (Table 10.3), and the cumulative net number of colonies from Figure 10.4. During the first wave of colonial expansion there is almost constant warfare. When the warfare ceases after 1815 there is a rapid decline in colonial activity. The Crimean War of 1854–1856 represents the only major conflict during the nineteenth century, and as you can

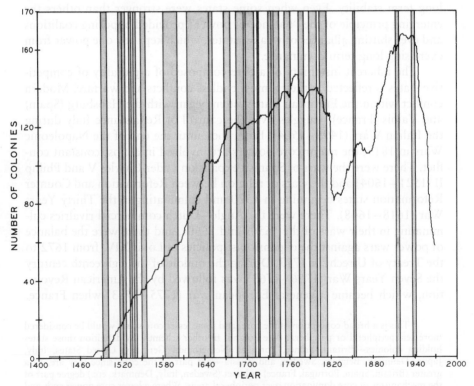

Figure 10.5. *The years of major European wars and the cumulative net number of colonies (war years taken from Table 9.2 and colonies from Figure 9.3).*

see in Figure 10.5 it is also associated with a short rise in colonial activity. While the second wave of colonialism took off during the 1870s there was no major war among the core powers until 1914. In this situation core instability did not manifest itself in warfare. This was, though, a period in which British hegemony was on the decline and the core was becoming increasingly unstable, with growing rivalry and friction among the major powers that would eventually result in World War. Then, with peace among the major powers after 1945 there is once again—like after 1815—a decline in colonialism.

Tightening Political Linkages: The First Wave of Colonialism

Although there were colonial holdings in the Philippines and along the coasts of Africa, India, and Asia, the first colonial expansion was located largely in the Americas. Spain nominally held what is today New Mexico, Arizona, California, Texas, Florida, Mexico (Neuva España), and all of South America except Brazil and the small French and Dutch settlements in Guiana. Portugal established bases in Brazil, Angola, Mozambique, Goa, Malacca, and Macao. By 1700, though, her holdings were mostly in the Atlantic, having lost much of her possessions in the East to the Dutch and English. Other Europeans also had holdings: The French had possessions in the Caribbean, like Martinique, Guadeloupe, and Grenada, and in North America from the Great Lakes and St. Lawrence down the Mississippi to Louisiana. British possessions in the Americas centered on the original 13 North American colonies, British Canada, Jamaica, Barbados and smaller holdings in the Caribbean. Russia, Sweden, Denmark, and the Netherlands also had colonial holdings during the first expansion (Fieldhouse, 1966).

Politically Regulated Economic Relations: The Mercantile Control of Colonial Trade

During this first period economic relations between core and periphery were also highly structured and explicitly regulated. The mercantile regulation of trade began in the sixteenth century with the Spanish and Portuguese empires, and by the latter seventeenth century these policies were more or less common to all core states holding colonies. As Fieldhouse (1968:9) notes, some regulations were common to all core states, such as: (a) the exclusion of foreign ships from colonial ports; (b) routing colonial imports and exports through the ports of the core country; and (c) limitations on manufacturing certain products in the colonies. Others, he points

Table 10.3

Dates and participants for major European wars since the inception
of the modern state system, 1495–1979

Major European Wars[a]	Years	Participants
1. Italian Wars	1495–1501	France, Spain, Florence, Milan, Naples, Papacy
2. First War against Charles V	1521–1526	France, Spain, Holy Roman Empire
3. Second War against Charles V	1526–1529	France, Spain, Holy Roman Empire, Naples, Papacy
4. Third War against Charles V	1536–1538	France, Netherlands, Spain, Holy Roman Empire, Papacy, Turkey
5. Fourth War against Charles V	1542–1544	France, Spain, Holy Roman Empire
6. Fifth War against Charles V	1552–1529	England, France, Spain, Holy Roman Empire, Saxony
7. War of the Armada	1585–1604	England, Spain
8. The Thirty Years War	1618–1648	Austria, France, Spain, Sweden, Netherlands, Denmark, the German States
9. Continuation of the Thrity Years War between Spain and France	1648–1659	Spain, France, England, Lorraine, Savoy
10. The War of the First Coalition against Louis XIV	1672–1679	France, Austria, Spain, Netherlands, Sweden, Denmark, Prussia
11. The War of the Second Coalition against Louis XIV	1688–1697	France, Austria, Spain, Netherlands, England, Savoy, Prussia
12. The War of the Spanish Succession	1701–1714	France, Austria, Spain, Netherlands, England, Prussia, Sardinia
13. The War of the Quadruple Alliance against Spain	1718–1720	France, Austria, England, Netherlands, Spain, Sardinia
14. The War of the Polish Succession	1733–1738	France, Austria, Spain, Prussia, Russia, Sardinia
15. The War of the Austrian Succession	1740–1748	Austria, France, England, Netherlands, Russia, Prussia, Spain, Sardinia
16. The Seven Years War	1756–1763	France, England, Prussia, Austria, Portugal, Sardinia, Russia, Sweden
17. The American Revolution[b]	1775–1783	England, France, Spain, Netherlands
18. The French Revolutionary Wars	1792–1802	France, Austria, England, Spain, Prussia, Netherlands, Sardinia, Naples, Portugal, Sweden, Turkey
19. The Napoleonic Wars	1805–1815	France, Austria, England, Netherlands, Sweden, Russia, Prussia, Spain, Portugal, Sardinia
20. The Crimean War	1854–1856	Turkey, France, England, Sardinia, Russia
21. World War I	1914–1919	Germany, Austria, Bulgaria, Turkey, Russia, France, Britain, Italy, Serbia, Belgium, Rumania, Greece, Portugal, Czechoslovakia, Poland[c]

Table 10.3 *(continued)*

Major European Wars[a]	Years	Participants
22. World War II	1939–1945	Germany, France, Britain, Poland, Denmark, Norway, Belgium, Luxembourg, Netherlands, Italy, Greece, Hungary, Rumania, Bulgaria, Czechoslovakia, Austria, Albania, Finland, Yugoslavia[c]

Source: From Q. Wright, *A Study of War,* Vol. 1 (1942): Tables 31, 32, 43.

[a] Wright (1942) defines a major war as having a minimum of 50,000 troops, lasting at least 2 years, and having at least one major power on each side.

[b] The American Revolution became a great-power war after France, the Netherlands, and Spain entered.

[c] Only the European participants in these two wars are listed.

out, were common only to Spain and Portugal, such as: (*d*) limiting the American trade to an annual convoy; and (*e*) allowing colonial imports to only enter one designated port. Finally, only Spain had the additional regulation of (*f*) banning intercolonial trade.

As Fieldhouse noted there are differences between core states in their degree of politically regulated colonial trade, and these are roughly correlated with the size and wealth of a core state's colonial holdings. Spain, with the largest and wealthiest empire, had all six of Fieldhouse's regulations. Portugal, which was probably next to Spain in the size and wealth of her empire (particularly during the earlier centuries), had only five, while France, Britain, and the Netherlands, whose holdings were substantially less than either Spain or Portugal, had only three regulations. If we consider these mercantile trade relations as a broad band of linkages tying core and periphery together, it appears that the center or "core" of the band, the links carrying the most weight—Spain—are the most heavily regulated. As we move outward from the center—Portugal—the ties become looser and weaker, until we reach the margins of the colonial linkage system—Britain, France, and the Netherlands—where the links are the weakest of all. This suggests a *horizontal* aspect to the strength of core–periphery ties. The links not only vary in strength *vertically,* the overtime expanding and contracting waves of colonialism, but also *horizontally* across this band of core–periphery relations, with the center of the linkage-system the most politically regulated and the margins the least.

This long period of a tightly linked world-system ends during the early nineteenth century. The core stabilizes with the emergence of British hegemony, the Americas are decolonized, and the mercantile regulation of trade gives way in the 1820s to the Era of Free Trade.

1815–1870: Core Stability and Less Politically Regulated Relations

Core Stability: British Hegemony and Pax Britannica

The incessant warfare from the emergence of the European state system in the late fifteenth century through the defeat of Napoleon in 1815 was followed by period of peace among the major core powers. Structurally, the core moved from being composed of a multiplicity of rival states to being dominated by one hegemonic power, Britain; as such, it became a much more stable molecular complex. British hegemony is most apparent up through the 1870s when the combined factors of her own increasingly sluggish growth and the dramatic expansion of German and American productivity once again began to transform the core into a plurality of competitive powers. There was, though, one short conflict involving core powers during this period, the Crimean War of 1854–1856. During this conflict the leading core powers did not oppose each other, but rather resisted the expansion of a more marginal core state, Russia.[5]

Contracting Political Linkages: The Decolonization of the Americas

The heart of the first colonial expansion, the Spanish and Portuguese empires in America, virtually disappeared between 1814 and 1824. After centuries of colonial expansion, the system contracted. This is not to say that all colonial activity ceased, or that all colonies became independent. But the first colonial wave was centered in the Americas and these empires did collapse. In this sense we can say the explicit political domination of the periphery temporarily receded, or from the point of view of the system as a whole, we can say the world-system relaxed or loosened its explicit political linkages.

The independence of the 13 British North American colonies occurs earlier in 1776, somewhat before the cessation of core conflicts in 1815. If we look at the British victory in the Seven Years War (1756–1763) as mark-

---

[5] The conflict began in 1853 when the Russians, who perennially had eyes on the Ottoman Empire, militarily occupied Wallachia and Moldavia. The Turks resisted and war broke out. The French and British joined the war in 1854 to prevent Russian expansion, and the Austrians took advantage of the situation to occupy Wallachia and Moldavia which the Russians soon evacuated. Czar Alexander II sued for peace in 1856 and the war ended.

ing the beginning of British hegemony (Frank, 1978), then the later French Revolutionary (1792–1802) and the Napoleonic Wars (1805–1815) can be seen as more of a by-product of the collapse of the Old Regime and the resultant ripples that sent through the core. In effect, if the Peace of Paris of 1763 marks the beginning of the early stages of British hegemony, and the later wars have more to do with France's internal collapse rather than general core instability, then we can see the independence of the 13 British colonies as the beginning of the general colonial contraction that will culminate with the collapse of Spanish and Portuguese empires during the first quarter of the nineteenth century.

Also if, as argued earlier, the British colonial links were more marginal to the colonial effort as a whole, and accordingly more loosely structured, then what we may be seeing in 1776 is the unraveling of the edges of the overall colonial linkage system. The system begins to collapse at the margins first, where it is the weakest and most loosely organized. Then, after the cessation of general core conflict in 1815, the heart of the system, the great bulk of the first colonial wave—Spanish and Portuguese Latin America—collapse. If we see the colonial ties as a rope holding core and periphery together, then in 1776 the outside edges began to unravel, and by 1824 the whole thing came apart. Regardless of how one interprets 1776, the great bulk of core–periphery linkages were in Latin America, and they did not begin to snap until there was peace and stability in the core.

Deregulated Trade Relations: The Decline of Mercantilism and the Rise of Free Trade

During the years after 1815 mercantile regulations of colonial trade largely disappeared and the era of Free Trade began (Kindleberger, 1975; Krasner, 1976). With the decolonization of the Americas, the periphery is now composed of both colonies—those still in existence and those yet to be established—and new states, which while independent, still occupy a dependent and peripheral position in the world-economy. The deregulation of trade, then, affected both independent, but peripheral states, and colonies.

The period from the 1820s to 1879 was basically one of decreasing tariff levels in Europe. The trend began in Great Britain in the 1820s, with reductions of duties and other barriers to trade. In 1846 the abolition of the Corn Laws ended agricultural protectionism. France reduced duties on some intermediate goods in the 1830s, and on coal, iron, and steel in 1852. The *Zollverein* established fairly low tariffs in 1834. Belgium, Portugal, Spain, Piedmont, Norway, Switzerland, and Sweden lowered imposts in the 1850s. The golden age of free trade began in 1860, when Britain and France signed the Cobden–

Chevalier Treaty, which virtually eliminated trade barriers. This was followed by a Series
of bilateral trade agreements between virtually all European states [Krasner, 1976:324–
325].

The mercantile regulation of colonial trade also disappeared in the early
nineteenth century.

British colonies were virtually open to the world by 1830 and by 1860 the last vestiges of
shipping controls and preferences on colonial products had gone. Other colonial powers
slowly followed suit. The Dutch threw open their colonial trade after 1815. . . . France
preserved the colonial shipping monopoly together with preferences and certain exclusive
regulations until the 1860s but had abolished them by 1870. Spain and Portugal never
completely removed mercantile controls but largely liberalized them for their few dependencies. By 1870 the era of mercantilism seemed over, in that no imperial power then
obtained economic advantages from its dependencies that were not available to the world
[Fieldhouse, 1968:10].[6]

In sum, during the first three quarters of the nineteenth century there
was peace in the core (except for the short Crimean War) and a deregulation
of core–periphery political and economic relations. The Spanish and Portuguese empires in the Americas collapsed, tariff levels dropped, and the mercantile regulation of the remaining colonial trade largely disappeared. During the last quarter of the century, though, the core again became
increasingly unstable, and once again the political regulation of core–periphery relations increased.

1870–1945: Core Instability and More
Politically Regulated Core–Periphery
Relations

Core Instability: New Powers, British Decline,
International Rivalry and World War

Although there were no major wars during the last quarter of the nineteenth century, the core as a whole became increasingly unstable. The transition from a core dominated by Britain to a world of many competitive
states probably begins somewhere around mid-century. By the 1870s the
shape of the core was becoming clear: Britain was no longer the preeminent
power she was at mid-century, as she was being challenged by the rapidly
growing industrial strength of Germany and the United States.

---

[6] This and subsequent quotes cited to Fieldhouse (1968) are reprinted with permission
from "Colonialism: Economic Aspects," by D. K. Fieldhouse, *International Encyclopedia of
the Social Sciences*, vol. 3, pp. 6–12. Copyright © 1968 by Macmillan Publishing Co., Inc.

This decomposition of the core into a multiplicity of competitive states occurred in a number of identifiable stages. The process began with the dramatic appearance of a number of new states during the relatively short period between 1859 and 1871. In 1865, following the Civil War, the United States emerged with a strengthened national government and proceeded to rapidly industrialize. In 1867 Italy was unified under Sardinian leadership, and the Germans of Austria–Bohemia merged with the Magyars of Hungary to form the Dual Monarchy of Austria–Hungary. Also in 1867, the British North America Act established the Dominion of Canada, and the last shogun abdicated, the Meiji restoration began, and a now politically centralized Japan began to industrialize on her way to becoming a major core power. Finally, in 1871, Germany was unified under Bismark with the formation of the German Empire.

The sheer appearance of so many new states was enough to place strains on the overall integration and stability of the core. The presence of new states, though, was only the beginning, for two of them, Germany and the United States, were to experience dramatic industrial expansion, which coupled with the increasing sluggishness of the British economy, transformed the core into an unstable molecular complex of multiple competitive powers. Britain fell behind in both new and old areas of industrial production. For example, in the newly emerging chemical industry Britain represented only 11% of world output in 1913 compared with 34% for the United States and 24% for Germany.

In the new electrical industry Britain's output in 1913 was little more than a third of Germany's (Hobsbawm, 1968:151). In the older areas of production Britain also lagged. In 1880 Germany produced only half as much steel as Britain, but by 1913 she produced more than twice as much. Similarly the United States went from producing about as much steel as Britain in 1880 to four times as much by 1913 (see Table 10.4). Whether this

Table 10.4

Volume of Steel Production as a Percentage of British Steel Production

	Years				
	1880	1890	1900	1910	1913
Germany	53.5	58.7	129.8	202.4	226.1
United States	96.9	119.6	208.0	409.6	408.6
World	324.0	343.0	568.0	931.4	981.1

Source: Adapted from "The Relative Decline of the Steel Industry, 1880–1913" by Peter Temin, in H. Rosovsky (ed.), *Industrialization in Two Systems:* Essays in Honor of Alexander Gerschenkron. New York: John Wiley & Sons, Inc., 1966, p. 143. Copyright © 1966 by John Wiley & Sons, Inc. Reprinted by permission.

change in relative industrial strength was more a function of the rapid growth of Germany and the United States or the decline of Britain remains an open question (Kindleberger, 1978). From the point of view of the core as a whole, though, the result was the same: There was a shift from a core dominated by one hegemonic state at mid-century to a core of many competitive powers by the end of the century.

With the stability of the core declining owing to the appearance and dramatic growth of new core powers, coupled with the increasing sluggishness of the past hegemonic power, the next development was an outpouring of alliances as individual states attempted to generate through treaties the peace and stability that the overall structure of the core could no longer provide. This web of alliances began with Bismark's German Empire, which as a new core power engaged in numerous alliances to protect itself, isolate enemies, and stabilize its position in the European state system. In 1879, Germany established a military alliance with Austria–Hungary, to which Italy was admitted in 1882. In 1887 Germany also signed a "reinsurance" treaty with Russia.

At this point the absence of the structural stability previously provided by British hegemony meant that the emergence of a unified Germany in alliance with Austria–Hungary and a unified Italy created a power imbalance to which other core states responded with countervailing alliance systems of their own. This initially took the form of the Franco–Russian alliance of 1894, which meant that by the mid-1890s the European core powers were now divided into two major camps. All that remained was the incorporation of Britain into this network of alliances. This occurred when Britain abandoned her diplomatic isolation and entered a military treaty with Japan in 1902. The decisive break with isolation came with the *entente cordiale* with France in 1904. Now all that was left was an alliance with Russia, and that came in 1907 with the Anglo–Russian Convention. The major European core powers were now grouped into two opposing camps, the Triple Alliance and the Triple Entente.

These alliances did not halt the core's increasing volatility. The core continued to decompose. The instability now reached a point where there was open friction and international crises that would bring Europe to the brink of war, and finally to overt conflict among the major powers. There were rivalries and disputes over territory such as the French and German designs on Morocco that erupted in the First (1906) and Second (1911) Moroccan Crises. There were also wars over territory, like the First Balkan War of 1912 when Serbia, Bulgaria, Greece, and Montenegro invaded the Ottoman Empire, and Turkey lost all her European possessions except the region around the straits, and then a Second Balkan War in 1913 when the victors of the first war fought over the Ottoman spoils. The resolution of this incident once again brought the core very near to general conflict among its major powers. The final stage of decomposition was the move from friction and crises to general war, starting in 1914 and ending in 1945.

In sum, the molecular structure of the core went from being composed of one dominant power in the early and middle nineteenth century to a collection of competitive states. This structural configuration was inherently unstable, and rivalry and competition led to friction, crises, and finally the overt conflict of the "Second Thirty Years War" of 1914–1945. This instability in the core generated a systemic response: the reassertion of explicit political domination of the periphery, which took the form of a second wave of colonialism, and increased political regulation of core–periphery trade.

Retightened Political Linkages: The Second Wave of Colonialism

Even though colonialism contracted with the decolonization of the Americas, this does not mean that colonial activity totally ceased. There was continuous colonial activity after 1815 (Gallagher and Robinson, 1953). The British were expanding their claims in India, the French were entering Algeria, the Dutch were developing Java, and the core powers were beginning to penetrate China. After 1870, though, the rate of colonial expansion dramatically increased, allowing us to speak of a second wave of colonialism beginning at this time. Where the first wave centered on the Americas, the second centered on Africa, India, Asia, and the Pacific. Colonial expansion was most dramatic in Africa, where the core powers began to penetrate inland from a few coastal outposts in the 1870s and by 1895 had literally partitioned the whole continent among themselves. The colonial empires established during the latter decades of the nineteenth century lasted until stability was restored to the core in 1945, at which point they also dissolved much like the first wave collapsed after 1815. This second wave of colonial expansion can be clearly seen in Figure 10.4.

Politically Regulated Economic Linkages: Rising Tariffs and Neo-Mercantile Protectionism

The Era of Free Trade gave way during the last quarter of the century to ever-rising tariffs and increased protectionism, as economic exchanges between core and periphery were again becoming more formal and explicitly regulated. Throughout the core tariffs began to rise in the 1870s.

The movement toward greater liberality [in trade policies] was reversed in the late 1870s. Austria–Hungary increased duties in 1876 and 1878, and Italy also in 1878; but the main breach came in Germany in 1879. France increased tariffs modestly in 1881, sharply in 1892, and raised them still further in 1910. . . . Although Britain did not herself impose duties, she began establishing a system of preferential markets in her overseas Empire in 1898. The United States was basically protectionist throughout the nineteenth century. . . . During the 1920s, tariff levels increased further. . . . Dramatic closure in terms of tariff levels began with the passage of the Smoot–Hawley Tariff Act in the United States in 1930. Britain raised tariffs in 1931 and definitively abandoned free trade at the Ottawa Conference of 1932, which introduced extensive imperial preferences. Germany and Japan established trading blocks within their own spheres of influence. All other major countries followed protectionist policies [Krasner, 1976:325–326].

The conscious regulation of trade also affected economic transactions between core states and their colonies.

The period of colonial free trade was very short-lived. The revival of protectionism in most parts of Europe in the last quarter of the century led naturally to its extension to the new tropical empires. France adopted a strongly protectionist domestic tariff in 1892 and extended it to all her colonies. . . . The United States incorporated most new dependencies in the Caribbean and Pacific within the metropolitan tariff . . . Portugal, Spain, and Italy either assimilated their colonies to the metropolis or imposed preferences . . . Britain . . . did not drop free trade until 1932, though the self-governing colonies indulged in protectionism and, after 1899, gave Britain unlimited preferences. During the last phase of European colonialism, therefore, most colonial powers adopted some form of preferential system . . . [Fieldhouse, 1968:10].

1945–1973: Core Stability and Less Politically Regulated Core–Periphery Relations

Core Stability: American Hegemony and Pax Americana

We have come full cycle. The core is again dominated by a hegemonic power, the United States, and there is peace among the major powers. Structurally the core now resembles the post-1815 configuration, with a Pax Americana replacing the earlier Pax Britannica. As the Americas were earlier decolonized now it is Africa, India, and Asia, and as free trade replaced mercantilism, a liberal free trading world-economy replaces the high tariffs, restrictions, and protectionism that skyrocketed during the years between the two world wars. Although there was tension generated by the emergence of the Soviet Union as the principal rival to American hegemony—the so-called "Cold War"—America's industrial and military capacity were overwhelming, and major conflicts among the core powers did not errupt. This is not to say there was not anxiety and tension during these years—there was—but the major core powers remained at peace.

Contracting Political Linkages: The Decolonization of India, Asia, and Africa

With stability in the core there was once again a movement toward decolonization, as the colonial empires constructed at the end of the nineteenth century dissolved in the relatively short period between 1947 and 1962. During these 15 years the British, French, Dutch, and Belgian colonial empires virtually disappeared. The British were out of India by 1947, and the Dutch recognized Indonesia as an independent republic in 1949. The French were defeated in Indochina in 1954 and Algeria voted for independence in 1962. Finally, during the 1950s and early 1960s most of Africa south of the Sahara became independent. Although some colonies remained, by the end of the 1960s most of the earlier colonial holdings had disappeared.

Deregulated Trade Relations: Lowered Tariffs, Free Trade, and GATT

The more formal regulation of trade came to an end shortly after 1945 with the General Agreement on Tariffs and Trade (GATT) negotiated in Geneva in 1947. This agreement reduced tariffs and prevented protectionism by making the most favored nation clause in trade agreements applicable to all member nations. A tariff reduction given to one nation must be given to all. Of the multiple rounds of tariff reductions, the initial one in Geneva and the Kennedy Round begun in 1964 were the most important. During that round quotas were largely abolished, tariffs reduced by about 35%, and the necessity of using national currencies to purchase goods was largely eliminated (Clough and Rapp, 1975:512).

Are We Beginning a Third Cycle?

By the mid-1970s though, conditions within the core, and relations between core and periphery, were again changing. We appear to be entering yet another global cycle. Some things are repeated once again—the decline of the hegemonic power and the rise of competitive states and the re-emergence for yet a third time of more politically regulated trade. Some things are also clearly different—most notably the disappearance of formal colonialism as we have known it over the past 500 years. This absence of colonialism combined with the increasing regulation of trade suggests some fundamental changes in these cycles that have implications for understanding some of the more long term trends in the development of the world-system. First, we will consider the mounting evidence that we are entering a third cycle.

Post-1973: Increasing Core Instability and More Politically Regulated Core—Periphery Relations

Increasing Core Instability: The Decline of American Hegemony

> Looking back, the pivotal year in the American decline was perhaps 1973, a year that began with the United States military withdrawal from Vietnam and the final collapse of the American-dominated monetary system of fixed foreign exchange rates. It closed with the quadrupling of oil prices by the Middle East-led oil cartel. American political and economic hegemony had been successfully challenged [Crittenden, 1979:1].

It is impossible to assign an exact date at which American hegemony reached its zenith, or began its decline. This is the same sort of problem we had with Britain a century ago. The year 1973, therefore, is not to be taken literally. The rise and fall of hegemonic states is a continuous process, and the relative decline of America became noticeable during the 1970s. The core is experiencing transformations similar to those that occurred after 1870: The dominant power began to face serious rivals, and her hegemony began to fade.

> The revival or rise of other capitalist economies, notably those in the EEC and Japan, puts the U.S. today in a similar relationship to them as Britain was from the end of the nineteenth century in relation to Germany and the USA. It is no longer true to think of the USA as the overwhelmingly dominant, or even the technologically dominant, country. . . . [T]he point is that we are once again in a situation of *international oligopoly*, whereas in the early nineteen-fifties the U.S. was overwhelmingly dominant in its wealth and productive capacity. International rivalry and tensions, therefore, revived as American hegemony declined. . . . The decline of the USA has once again led to a much more explosive or potentially explosive international situation, from which once again major international conflicts may spring. . . . In this sense, once again, a period of economic difficulties and a period of political and international tensions combine and coincide [Hobsbawm, 1976:93,95].

ECONOMIC DECLINE

The transformation of the core from one dominant state to a plurality of competing states appears to involve the same general set of factors that

Table 10.5
Steel Production as a Percentage of United States Steel Production

	Years				
	1950	1955	1960	1965	1970
France	9.9	11.9	19.2	16.4	19.9
West Germany	15.9	23.2	37.8	30.8	37.7
Italy	2.6	5.1	9.1	10.6	14.5
Japan	5.5	8.9	24.5	34.5	78.2
United Kingdom	18.9	18.9	27.4	23.0	23.7
USSR	30.5	42.7	72.5	76.3	97.2
USA–World	54.5	39.4	26.1	26.0	20.1

Source: United Nations, *U.N. Statistical Yearbook,* various years, as reported in Szymanski, *Social Policy,* Vol. 4, 1974. Reprinted with permission of the publishers, Social Policy Corporation, New York, New York 10036. Copyright 1974 by Social Policy Corporation.

characterized the core a hundred years earlier: The economy of the old power grows increasingly sluggish and the industrial capacity of other core states rapidly expands. Consider American productivity. From 1960 to 1970 labor productivity in the United States grew only 35%, while that of Japan grew 188%, and West Germany 74%. Even the supposedly laggard United Kingdom grew by 40% during this period (Brooks, 1972:113). Steel production provided a good indicator of Britain's changing position in the late nineteenth century and it also reflects the declining industrial dominance of the United States, as America went from producing a little over half of the world's steel in 1950 to only 20% in 1970 (Table 10.5). The rise in steel production of other core states has been dramatic—reminiscent again

Table 10.6
Exports as a Percentage of United States Exports

	Years					
	1948	1953	1959	1965	1969	1972
France	16.8	25.7	32.4	37.0	39.7	53.8
West Germany	6.2	30.3	57.1	65.8	77.6	95.1
Italy	8.6	9.6	16.7	26.5	31.3	37.8
Japan	2.1	8.1	19.8	31.1	42.7	58.4
United Kingdom	50.2	45.7	54.9	48.7	45.1	49.6
EEC (Original 6)	53.2	93.7	146	176	202	254
Centrally planned economies	29.5	50.4	81.3	79.8	79.3	—

Source: Yearbook of International Trade Statistics, various years; and International Monetary Fund, *International Financial Statistics,* April 1973, as reported in Szymanski, *Social Policy,* Vol. 4, 1974. Reprinted with permission of the publishers, Social Policy Corporation, New York, New York 10036. Copyright 1974 by Social Policy Corporation.

of the challenge of German and American steel production to Britain earlier. Japan, for instance, went from producing only 6% of the American output in 1950 to almost 80% in 1970; the Soviet Union went from producing a third of the American total to equaling her output in 1970.

Along with steel, shifting patterns of world trade also reflect the decline of American supremacy. West Germany went from exporting 6% as much as the United States in 1948 to equaling her total by 1972, and Japan went from 2% to 58% of the American total during the same years. More generally, the EEC went from doing about half as much exporting as the United States in 1948 to more than twice as much by 1972 (Table 10.6). In short, other core states have made dramatic gains on the United States: The 1950 combined Gross Domestic Product of France, West Germany, Italy, Japan, and Britain went from less than 40% of American GDP to some 86% by 1972 (Table 10.7).

MILITARY DECLINE

Along with industrial dominance, America also enjoyed military supremacy, and this too began to wane as the Soviet Union approached, or attained, military parity by the late 1970s. During the years immediately after 1945 the United States possessed a clear nuclear monopoly, and through the 1950s and mid-1960s a clear advantage in both the quality and quantity of strategic nuclear weapons. By the late 1970s that quantitative gap had been removed and the qualitative edge was being rapidly narrowed.

Although nuclear weapons are the most apparent aspect of the Soviet–American arms race, the expansion of the Soviet navy and her increasing arms sales to the third world (peripheral states) have been equally dramatic.

Table 10.7
Gross Domestic Products as a Percent of United States GNP

	Years					
	1950	1955	1960	1965	1969	1972
France	9.7	12.3	12.0	14.3	15.1	16.5
West Germany	8.1	10.7	14.1	16.7	16.5	22.2
Italy	4.9	5.6	6.8	8.5	8.8	10.1
Japan	3.8	5.7	8.5	12.8	18.0	23.9
United Kingdom	12.6	13.5	14.0	14.3	11.7	13.6
All five	39.1	47.8	55.4	66.6	70.1	86.3

Source: United Nations, *Yearbook of National Account Statistics,* various years; and International Monetary Fund, *International Financial Statistics,* April 1973, as reported in Szymanski, *Social Policy,* Vol. 4, 1974. Reprinted with permission of the publishers, Social Policy Corporation, New York, New York 10036. Copyright 1974 by Social Policy Corporation.

Speaking of the post-1945 era, the Stokholm International Peace Research Institute concluded that

> the most significant changes [in the world stock of fighting vessels] has been the emergence of the WTO [Warsaw Treaty Organization]—in essence the Soviet Union—as a major naval power. Over the period 1950–1974, the WTO's naval stock has, on the average, increased twice as fast as the world total and three times as fast as that of NATO [SIPRI, 1976:25].

During the previous destabilization of the core, there emerged a naval arms race between the declining hegemonic power, Britain, and one of the ascending competitors, Germany. This sort of naval arms race appears possible again.

> There is every indication that the USA and the USSR are on the verge of a naval arms race if, indeed, it has not already begun. . . . For the first time in the post-war period there is now a serious rival. Soviet naval strength has now reached the point at which it is possible to argue that further (unmatched) expansion will threaten US naval superiority. In other words, a necessary condition for a naval arms race, previously lacking, now exists [SIPRI, 1976:26].

There has also been a dramatic change in the Soviet proportion of world arms sales to peripheral states. Throughout the 1950s, the Soviet Union accounted for a little less than 10% of world arms sales to the third world. As late as 1960 they accounted for only 14% of world expenditures compared with 47% for the United States (Table 10.8). By 1965 they reached parity, with each nation accounting for some 34% of the world total. By the 1970s they had surpassed the United States: during the 1970–1975 period the Soviet Union accounted for 37.6% compared with 34.5% for the United States (SIPRI, 1976:51).

The growth of Soviet nuclear weapons, navy, and arms sales, while cer-

Table 10.8

Percentage Distribution of World Expenditures on Major Weapons Systems Exported to the Third World for Selected Suppliers, 1950–1975

	Years								
	1950	1955	1960	1965	1970	1972	1973	1974	1975
United States	31.0	39.9	47.0	34.6	42.8	35.8	30.4	29.5	36.5
Soviet Union	8.5	8.6	14.2	34.2	37.2	27.2	53.0	37.8	34.1
Britain	32.7	22.9	16.7	17.0	6.3	10.6	8.3	11.8	10.4
France	1.0	9.2	3.2	6.2	6.9	10.1	14.1	8.8	9.8

Source: Adapted from Stockholm International Peace Research Institute (Atlantic Highlands, N.J.: Humanities Press Inc., 1976), Table IC2, p. 51.

tainly the most obvious example of the decline of American military hegemony, is not, though, the only instance of the increasing distribution of military strength across the major core powers. Japan, for instance, appears to be increasing her military capacity. While the expenditures are small compared to other core states, what appears to be a changing Japanese attitude is significant in the context of the 1946 Constitution that explicitly forbids armed forces.

> For the first time in 30 years the Japanese are not being shy about defense. . . . There was public discussion in Tokyo during 1978 of plans to acquire longer-range, modern weapons, including four small aircraft carriers, air-to-air refueling tankers, and more antisubmarine patrol aircraft and fighter-bombers. . . . On a more concrete level the Japanese . . . also announced that they were sending pilots to the United States for "defensive" air combat training—a decision that once would have been highly controversial. What is more, incremental steps to upgrade the role of tanks and paratroopers in the ground forces have been announced, as have increases in the operations range limits of air and naval patrols for surveillance around Japan [Pillsbury, 1979:6, 12].[7]

The decline in American power is the beginning of the more general decomposition of the core as a whole. Other core states, like Japan and West Germany, begin to question their security as the reach of American power contracts. Not only individual states begin to rearm, but larger blocs of nations within the core also continue to decompose. The Soviet Union and China for example, have gone from ideological bickering in the 1960s to border skirmishes and fighting proxy wars through their support of antagonistic client states (the Vietnamese invasion of Cambodia in 1979). The international situation increasingly resembles the pre-1914 period. With the previous stability provided by a Pax Americana fading, core nations once again begin to reach out to form alliances for support and stability. Some of these would have seemed improbable, to say the least, during the early postwar period.

The Chinese established a peace and friendship treaty with the Japanese in 1978 and established diplomatic relations with the United States in 1979. The Chinese suggestion to the Americans, made by Premier Deng Xiaoping in 1979, that, "If we want to be able to place curbs on the polar bear [Soviet Union], the only realistic thing for us is to unite [*Time,* 1979:34]," represents some of the strange realignment of forces that the decline in American hegemony is generating. The divisions and bickering are not limited to the Soviet Union and China, as the 1970s brought increased friction over trade, monetary policies, and the status of NATO among the United States, Japan,

---

[7] Reprinted with permission from *Foreign Policy* No. 33 (Winter), 1978–1979. Copyright 1978 by the Carnegie Endowment for International Peace.

and Western Europe (Kaldor, 1978). Whether the continuing decomposition of the core will result in a series of alliances like the Triple Entente and Triple Alliance remains to be seen, although charges by Moscow radio that a United States–Chinese–Japanese military axis is being directed against the Soviet Union (Pillsbury, 1979) is certainly reminiscent of earlier periods of instability.

In sum, then, the core appears once again to be moving from being dominated by one hegemonic power to being composed of a plurality of competitive and rivalrous powers. As such the core should also be moving toward increased instability, and as a consequence core–periphery relations should once again become more tightly politically regulated as a systemic response to this growing instability.

The Political Regulation of Trade: Import Restrictions and Protectionism

> The one thing that is clear . . . is that the liberal world economy, as it existed for a quarter of a century after 1945, is on the way out. . . . What we have to expect in its place . . . is a world of regional blocs or superblocs . . . of exclusive trading areas, hedged in by protective tariff areas, in which groups of developed and underdeveloped countries are linked together by mutual interests and stand opposed to other groups of developed and developing countries similarly linked [Barraclough, 1978:56].

Perhaps the clearest sign of rigidifying core–periphery relations is the emergence once again of protectionist trade policies during the 1970s. The GATT annual report for 1978 notes that import restrictions by developed countries (core) have increased not only on goods where core producers are at a clear competitive disadvantage (textiles, clothing, footwear), but also on goods where they compete equally, and even for goods, like chemicals, where core countries hold a clear competitive advantage. Growing import restrictions are most dramatically seen in the declining share of core countries' manufactured imports that are accounted for by peripheral and semi-peripheral states. For the past 20 years the developing countries' share of the imports of the rich countries has shown uninterrupted growth, but in 1977 it came to a virtual halt. While the reasons for this are not entirely clear, GATT suggests that

> one major factor is painfully apparent: the significant slowing down of imports of textiles and clothing from the third world which occurred last year [1977]. These goods have been singled out for the most enthusiastic pieces of protectionism. And it worked. In the case of clothing, the share of the developing countries stood still in North America, and actually fell in western Europe and Japan, after 20 years of unstopped growth [The Economist, 1978:10].

The earlier free trade policies, which allowed peripheral and semiperipheral exporters to continually increase their share of core manufactured imports, are, like the last quarter of the nineteenth century, in decline.

The growth of import restrictions is nowhere more apparent than in the trading policies of the leading core state. The United States demanded "voluntary" export quotas on Far Eastern textile products in 1970–1971, and in 1973 imposed export embargoes on soybeans, cottonseed, and their related products. Later that year export controls were extended to 41 more farm products, including livestock feed, edible oils, animal fats, peanuts, lard, tallow, and scrap metal. These moves along with inflationary pressures experienced by western countries in general led Italy, Finland, and Portugal to impose import regulations themselves in 1973 (Hudson, 1977). A more dramatic American move was made in 1975 with the passage of the Trade Act that gave the President authority to impose import quotas whenever imports were a "substantial cause of serious injury" to American industry or employment. In the same year the steel industry applied for protection and the Trade Commission recommended a unilateral import quota of 147,000 tons annually (Hudson, 1977:137). The Customs Court of the United States International Trade Commission has also ruled in favor of higher tariffs on shoe and electronic imports, and the United States has demanded that Japan curtail its color TV imports.

The European Economic Community has also moved toward protectionism in the 1970s. In 1975 France advanced a plan for a "Latin African" bloc tied to the French monetary system and in opposition to English-speaking countries. At the same time the Common Market began talking to Arab countries, especially Egypt, Lebanon, Syria, and Jordan about trade preferences. There was also talk with Mediterranean countries outside the EEC, like Spain, Portugal, Turkey, and Greece about creating a Mediterranean Free Trade Area, "which—as Washington immediately perceived—would virtually close the market to American exports [Barraclough, 1978:50]."

One example of the formal links emerging between core and periphery is the Lomé Convention which was signed in 1975 replacing the earlier Yaoundé Convention. This agreement set up a preferential trading zone composed of 46 African, Caribbean, and Pacific developing countries linked to the EEC through reciprocal trade preferences and aid from the European Economic Development Fund. One of the essential features of this agreement is the "Stabex Scheme," which provides compensations for peripheral exporters when certain commodities fall below an agreed-upon level, and illustrates the increasingly explicit political regulation of core–periphery transactions.

Along with the United States and the EEC, the third major manufacturing and trading area, Japan, is also involved in protectionist policies, although with Japan protectionism has long been a center piece of their economic policy.[8]

> For a very long time and until very recently, Japan was utterly protectionist in every aspect of international economic interaction. All transactions—goods in trade, technology sale and purchase, capital inflow and outflow—were closely regulated and circumscribed [Abegglen and Hout, 1978:146].

Protectionism, then, seems clearly on the rise. Throughout the 1970s, it was a growing reality in the trade policies of the United States and the EEC, and it has always been the cornerstone of Japanese policy. In this sense we can speak of a growing formalization and political regulation of core–periphery economic transactions, much like the growth of protectionism a century earlier. This, we argued, was a systemic response to the decline of British hegemony and the ever increasing instability in the core. The argument is the same today. The decline of American hegemony, both economically and militarily, is part of the transformation of the core into an increasingly unstable amalgam of competitive states, which results in a growing rigidity of core–periphery relations as the system as a whole moves to reestablish its basic social relations.

Increasing Political Control of the Periphery

> Does the Third World still exist? In its poverty and underdevelopment more than ever; in its "nonalignment" less and less. Most of Asia has already been divided into Soviet, American, and Chinese spheres of influence . . . [and] . . . now that Africa has entered the storm zone, its internal political and social conflicts are largely overshadowed by the politics of the great powers. The few years of relative national autonomy that followed decolonization are, for the weaker and more artificial of these new countries, now little more than a memory [Julliard, 1978:3].

Colonialism, as the primary means of core political domination of peripheral areas, has passed and this raises the question of alternative forms of control. The declining hegemony of the United States and the rise in protectionism during the 1970s suggest that we are entering another cycle. But

---

[8] In this sense Japan resembles the United States during the nineteenth century, whose tariff levels remained high while others dropped during the mid-century Era of Free Trade.

what of the more political means of core control that have been historically managed by colonialism? There are two trends in world politics which can be viewed as signals of a reimposition of more explicit political control over peripheral areas. One is the increase in arms sales by core states and the political dependence this implies; the other is the declining "nonaligned" status of the Third World as it is increasingly divided into spheres of influence by the major core powers. These two trends are obviously interconnected, since arms dependence, along with foreign aid of a nonmilitary character, provide the principal means through which core influence and control are exercised.

Peripheral states are almost entirely dependent upon four core states for their major weapons systems. Between 1950 and 1969 the United States, the Soviet Union, Britain, and France provided an average of 87% of the major weapons for the Third World. Virtually all of these sales are handled on a government to government basis, which more easily facilitates their use as extensions of state policy. Less than 5% of the weapons business is in private hands, and only a small fraction of these operate without government approval. Weapons are also relatively easy to acquire. The United States and the Soviet Union, who over the past 20 years have accounted for two-thirds of third world arms sales, provide arms free of charge or at subsidized prices with low interest rates (SIPRI, 1976). With weaponry so easy to acquire and such a massive dependence on only a few suppliers, the conditions for at least dependence, if not influence and outright control, are clearly present. If we are experiencing another cycle, then sales of arms to peripheral states should be increasing—and they are. "The cumulative value of major weapon transfers in the six years 1970–1975 ($19.2 billion) is already larger than that for the decade of 1960–1969 ($14.2 billion) and nearly three times that for the decade 1950–1959 ($6.8 billion) [SIPRI, 1976:34]." Arms expenditures by the third world have gone from 6.2% of the world total in 1955 to 18.0% in 1974. By comparison for the same years the United States' expenditures declined from 46.2 to 31.5% and the Soviet Union increased from 27.4 to 29.4%. Arms sales are growing on a world scale, but they are growing the fastest in the Third World.

Along with increasing dependence upon arms from the core, another indicator of the reimposition of political control is the decline in the nonaligned status of the third world. As Julliard noted, the sense of autonomy of the newer states of Africa and Asia seemed to be fading in the late 1970s. Like the late-nineteenth century we see in the 1970s core states extending their influence into the affairs of the periphery. Perhaps the most dramatic newcomer is the Soviet Union, whose relations with the Third World have changed dramatically in the 1970s. Earlier, during the 1950s, Soviet strategy centered on support for the national bourgeoisie, like India's Nehru,

Egypt's Nasser, Indonesia's Sukarno, Guinea's Sekou Toure, and Algeria's Ben Bella.

By the mid-1970s, the policy changed to helping local communist parties gain state power and then becoming much more directly linked to them through a combination of friendship treaties, arms, and Soviet, Cuban, or East European advisors. This, obviously, provides a much firmer foothold in the Third World, particularly when it is "supported by the modern equivalents of the nineteenth century coaling stations—missile depots, airfields, logistic bases, and naval facilities in . . . South Yemen, Cuba, Iraq, Angola, and Guinea . . . [Luttwak, 1977:58]." As an example of this changing Soviet strategy, during the years 1975–1979 seven pro-Soviet parties seized power in peripheral states with Soviet aid (Zagoria, 1979). In 1975 Soviet aid contributed heavily to the Vietnamese victory, and to the ascension of the Pathet Lao in Laos. Aid has continued to Vietnam, and Soviet ships use the naval base at Cam Ranh Bay, fly reconnaissance flights regularly between Vladivostock and the U.S. built airbase in Danang, and are building a large communication facility for listening to China at Cam Ranh Bay (Reston, 1979). In 1976, Soviet airlifts of arms and 10,000 Cuban advisors were instrumental in the MPLA victory in Angola.

In 1977, after officers seized power in Ethiopia there was a massive airlift of $2 billion worth of arms, 20,000 Cuban advisors, 300 tanks, and 3000 Soviet military technicians which then enabled Ethiopia to route the Somali-led insurgents in the Ogaden and the Eritrean secessionists. In 1978, before the coups in Afganistan and South Yemen, Soviet advisors were entrenched in the army and were the leading arms suppliers to Afganistan, which they later occupied with Soviet troops in 1979. Cubans were also training the peoples' militia and East Germans were training the security forces in South Yemen. The Soviets consider these new regimes allies and aid for most of them has increased so they can consolidate power against both internal and external enemies (Zagoria, 1979).

The point here is not that increased Soviet presence in and of itself constitutes the reimposition of colonial control. American arms, friendship treaties, and advisors remain in the Third World. The Soviets are simply the most dramatic newcomer. The situation is in some sense analogous to core–periphery relations a century earlier. Britain had colonies, and intervened to protect her interests during the years of her hegemony, in a practice referred to as the "Imperialism of Free Trade" (Gallagher and Robinson, 1953). The same is true for the United States of the 1945–1973 years. It was a free trade world economy, dominated by the United States; there were also American interventions, arms sales, and bases throughout the periphery. What is different about the 1970s is what was different about the 1870s: Other core states began to engage in the same practices and as such the rate of core domination increased, creating the second wave of colonialism, and now the third wave of core domination of peripheral areas.

It is the end of the nineteenth century all over again, only new actors. Rather than Britain, France, Germany, Belgium, and Italy fighting over territory, it is now the United States and the Soviet Union with lesser roles being played by China and some European states. It is not colonialism in the old sense, but the autonomy of the recently independent Third World is not growing. The informal hegemony of the Pax Americana is being replaced by the more explicit presence of the major core states, notably the United States and the Soviet Union. We may be witnessing yet another "Rush for Africa," this time in the 1970s and 1980s rather than the 1870s and 1880s.

To the extent, then, that American hegemony is declining—and all indicators suggest it is—and to the extent that protectionism is rising and political control over the periphery is being reasserted—albeit in new and different forms—then we can speak of yet a third global cycle of tightened core–periphery relations. There is, though, a major difference. Colonialism is gone. We are clearly speaking more of dependence and influence than overt domination and explicit political control. Arms dependence is simply not the same as being a colony. So far we have been looking at a model of more cyclical or repetitive processes—core instability generating a tighter core–periphery control structure. The disappearance of colonialism, though, raises fundamental questions. If the third wave is different from the second (no formal colonies), is the second different from the first and more importantly are the differences systematic? Do they constitute a pattern of some sort which can tell us something about the more long term secular trends of the system, as opposed to the cyclical rhythms we have been dealing with.

Long-Term Trends

If we can speak of a third wave or cycle of control that is more a matter of dependence and influence than over political domination (colonies), then it would seem that the means of extending core control has become less overt and more indirect in its effect upon peripheral peoples and social formations. If the third wave is more indirect and less severe than the second, is the second less disruptive than the first? In effect, is there a trend toward decreasing severity and more indirect means of core control with each successive wave? If we focus upon the disruptive aspects of colonialism, including the brutality involved in the uprooting of local peoples and the destruction of local social arrangements that is involved in establishing colonial control, then the first wave seems to have been more severe than the second.

The difference is caught in the characterization of the first wave as "settler" colonies and the second wave as colonies of "occupation." Settler means not only the transportation of core-like societies to peripheral areas, but the destruction of local social formations, and in the case of the Indians of Mexico and Peru their virtual annihilation through enslavement and Spanish diseases for which they had no defense (Frank, 1978). There was also the destruction of local social arrangements and the enslavement and transportation of Africans to the Americas as a coerced labor force. The second wave did not involve the same degree of enslavement, transplanting of core societies, and destruction of local societies and anihilation of local peoples. This is not to say that there was not brutality, killing, or that local social arrangements were not destroyed. The scale and amount of disruption seems less; the second colonization was more a matter of occupation than replacing one people and social arrangement with another.

The degree of internal transformation of peripheral areas can be seen when they are examined after colonial control has been withdrawn. When the Europeans leave Africa and Asia after 1945, local Africans and Asians remain to organize and manage their newly independent states. When the Europeans left the Americas, the Indians did not assume control. In North America they were replaced by Europeans themselves; in Latin America there was a fusion of Spaniards and Indians that formed the nucleus of local nationalist forces (Wolf, 1959). The racial composition of the Americas is also premanently altered, as Africans become a constituent group in North and South American racial and ethnic stratification systems.

Does this pattern of more indirect and subtle means of exercising core control also hold for the political regulation of trade? The answer appears to be yes. The second wave of mercantilism

> never approximated in its severity the mercantilism of the first period. No power excluded foreign ships or goods from its colonies, forced colonial trade to pass through metropolitan ports, forbade colonial manufactures that might compete with its own or, with the sole exception of Holland between 1830 and 1877, transferred colonial revenues to the metropolitan treasury [Fieldhouse, 1968:10].

The mercantilism of the 1970s and 1980s appears to be even more indirect and subtle than that of the second wave of mercantilism.

> In the new mercantilism . . . nations are not relying on tariffs or quotas to protect jobs and profits. Instead, they use new and more subtle market restrictions such as currency manipulation, cartel-like schemes, direct subsidies to industries, and voluntary export restraint agreements [Business Week, 1979:50].

There are two other important trends. First, the waves are becoming shorter: The first wave lasted some 300 years while the second lasted a little over 100 years. If this trend continues we expect the third wave to be even shorter. Second, with each wave, more of the world is included and brought within the web of the world-economy. The first wave reached a peak of 147 colonies in 1770 and the second climbed to a peak of 168 in 1921. The third wave seems to be more extensive than the second; today's arms sales include Latin America, an area that was not included during the second wave of colonialism. We have not only the excolonies of the second wave, but also the independent states of Latin America making up the third wave of peripheral areas susceptible to dependence on core armaments. We have, then, three long term trends: The waves of core domination are (a) more indirect, milder, and less disruptive, (b) shorter, and (c) more extensive.

Primitive Accumulation on a World Scale

The fact that these waves of core domination over peripheral areas are becoming less disruptive, shorter, and more extensive, reflects the long term extensive and intensive development of the world-economy. As the world division of labor has expanded and become institutionalized there is less and less need for extra-economic linkages—like colonialism—to bind the system together. The first wave was the most disruptive and lasted the longest. The severity represented the initial phase of destroying and reconstituting the social formations of unincorporated areas in the process of assigning them peripheral positions in the world division of labor. The reconstitution of local modes of production into functioning components of a worldwide division of labor, representing primitive accumulation on a world scale, involved a tremendous exertion of energy and force. Conquest, plunder, slavery, and the annihilation of indigenous peoples all played a part in the realignment of different social formations on different continents, into one integrated social formation on a world scale—the capitalist world-economy that emerged during the sixteenth century.

During the early centuries this worldwide social formation was "held together," or constructed out of, social relations that were more political than economic. The self-perpetuating mechanisms of a world market and unequal exchange could not take hold as well during the earlier centuries because the infrastructure of peripheral regions were still being "hammered" into the appropriate shape required for their dependent position in the emerging world economy. In this sense colonialism truly represents a

means of primitive accumulation that precedes the more organic functioning of the self-perpetuating and self-reproducing core–periphery division of
labor. To overcome the resistance of social formations, which had been outside the developing European world-economy, colonialism crushed the local
social formations of the Americas and uprooted, enslaved, and transplanted
Africans, as it reached out to peripheralize isolated and more or less independent regions into one interrelated world economy.[9]

As the infrastructure of peripheral regions became more and more in
sync with their role in the world division of labor, the more distinctly economic relations, such as unequal exchange (Emmanuel, 1972), could grow,
expand, and increasingly assume responsibility for overall system integration. The stronger the world-economy grows, the more it carries the collective reality of a world-system, and the less extra-economic linkages, are required, so that these waves of colonialism and politically regulated trade
have become progressively milder, and shorter in length. Their growing extensiveness also reflects the overall expansion of the system as a whole, and
each time a wave of extra-economic linkages appears it covers more of the
world than before.

If the world-economy has been more or less continually growing and
expanding, why do extra-economic linkages appear in waves or cycles?
Why didn't colonialism die off more gradually? One possible answer lies in
examining the troughs of these waves. While the growth of the world economy is probably continuous, there can still be periods of accelerated expansion—booms—that periodically punctuate the long term trend of continuous growth. If the system is continuously growing and expanding, it may
be that the wave-like effects we have been dealing with so far are generated
by periods of rapid economic growth which temporarily heighten the more
distinctly economic linkages—as reflected in the growth of free trade policies during the 1815–1870, and 1947–1973 periods—and temporarily
dissolve or replace the more explicit political links. What appears as waves
of political linkages may be a by-product of the periodic boom periods of
the world-economy.

In the previous sections we have focused upon the ebb and flow of colo-

---

[9] Critics of the world-system perspective (Brenner, 1977) have argued that more attention has been paid to the world division of labor than the class struggles which made such trade
and exchange possible. The world economy is a product of class struggle—but struggle on a
world scale. Colonialism, with its plunder and destruction of local social formations, represents
just such a struggle as it precedes, and makes possible, the hierarchial world-economy of unequal exchange and unequal development.

nialism, linking it to stability and instability within the core. What we are suggesting here is that these political linkages may be more of a constant that is gradually diminishing as the world-economy continues to grow and expand. The two dips in colonialism may actually reflect the two "boom" periods of world capitalism, which by punctuating the long term decline in political linkages creates the wave-like effect of colonialism. The mid-nineteenth century boom (Hobsbawm, 1975), by increasing the more distinctly economic ties between core and periphery, dramatically lessens the needs for the system to be bound together through the more heavy handed means of colonialism. Hence the decline in colonies, along with the rapid growth of world capitalism.

These are but two sides of the same social coin, and we can just as easily read Figure 10.4 in terms of two waves of expanded growth, our 1815–1870 and 1945–1973 periods, rather than as three waves of expanded political relations: 1500–1815, 1870–1945, and the possible third cycle beginning in the 1970s (1973–). The first boom comes to an end during the 1870s, "for then began what a contemporary observor called 'a most curious and in many respects unprecedented disturbance and depression of trade, commerce and industry' which contemporaries called the 'Great Depression,' and which is usually dated 1873–1896 [Hobsbawm, 1975:5]." As the world economy begins to experience difficulties, there is a shift toward the extra-economic linkages of colonialism, and more of the burden for system integration is passed to the more explicit political ties of the second wave of colonialism. This new wave of colonization, as noted earlier, is less disruptive, and will last for a shorter time than the first wave.

The world-system does not return to its original state. There has been both long term growth and the spurt of the mid-nineteenth century, such that when the extra-economic linkages pick up the slack of a world economic downturn, they need not be as intense and severe as the first time around for now the capitalist world-economy is stronger and as such it requires less extra-economic effort to perpetuate it. After 1945 we experience a second major boom and once again colonial ties melt away as the expanding capitalist world-economy again assumes more responsibility for integrating and reproducing the core–periphery division of labor. Now, 100 years after the end of the first boom, the second one is passing. "Beginning in some countries in late 1973, in others during the following year, the long trend of growth came to an abrupt halt. In the United States, output declined by 9% from 1974 to 1975. In Germany and France, production fell by a percentage point less; in Italy and Japan by a percentage point more (Heilbroner 1978:13)." With this economic downturn core–periphery relations once again become more political. The continued growth of the world-

economy since the late-nineteenth century is reflected in the fact that core
domination is now more a question of arms dependence, political influence,
and client states.

The long term movement of the world-system is toward a full blown,
self-perpetuating capitalist world-economy, such that noneconomic linkages, like colonialism, are increasingly unnecessary. The world-economy
has experienced spurts of growth and expansion—the mid-nineteenth century boom ending in the 1870s, and the post-1945 boom ending in the
1970s—that temporarily dissolved colonial relations. When the economic
expansion subsides the extra-economic linkages again appear, except that
they are less necessary and hence each wave is milder and shorter in length.
If the capitalist world-economy continues to grow and expand, we should

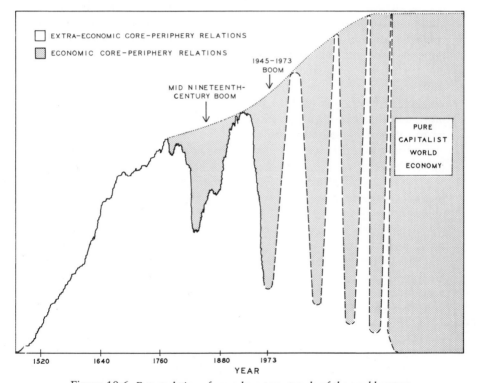

Figure 10.6. *Extrapolation of some long term trends of the world-system.*

expect the trend of milder, shorter, and more extensive waves of extra-economic political domination to continue.

As most of the world becomes implicated in the world-economy there is probably a ceiling for the extensive development of the system, although intensive development would continue. How many more waves are necessary before we have realized the pure form of a self-generating and self-reproducing world-economy is unknown. The waves could eventually become so short and mild that they virtually disappear (see Figure 10.6). Alternatively, the periodic crises of capitalism may continue to require some sort of "primitive accumulation" to put the system back on its feet, or to overcome the structural blockage, which caused the crisis in the first place (Frank, 1967; Gordon, 1978; Heilbroner, 1978). In this case whenever we have a major downturn in the world-economy, political regulation will reappear to reset the mechanisms and restart the system.

Finally, there is the position we started with. As long as we have rising and falling hegemonic powers, as long as we have unicentric and stable, and multicentric and unstable cores, then we will continue to see political regulation and domination as a systemic response to instability, confusion, and conflict within the center of the system. While the original model seems to be supported by the growing protectionism and arms dependence, which is accompanying the decline of American hegemony, it does not provide an explanation for the three long term trends we have just discussed. It may very well be that as the system grows and deepens in its relations it responds more quickly to problems within the core. As the system is progressively more tightly integrated it can go through a cycle quicker. Also if the system is more integrated it may require less explicit domination to achieve the same effect that was accomplished earlier with greater force and violence. With world interdependencies growing, the withholding of spare parts may provide the leverage that planting the flag and formal occupation accomplished a century before.

Repetitive processes like waves and cycles and long term secular trends are all part of the dynamics of the world-system, and are undoubtedly causally interconnected and interdependent. The next task is to find the common underlying structural dynamics that explain both cycles and secular trends.

Acknowledgments

Earlier versions of these ideas were presented at the American Academy of Arts and Sciences World-System Conference, Stanford University, April 3, 1976, and at the Annual Meetings of the American Sociological Association, San Francisco, California, September 4–8, 1978. We would like to thank Beverly Duncan, Otis Dudley Duncan, and Michael Hout for suggestions on coding colonialism and presenting the data. We would also like to thank Bill Lockwood for computer assistance and Sandy Goers for graphic work.

Appendix

Number of Colonies Established (E) and Terminated (T) Each Year and the Cumulative Net Number, 1415–1969

Year	E	T	Cum. Net	Year	E	T	Cum. Net	Year	E	T	Cum. Net	Year	E	T	Cum. Net
1415	1	0	1	1465	0	0	1	1515	1	0	16	1565	2	0	43
1416	0	0	1	1466	0	0	1	1516	0	0	16	1566	0	0	43
1417	0	0	1	1467	0	0	1	1517	0	0	16	1567	1	0	44
1418	0	0	1	1468	0	0	1	1518	1	0	17	1568	1	0	45
1419	0	0	1	1469	0	0	1	1519	0	0	17	1569	1	0	46
1420	0	0	1	1470	0	0	1	1520	0	0	17	1570	0	0	46
1421	0	0	1	1471	0	0	1	1521	1	0	18	1571	0	0	46
1422	0	0	1	1472	0	0	1	1522	1	0	19	1572	0	0	46
1423	0	0	1	1473	0	0	1	1523	0	0	19	1573	0	0	46
1424	0	0	1	1474	0	0	1	1524	1	0	20	1574	1	0	47
1425	0	0	1	1475	0	0	1	1525	1	0	21	1575	2	0	49
1426	0	0	1	1476	0	0	1	1526	2	0	23	1576	0	0	49
1427	0	0	1	1477	0	0	1	1527	1	0	24	1577	0	0	49
1428	0	0	1	1478	0	0	1	1528	0	0	24	1578	0	0	49
1429	0	0	1	1479	0	0	1	1529	0	0	24	1579	1	0	50
1430	0	0	1	1480	1	0	2	1530	0	0	24	1580	0	0	50
1431	0	0	1	1481	0	0	2	1531	1	0	25	1581	1	0	51
1432	0	0	1	1482	1	0	3	1532	0	0	25	1582	2	0	53
1433	0	0	1	1483	0	0	3	1533	1	0	26	1583	0	0	53
1434	0	0	1	1484	0	0	3	1534	1	0	27	1584	0	0	53
1435	0	0	1	1485	1	0	4	1535	2	0	29	1585	0	0	53
1436	0	0	1	1486	0	0	4	1536	2	0	31	1586	0	0	53
1437	0	0	1	1487	0	0	4	1537	0	0	31	1587	0	0	53
1438	0	0	1	1488	0	0	4	1538	1	0	32	1588	0	0	53
1439	0	0	1	1489	0	0	4	1539	0	0	32	1589	1	0	54
1440	0	0	1	1490	0	0	4	1540	1	0	33	1590	1	0	55
1441	0	0	1	1491	0	0	4	1541	0	0	33	1591	1	0	56
1442	0	0	1	1492	0	0	4	1542	0	0	33	1592	0	0	56
1443	0	0	1	1493	0	0	4	1543	0	0	33	1593	1	0	57
1444	0	0	1	1494	0	0	4	1544	0	0	33	1594	0	0	57
1445	0	0	1	1495	0	0	4	1545	0	0	33	1595	0	0	57
1446	0	0	1	1496	2	0	6	1546	0	0	33	1596	0	0	57
1447	0	0	1	1497	0	0	6	1547	0	0	33	1597	0	0	57
1448	0	0	1	1498	0	0	6	1548	0	0	33	1598	2	0	59
1449	0	0	1	1499	0	0	6	1549	1	0	34	1599	0	0	59
1450	0	0	1	1500	0	0	6	1550	2	0	36	1600	0	0	59
1451	0	0	1	1501	1	0	7	1551	0	0	36	1601	0	0	59
1452	0	0	1	1502	0	0	7	1552	0	0	36	1602	0	0	59
1453	0	0	1	1503	0	0	7	1553	0	0	36	1603	0	0	59
1454	0	0	1	1504	1	0	8	1554	0	0	36	1604	1	0	60
1455	0	0	1	1505	1	0	9	1555	0	0	36	1605	0	0	60
1456	0	0	1	1506	0	0	9	1556	2	0	38	1606	0	0	60
1457	0	0	1	1507	0	0	9	1557	1	0	39	1607	1	0	61
1458	0	0	1	1508	1	0	10	1558	0	0	39	1608	1	0	62
1459	0	0	1	1509	2	0	12	1559	1	0	40	1609	2	0	64
1460	0	0	1	1510	0	0	12	1560	0	0	40	1610	0	0	64
1461	0	0	1	1511	1	0	13	1561	0	0	40	1611	1	0	65
1462	0	0	1	1512	1	0	14	1562	1	0	41	1612	2	0	67
1463	0	0	1	1513	0	0	14	1563	0	0	41	1613	1	0	68
1464	0	0	1	1514	1	0	15	1564	0	0	41	1614	1	0	69

(cont.)

Albert B   *and Ronald Schoenberg*

APPENDIX (*continued*)

Year	E	T	Cum. Net	Year	E	T	Cum. Net	Year	E	T	Cum. Net	Year	E	T	Cum. Net
1615	1	0	70	1665	2	0	110	1715	0	0	123	1765	2	0	142
1616	2	0	72	1666	1	0	111	1716	1	0	124	1766	2	1	143
1617	0	0	72	1667	1	1	111	1717	0	0	124	1767	2	0	145
1618	3	1	74	1668	2	0	113	1718	0	0	124	1768	1	0	146
1619	0	0	74	1669	0	0	113	1719	0	0	124	1769	0	0	146
1620	2	0	76	1670	2	1	114	1720	2	0	126	1770	1	0	147
1621	0	0	76	1671	2	0	116	1721	0	1	125	1771	0	0	147
1622	0	1	75	1672	2	0	118	1722	1	0	126	1772	0	0	147
1623	1	0	76	1673	1	0	119	1723	0	0	126	1773	0	0	147
1624	3	0	79	1674	2	2	119	1724	0	0	126	1774	0	0	147
1625	0	2	77	1675	0	0	119	1725	0	0	126	1775	0	5	142
1626	0	0	77	1676	0	0	119	1726	0	0	126	1776	0	5	137
1627	0	0	77	1677	0	0	119	1727	0	0	126	1777	1	1	137
1628	4	0	81	1678	0	0	119	1728	0	0	126	1778	1	1	137
1629	1	0	82	1679	0	0	119	1729	0	1	125	1779	0	1	136
1630	2	0	84	1680	1	0	120	1730	0	0	125	1780	0	0	136
1631	0	0	84	1681	1	0	121	1731	0	0	125	1781	1	1	136
1632	1	0	85	1682	0	0	121	1732	0	0	125	1782	0	2	134
1633	0	0	85	1683	1	0	122	1733	1	0	126	1783	0	2	132
1634	2	0	87	1684	0	1	121	1734	1	0	127	1784	3	0	135
1635	4	0	91	1685	1	0	122	1735	1	0	128	1785	0	0	135
1636	1	0	92	1686	0	0	122	1736	0	0	128	1786	2	1	136
1637	1	1	92	1687	0	1	121	1737	1	0	129	1787	0	0	136
1638	4	0	96	1688	0	0	121	1738	0	0	129	1788	2	0	138
1639	1	0	97	1689	0	1	120	1739	1	0	130	1789	0	0	138
1640	1	0	98	1690	0	0	120	1740	1	0	131	1790	1	0	139
1641	5	3	100	1691	0	0	120	1741	1	0	132	1791	0	0	139
1642	2	0	102	1692	0	1	119	1742	0	0	132	1792	1	1	139
1643	1	0	103	1693	0	0	119	1743	0	0	132	1793	0	0	139
1644	0	0	103	1694	0	0	119	1744	0	0	132	1794	0	0	139
1645	0	1	102	1695	0	0	119	1745	0	0	132	1795	1	1	139
1646	0	0	102	1696	0	0	119	1746	1	0	133	1796	1	1	139
1647	0	0	102	1697	0	0	119	1747	0	0	133	1797	1	1	139
1648	0	1	101	1698	0	0	119	1748	0	0	133	1798	0	0	139
1649	1	0	102	1699	1	0	120	1749	1	0	134	1799	1	0	140
1650	0	0	102	1700	1	0	121	1750	1	0	135	1800	0	0	140
1651	1	0	103	1701	0	0	121	1751	3	0	138	1801	0	0	140
1652	1	1	103	1702	1	1	121	1752	0	0	138	1802	1	1	140
1653	0	0	103	1703	0	0	121	1753	0	0	138	1803	2	5	137
1654	0	2	101	1704	1	0	122	1754	0	0	138	1804	0	0	137
1655	1	1	101	1705	0	0	122	1755	0	0	138	1805	0	0	137
1656	0	0	101	1706	0	0	122	1756	1	0	138	1806	0	1	136
1657	1	0	102	1707	0	0	122	1757	0	0	138	1807	1	0	137
1658	0	1	101	1708	1	0	123	1758	2	3	137	1808	0	1	136
1659	2	0	103	1709	0	0	123	1759	1	0	138	1809	0	0	136
1660	0	1	102	1710	2	2	123	1760	0	2	136	1810	2	7	131
1661	2	0	104	1711	0	0	123	1761	0	0	136	1811	1	4	128
1662	1	1	104	1712	0	0	123	1762	1	2	135	1812	0	1	127
1663	1	0	105	1713	0	1	122	1763	4	1	138	1813	0	0	127
1664	4	1	108	1714	1	0	123	1764	2	0	140	1814	0	1	126

(*cont.*)

APPENDIX (continued)

Year	E	T	Cum. Net	Year	E	T	Cum. Net	Year	E	T	Cum. Net	Year	E	T	Cum. Net
1815	1	0	127	1855	2	0	107	1895	3	1	139	1935	1	0	166
1816	0	0	127	1856	2	0	109	1896	2	1	140	1936	1	0	167
1817	0	2	125	1857	0	0	109	1897	1	0	141	1937	0	0	167
1818	0	0	125	1858	2	0	111	1898	5	4	142	1938	0	0	167
1819	2	0	127	1859	1	1	111	1899	2	1	143	1939	0	0	167
1820	0	5	122	1860	0	1	110	1900	5	1	147	1940	0	0	167
1821	0	31	91	1861	1	0	111	1901	5	5	147	1941	0	1	166
1822	1	7	85	1862	0	0	111	1902	4	0	151	1942	0	3	163
1823	0	0	85	1863	1	0	112	1903	1	0	152	1943	0	1	162
1824	1	2	84	1864	0	1	111	1904	2	0	154	1944	0	1	161
1825	0	3	81	1865	0	0	111	1905	1	0	155	1945	1	7	155
1826	3	0	84	1866	0	2	109	1906	2	1	156	1946	3	6	152
1827	0	0	84	1867	0	2	107	1907	3	0	159	1947	2	18	136
1828	1	0	85	1868	1	0	108	1908	0	0	159	1948	0	3	133
1829	0	0	85	1869	1	0	109	1909	0	0	159	1949	1	3	131
1830	1	0	86	1870	0	2	107	1910	1	3	157	1950	0	1	130
1831	0	1	85	1871	1	1	107	1911	0	0	157	1951	0	1	129
1832	0	0	85	1872	0	1	106	1912	5	0	162	1952	0	1	128
1833	0	0	85	1873	1	1	106	1913	1	1	162	1953	1	2	127
1834	0	1	84	1874	1	1	106	1914	3	5	160	1954	1	4	124
1835	0	0	84	1875	0	0	106	1915	0	1	159	1955	0	1	123
1836	2	0	86	1876	0	0	106	1916	4	1	162	1956	0	4	119
1837	0	0	86	1877	2	1	107	1917	1	1	162	1957	1	3	117
1838	1	0	87	1878	2	2	107	1918	0	1	161	1958	2	2	117
1839	1	0	88	1879	1	1	107	1919	2	0	163	1959	1	3	115
1840	3	0	91	1880	1	0	108	1920	2	0	165	1960	0	22	93
1841	2	0	93	1881	1	0	109	1921	3	0	168	1961	0	6	87
1842	0	0	93	1882	3	1	111	1922	0	1	167	1962	0	9	78
1843	5	0	98	1883	1	0	112	1923	1	0	168	1963	0	4	74
1844	0	0	98	1884	6	0	118	1924	0	0	168	1964	0	4	70
1845	2	3	97	1885	5	0	123	1925	0	0	168	1965	1	3	68
1846	0	0	97	1886	4	0	127	1926	0	1	167	1966	0	4	64
1847	2	0	99	1887	3	0	130	1927	0	0	167	1967	0	1	63
1848	1	0	100	1888	2	0	132	1928	0	0	167	1968	0	4	59
1849	2	0	102	1889	0	0	132	1929	0	0	167	1969	0	1	58
1850	0	1	101	1890	1	2	131	1930	0	1	166				
1851	0	0	101	1891	1	0	132	1931	0	0	166				
1852	1	0	102	1892	1	0	133	1932	0	1	165				
1853	1	0	103	1893	2	0	135	1933	0	0	165				
1854	2	0	105	1894	2	0	137	1934	0	0	165				

References

Abegglen, J. C., and T. H. Hout
    1978 "Facing up to the trade gap with Japan." *Foreign Affairs* 57(Fall):146–168.
Anderson, P.
    1974 *Lineages of the Absolutist State.* London: New Left Books.

Barraclough, G.
   1978   "The struggle for the third world." *New York Review of Books* 25 (November 9).
Brenner, R.
   1977   "The origins of capitalist development: A critique of neo-Smithian Marxism." *New Left Review* 104 (July–August):25–92.
Brooks, H.
   1972   "What's happening to the U.S. lead in technology?" *Harvard Business Review* (May–June):110–118.
Business Week
   1979   "Neo-Mercantilism in the 80s." (July 9):50–54.
Clough, S. B., and R. T. Rapp
   1975   *European Economic History.* New York: McGraw-Hill.
Crittenden, A.
   1979   "A new world disorder." *New York Times,* Sec. 12, p. 1, February 4.
The Economist
   1978   "Hurt the poor, hurt yourselves." *Arizona Daily Star,* September 18, Sec. A, p. 10.
Emmanuel, A.
   1972   *Unequal Exchange: A Study of the Imperialism of Trade.* New York: Monthly Review Press.
Fieldhouse, D. K.
   1966   *The Colonial Empires.* New York: Dell.
   1968   "Colonialism: Economic aspects." Pp. 6–12 in D. Sills (ed.), *Encyclopedia of the Social Sciences,* Vol. 3. New York: Macmillan and the Free Press.
   1973   *Economics and Empire, 1830–1914.* New York: Cornell University Press.
Frank, A. G.
   1977   "Long live transidelogical enterprise." *Review* 1 (Summer):91–140.
   1978   *World Accumulation, 1492–1789.* New York: Monthly Review Press.
Gallagher, J., and R. Robinson
   1953   "The imperialism of free trade." *Economic History Review,* Second Series, 5:1–15.
Gordon, D.
   1978   "Up and down the long roller coaster." Pp. 22–35 in Crisis Editorial Collective (ed.), *U.S. Capitalism in Crisis.* New York: U.R.P.E.
Heilbroner, R. L.
   1978   *Beyond Boom and Crash.* New York: Norton.
Heinge, D.
   1970   *Colonial Governors.* Madison: University of Wisconsin Press.
Hobsbawm, E. J.
   1968   *Industry and Empire.* Harmondsworth: Penguin.
   1975   *The Age of Capital, 1848–1875.* London: Weidenfeld and Nicolson.
   1976   "The crisis of capitalism in historical perspective." *Socialist Revolution* 6(Oct.–Dec.):77–96.
Hudson, M.
   1977   *Global Fracture: The New International Economic Order.* New York: Harper and Row.
Julliard, J.
   1978   "For a new 'Internationale.'" *New York Review of Books,* July 20.
Kaldor, M.
   1978   *The Disintegrating West.* London: Penguin Books.
Kindleberger, C. P.

1975 "The rise of free trade in western Europe 1820–1875." *The Journal of Economic History* 35(March):20–55.

1978 "Germany's overtaking of England, 1806–1914." Pp. 185–274 in C. P. Kindleberger (ed.), *Economic Response.* Cambridge: Harvard University Press.

Krasner, S.

1976 "State power and the structure of International Trade." *World Politics* 28(April):317–347.

Luttwak, E. N.

1977 "Defense reconsidered." *Commentary* 63(March):51–58.

Pillsbury, M.

1979 "A Japanese card?" *Foreign Policy* 33(Winter):3–30.

Reston, J.

1979 "Toward a sensible world order." *Tucson Daily Star,* May 23.

Szymanski, A.

1974 "The decline and fall of the U.S. eagle." *Social Policy 4* (March/April):5–13.

Stockholm International Peace Research Institute

1976 *Armaments and Disarmament in the Nuclear Age.* Atlantic Highlands, N. J.: Humanities Press.

Temin, P.

1966 "The relative decline of the British steel industry, 1880–1913." Pp. 140–155 in Henry Rosovsky (ed.), *Industrialization in Two Systems: Essays in Honor of Alexander Gerschenkron.* New York: John Wiley.

Time Magazine

1979 "An interview with Deng Xiaoping." February 5, pp. 32–35.

Wallerstein, I.

1974 *The Modern World-System.* New York: Academic Press.

Wolf, E.

1959 *Sons of the Shaking Earth.* Chicago: University of Chicago Press.

Wright, Q.

1942 *The Study of War.* Chicago: University of Chicago Press.

Zagoria, D. S.

1979 "Into the breach: New Soviet alliances in the Third World." Foreign Affairs 57(Spring):733–754.

Subject Index

STUDIES IN SOCIAL DISCONTINUITY

Under the Consulting Editorship of:

CHARLES TILLY
University of Michigan

EDWARD SHORTER
University of Toronto

In preparation

Evelyne Huber Stephens. The Politics of Workers' Participation: The Peruvian Approach in Comparative Perspective

Paul Oquist. Violence, Conflict, and Politics in Columbia

John R. Hanson II. Trade in Transition: Exports From The Third World, 1840-1900

Fred Weinstein. Germany's Discontents, Hitler's Visions: The Claims of Leadership and Ideology in the Nazi Movement

The list of titles in this series continues on the last page of this volume

Published

Albert Bergesen (Ed.). Studies of the Modern World-System

Lucile H. Brockway. Science and Colonial Expansion: The Role of the British Royal Botanic Gardens

James Lang. Portuguese Brazil: The King's Plantation

Elizabeth Hafkin Pleck. Black Migration and Poverty: Boston 1865-1900

Harvey J. Graff. The Literacy Myth: Literacy and Social Structure in the Nineteenth-Century City

Michael Haines. Fertility and Occupation: Population Patterns in Industrialization

Keith Wrightson and David Levine. Poverty and Piety in an English Village: Terling, 1525-1700

Henry A. Gemery and Jan S. Hogendorn (Eds.). The Uncommon Market: Essays in the Economic History of the Atlantic Slave Trade

Tamara K. Hareven (Ed.). Transitions: The Family and the Life Course in Historical Perspective

Randolph Trumbach. The Rise of the Egalitarian Family: Aristocratic Kinship and Domestic Relations in Eighteenth-Century England

Arthur L. Stinchcombe. Theoretical Methods in Social History

Juan G. Espinosa and Andrew S. Zimbalist. Economic Democracy: Workers' Participation in Chilean Industry 1970-1973

Richard Maxwell Brown and Don E. Fehrenbacher (Eds.). Tradition, Conflict, and Modernization: Perspectives on the American Revolution

Harry W. Pearson. The Livelihood of Man by Karl Polanyi

Frederic L. Pryor. The Origins of the Economy: A Comparative Study of Distribution in Primitive and Peasant Economies

Charles P. Cell. Revolution at Work: Mobilization Campaigns in China

Dirk Hoerder. Crowd Action in Revolutionary Massachusetts, 1765-1780

David Levine. Family Formations in an Age of Nascent Capitalism

Ronald Demos Lee (Ed.). Population Patterns in the Past

Michael Schwartz. Radical Protest and Social Structure: The Southern Farmers' Alliance and Cotton Tenancy, 1880-1890

Jane Schneider and Peter Schneider. Culture and Political Economy in Western Sicily

Daniel Chirot. Social Change in a Peripheral Society: The Creation of a Balkan Colony

Stanley H. Brandes. Migration, Kinship, and Community: Tradition and Transition in a Spanish Village

James Lang. Conquest and Commerce: Spain and England in the Americas

Kristian Hvidt. Flight to America: The Social Background of 300,000 Danish Emigrants

D. E. H. Russell. Rebellion, Revolution, and Armed Force: A Comparative Study of Fifteen Countries with Special Emphasis on Cuba and South Africa

John R. Gillis. Youth and History: Tradition and Change in European Age Relations 1770-Present

Immanuel Wallerstein. The Modern World-System I: Capitalist Agriculture and the Origins of the European World-Economy in the Sixteenth Century; II: Mercantilism and the Consolidation of the European World-Economy, 1600-1750

John W. Cole and Eric R. Wolf. The Hidden Frontier: Ecology and Ethnicity in an Alpine Valley

Joel Samaha. Law and Order in Historical Perspective: The Case of Elizabethan Essex

William A. Christian, Jr Person and God in a Spanish Valley